Practical Windows Forensics

Leverage the power of digital forensics for Windows systems

Ayman Shaaban

Konstantin Sapronov

BIRMINGHAM - MUMBAI

Practical Windows Forensics

Copyright © 2016 Packt Publishing

All rights reserved. No part of this book may be reproduced, stored in a retrieval system, or transmitted in any form or by any means, without the prior written permission of the publisher, except in the case of brief quotations embedded in critical articles or reviews.

Every effort has been made in the preparation of this book to ensure the accuracy of the information presented. However, the information contained in this book is sold without warranty, either express or implied. Neither the authors, nor Packt Publishing, and its dealers and distributors will be held liable for any damages caused or alleged to be caused directly or indirectly by this book.

Packt Publishing has endeavored to provide trademark information about all of the companies and products mentioned in this book by the appropriate use of capitals. However, Packt Publishing cannot guarantee the accuracy of this information.

First published: June 2016

Production reference: 2220616

Published by Packt Publishing Ltd.
Livery Place
35 Livery Street
Birmingham
B3 2PB, UK.
ISBN 978-1-78355-409-6

www.packtpub.com

Credits

Authors

Ayman Shaaban

Konstantin Sapronov

Reviewers

Jim Swauger

Dr. Stilianos Vidalis

Zhouyuan Yang

Acquisition Editor

Manish Nainani

Content Development Editor

Rashmi Suvarna

Technical Editor

Vivek Arora

Copy Editor

Priyanka Ravi

Project Coordinator

Judie Jose

Proofreader

Safis Editing

Indexer

Monica Ajmera Mehta

Graphics

Disha Haria

Production Coordinator

Arvindkumar Gupta

Cover Work

Arvindkumar Gupta

About the Authors

Ayman Shaaban (`@aymanshaaban`) has been working as a security researcher for Kaperksy Lab since May 2014. He worked in the Egyptian national CERT as a digital forensics engineer for 5 years. During his career, Ayman has participated in building digital forensics labs, provided analysis for cases with national and international scopes, and delivered training courses on digital forensics analysis for different high-profile entities.

Ayman is a certified GSEC, GCIH, GCFA, and CFCE. He also has a BSc in communication and electronics, an information security diploma from ITI, and is working on his master's degree in information security. Ayman can be found on LinkedIn at `http://eg.linkedin.com/in/aymanshaaban`.

> *I would like to thank my family and my friends for their continuous support. Also, I want to thank all my current and past colleagues in Kaspersky Lab, EG-CERT, and Nile University for their support and dedication.*

Konstantin Sapronov works as the deputy head of the Global Emergency Response Team at Kaspersky Lab. He joined Kaspersky Lab in 2000 and has been in his current position since August 2011. His previous position was group manager of the virus lab in China since 2007, and he has been responsible for establishing and developing the virus lab at Kaspersky Lab's office in China. Prior to this, he worked as a virus analyst and head of the Non-Intel Platform Group in the virus lab at Kaspersky Lab's HQ in Moscow, specializing in reverse engineering and the analysis of malware, exploits, and vulnerabilities. Konstantin is the author of several analytical articles on malware for Unix and other information security topics.

Konstantin holds degrees from the Moscow Power Engineering Institute (a technical university) and the Moscow State University of Economics, Statistics and Information Technology.

> *First of all, many thanks to all my family—my parents, my wife, and my daughter, who have always supported me. Also, I would like to thank all the people I have worked with all these years at our company for their support, professionalism, and willingness to help.*

About the Reviewers

Jim Swauger has over 18 years of experience in the digital forensics field, starting as a computer forensics specialist with the Ohio Attorney General's Computer Crime Unit and then moving on to being the technical security investigator for a top financial institution before becoming an expert consultant with Binary Intelligence. At Binary Intelligence, a firm that specializes in complex cellphone forensic services, Jim manages advanced mobile device Chip-Off, JTAG, and ISP extractions and subsequent forensic data analyses. Jim is an avid Linux user and proponent of using open source resources in digital forensic investigations. His clients include law enforcement and government agencies, corporations, and law firms.

Dr. Stilianos Vidalis was born and raised in Mykonos, a Greek island in Cyclades. He moved to the UK in 1995 to study computer science. He holds a PhD in the threat assessment of micro-payment systems. He is currently the Director of Training for the Cyber Security Centre at the University of Hertfordshire. He lectures on the subjects of cyber security and digital forensics and undertakes consultancy for a number of private and public organizations.

His involvement in the information operations arena began in 2001. Since then, he has participated in high-profile, high-value projects for large international organizations and governments. He has collected and analyzed information for prestigious European financial institutions, applying international standards under the context of risk and threat assessment. He trained the British Armed Forces (Tri-Service) in penetration testing and digital forensics for a number of years.

During his career, Dr. Vidalis has developed and published in peer-reviewed scientific journals his own threat-assessment methodology and other aspects of his work on threat agent classification, vulnerability assessment, early warning systems, deception in CNO, identity theft, and computer criminal profiling.

Zhouyuan Yang has a master's degree in advanced security and digital forensics. His research areas include host- and network-based security, forensics, penetration testing, and IDP/S systems.

Currently, he is a researcher at Fortinet's Fortiguard Labs on the zero-day team, focusing on network security and vulnerability research.

I would like to thank my father, Qisheng Yang, who gives his full love supporting my career dreams.

www.PacktPub.com

For support files and downloads related to your book, please visit www.PacktPub.com.

Did you know that Packt offers eBook versions of every book published, with PDF and ePub files available? You can upgrade to the eBook version at www.PacktPub.com and as a print book customer, you are entitled to a discount on the eBook copy. Get in touch with us at service@packtpub.com for more details.

At www.PacktPub.com, you can also read a collection of free technical articles, sign up for a range of free newsletters and receive exclusive discounts and offers on Packt books and eBooks.

https://www2.packtpub.com/books/subscription/packtlib

Do you need instant solutions to your IT questions? PacktLib is Packt's online digital book library. Here, you can search, access, and read Packt's entire library of books.

Why subscribe?

- Fully searchable across every book published by Packt
- Copy and paste, print, and bookmark content
- On demand and accessible via a web browser

Free access for Packt account holders

If you have an account with Packt at www.PacktPub.com, you can use this to access PacktLib today and view 9 entirely free books. Simply use your login credentials for immediate access.

Table of Contents

Preface	1
Chapter 1: The Foundations and Principles of Digital Forensics	7
What is digital crime?	8
Digital forensics	8
Digital evidence	10
Digital forensic goals	11
Analysis approaches	12
Summary	12
Chapter 2: Incident Response and Live Analysis	13
Personal skills	14
Written communication	14
Oral communication	14
Presentation skills	14
Diplomacy	15
The ability to follow policies and procedures	15
Team skills	15
Integrity	15
Knowing one's limits	15
Coping with stress	16
Problem solving	16
Time management	16
Technical skills	16
Security fundamentals	17
Security principles	17
Security vulnerabilities and weaknesses	17
The Internet	18
Risks	18
Network protocols	18
Network applications and services	19
Network security issues	19
Host or system security issues	19
Malicious code	20
Programming skills	21
Incident handling skills	21

The hardware for IR and Jump Bag	21
Software	25
Live versus mortem	25
Volatile data	26
Nonvolatile data	29
Registry data	30
Remote live response	35
Summary	36
Chapter 3: Volatile Data Collection	**37**
Memory acquisition	38
Issues related to memory access	39
Choosing a tool	39
DumpIt	41
FTK Imager	43
Acquiring memory from a remote computer using iSCSI	44
Using the Sleuth Kit	46
Network-based data collection	47
Hubs	47
Switches	48
Tcpdump	49
Wireshark	50
Tshark	51
Dumpcap	52
Summary	52
Chapter 4: Nonvolatile Data Acquisition	**53**
Forensic image	54
Incident Response CDs	54
DEFT	55
Helix	57
Live imaging of a hard drive	58
FTK imager in live hard drive acquisition	58
Imaging over the network with FTK imager	61
Incident response CDs in live acquisition	63
Linux for the imaging of a hard drive	65
The dd tool	66
dd over the network	67
Virtualization in data acquisition	69
Evidence integrity (the hash function)	70
Disk wiping in Linux	73

Summary	73

Chapter 5: Timeline — 75

Timeline introduction	75
The Sleuth Kit	79
Super timeline – Plaso	82
Plaso architecture	82
Preprocessing	83
Collection	83
Worker	83
Storage	84
Plaso in practice	84
Analyzing the results	88
Summary	95

Chapter 6: Filesystem Analysis and Data Recovery — 97

Hard drive structure	98
Master boot record	98
Partition boot sector	99
The filesystem area in partition	99
Data area	99
The FAT filesystem	100
FAT components	100
FAT limitations	102
The NTFS filesystem	103
NTFS components	103
Master File Table (MFT)	104
The Sleuth Kit (TSK)	104
Volume layer (media management)	105
Filesystem layer	107
The metadata layer	108
istat	109
icat	110
ifind	111
The filename layer	112
Data unit layer (Block)	115
blkcat	115
blkls	118
Blkcalc	118
Autopsy	119
Foremost	128

Summary	131
Chapter 7: Registry Analysis	**133**
The registry structure	133
Root keys	135
HKEY_CLASSES_ROOT or HKCR	135
HKEY_LOCAL_MACHINE	137
HKEY_USERS or HKU	138
HKEY_CURRENT_USER or HKCU	140
Mapping a hive to the filesystem	141
Backing up the registry files	141
Extracting registry hives	143
Extracting registry files from a live system	143
Extracting registry files from a forensic image	147
Parsing registry files	149
The base block	149
Hbin and CELL	151
Auto-run keys	157
Registry analysis	158
RegistryRipper	158
Sysinternals	161
MiTeC Windows registry recovery	164
Summary	164
Chapter 8: Event Log Analysis	**165**
Event Logs – an introduction	165
Event Logs system	166
Security Event Logs	168
Extracting Event Logs	171
Live systems	171
Offline system	172
Event Viewer	174
Event Log Explorer	174
Useful resources	175
Analyzing the event log – an example	176
Summary	180
Chapter 9: Windows Files	**181**
Windows prefetch files	181
Prefetch file analysis	183
Windows tasks	185

Windows Thumbs DB	186
Thumbcache analysis	188
Corrupted Windows.edb files	190
Windows RecycleBin	191
RECYCLER	192
$Recycle.bin	194
Windows shortcut files	195
Shortcut analysis	196
Summary	198
Chapter 10: Browser and E-mail Investigation	199
Browser investigation	199
Microsoft Internet Explorer	200
History files	200
History.IE5	201
IEHistoryView	206
BrowsingHistoryView	206
MiTeC Internet History browser	207
Cache	208
Content.IE5	209
IECacheView	210
Msiecf parser (Plaso framework)	211
Cookies	211
IECookiesView	213
Favorites	213
FavoritesView	214
Session restore	214
MiTeC SSV	215
Inprivate mode	216
WebCacheV#.dat	217
ESEDatabaseView	219
Firefox	220
Places.sqlite	221
MozillaHistoryView	222
Cookies.sqlite	222
MozillaCookiesView	223
Cache	224
MozillaCacheView	224
Other browsers	225
E-mail investigation	225
Outlook PST file	225

Outlook OST files	226
EML and MSG files	226
DBX (Outlook Express)	228
PFF Analysis (libpff)	228
Other tools	230
Summary	231
Chapter 11: Memory Forensics	**233**
Memory structure	233
Memory acquisition	234
The sources of memory dump	234
Hibernation file	234
Crash dump	235
Page files	236
Processes in memory	237
Network connections in memory	238
The DLL injection	239
Remote DLL injection	239
Remote code injection	239
Reflective DLL injection	240
API hooking	240
Memory analysis	240
The volatility framework	240
Volatility plugins	241
imagecopy	241
raw2dmp	241
imageprofile	241
pslist	242
psscan	242
pstree	242
psxview	243
getsids	243
dlllist	243
handles	244
filescan	244
procexedump	245
memdump	245
svcscan	246
connections	246
connscan	246
sockets	247

sockscan	247
Netscan	247
hivelist and printkey	247
malfind	248
vaddump	249
apihooks	249
mftparser	250
Summary	250
Chapter 12: Network Forensics	**251**
Network data collection	251
Exploring logs	253
Using tcpdump	255
Using tshark	257
Using WireShark	258
Fields with more information	260
Knowing Bro	261
Summary	267
Appendix A: Building a Forensic Analysis Environment	**269**
Factors that need to be considered	270
Size	270
Environment control	270
Security	271
Software	272
Hardware	273
Virtualization	273
Virtualization benefits for forensics	274
The distributed forensic system	275
GRR	276
Server installation	276
Client installation	277
Browsing with the newly-connected client	278
Start a new flow	279
Appendix B: Case Study	**283**
Introduction	283
Scenario	283
Acquisition	284
Live analysis	284
The running processes	284
Network activities	287

Autorun keys	288
Prefetch files	289
Browser analysis	290
Postmortem analysis	291
Memory analysis	291
Network analysis	295
Timeline analysis	296
Summary	298
Index	299

Preface

Regardless of your level of experience in the field of information security in general, *Practical Windows Forensics* will fully introduce you to digital forensics. It will provide you with the knowledge needed to assemble different types of evidence properly, and walk you through the various stages of the analysis process.

We start by discussing the principles of the digital forensics process and move on to learning about the approaches that are used to conduct analysis. We will then study various tools to perform live analysis, and go through different techniques to analyze volatile and nonvolatile data. This will be followed by recovering data from hard drives and learning how to use multiple tools to perform registry and system log analyses.

Next, you will be taught how to analyze browsers and e-mails as they are crucial aspects of investigations. We will then go on to extract data from a computer's memory and investigate network traffic, which is another important checkpoint. Lastly, you will learn a few ways in which you can present data, because every investigator needs a work station where they can analyze forensic data.

What this book covers

Chapter 1, *The Foundations and Principles of Digital Forensics*, explains the importance of the principles of the digital forensics process and the approaches that are usually used to conduct an analysis.

Chapter 2, *Incident Response and Live Analysis*, discusses the hardware and software that the responder should have to perform incident response properly. Incident response is a very important process that needs to be conducted carefully to properly collect all the available evidence, which will be analyzed in the analysis phase.

Chapter 3, *Volatile Data Collection*, discusses how to collect the volatile data of the system. Volatile data, such as system memory, is very important and can tell what is happening in the system in the running time. So, to conduct post mortem analysis on this kind of evidence, we need to acquire the evidence first. Also, it changes very quickly, and collecting it in the right way is a very important issue.

Chapter 4, *Nonvolatile Data Acquisition*, talks about the acquisition of nonvolatile data, such as the hard drive, and how to collect such data forensically in order to not change the integrity of this evidence.

Chapter 5, *Timeline*, discusses Timeline, which shows all the system and user activities on the system in chronological order. It helps building the whole picture of the incident. And we will show you how to do it with the plaso framework.

Chapter 6, *Filesytem Analysis and Data Recovery*, gives you a good understanding of the most famous file systems. To perfectly understand how the tools work, either for analysis or recovery, the reader needs to understand how the files are stored in the file system in the partitioned hard drive.

Chapter 7, *Registry Analysis*, discusses the structure of the registry and some tools used to perform analyses. When MS Windows operates, almost all actions are mapped in the registry. The registry files are considered the Windows database. Registry forensics can help answer a lot of issues, from what kind of application has been installed on the system to user activities, and many more.

Chapter 8, *Event Log Analysis*, explains that the MS Windows system has good features out of the box, we just need to know how to use them. One of these features is logging. Logging can help to figure out what has happened on the system. It logs all the events on the system including security events or other events related to the applications within the system.

Chapter 9, *Windows Files*, tell us that MS Windows has a lot of artifacts, which are created in the currently running Windows. During analysis, these artifacts can be used to prove or refute hypotheses, or in some cases uncover new interesting information with evidential value.

Chapter 10, *Browser and E-mail Investigation*, talks about the Internet, and the World Wide Web of course, is the main channel of information that users use to exchange data. Browsers are the most common tools that are used to do that. So, the investigation of browsers is important when analysts try to investigate user's activity. There are a lot of browsers and we will cover the most popular among them: IE, FF, and Chrome.

E-mail still remains a way to communicate with people in the computer world, especially in a corporate environment. This chapter will cover e-mail formats and explain how to read e-mails from PFF files for analysis and to trace senders.

Chapter 11, *Memory Forensics*, discusses how memory is the working space for the operating system. It the past, memory forensics was optional, but now there are a few very powerful tools that allow us to extract a lot of evidential information from the memory and take digital forensics to a new level.

Chapter 12, *Network Forensics*, discusses how network forensics provides another perspective to the incident. Network traffic can reveal a lot of information about the behavior of malicious activity. Together with other sources of information, networks will speed up the investigation process. You will also learn not only about the traditional tools, such as Wireshark, but also about the powerful Bro framework.

Appendix A, *Building a Forensic Analysis Environment*, discusses the creation of convenient work environment to conduct the digital forensics analysis in the digital forensics lab at an enterprise scale. After the previous chapters we should now have realized how important incident response is for digital forensics processes and how necessary it is to deal with both of them accurately.

Appendix B, *Case Study*, uses an infected machine to illustrate how to conduct primary analysis on different types of evidences and we will go through live analysis along with the post-mortem analysis.

What you need for this book

There are no special requirements for this book.

Who this book is for

If you have previous experience in information security or did some digital forensic analysis before and want to extend your skill set about digital forensics this is the perfect guide for you. This book will provide you with the knowledge and core skills necessary to use free and open source tools mostly under Linux operating system and undertake forensic analysis of digital evidence with them.

Conventions

In this book, you will find a number of text styles that distinguish between different kinds of information. Here are some examples of these styles and an explanation of their meaning.

Code words in text, database table names, folder names, filenames, file extensions, pathnames, dummy URLs, user input, and Twitter handles are shown as follows: "In the destination machine, which is the handler machine, you need to run the network listener from the same `receiver.exe` folder."

Any command-line input or output is written as follows:

```
dd conv=sync, noerror bs=64K if=/dev/sda | pv | dd
    of=/media/Elements/HD_image/image.dd
```

New terms and **important words** are shown in bold. Words that you see on the screen, for example, in menus or dialog boxes, appear in the text like this: "Now from the source machine, run the FTK Lite program, and then open **Create Disk image** from **File**."

Warnings or important notes appear in a box like this.

Tips and tricks appear like this.

Reader feedback

Feedback from our readers is always welcome. Let us know what you think about this book-what you liked or disliked. Reader feedback is important for us as it helps us develop titles that you will really get the most out of.

To send us general feedback, simply e-mail feedback@packtpub.com, and mention the book's title in the subject of your message.

If there is a topic that you have expertise in and you are interested in either writing or contributing to a book, see our author guide at www.packtpub.com/authors.

Customer support

Now that you are the proud owner of a Packt book, we have a number of things to help you to get the most from your purchase.

Downloading the color images of this book

We also provide you with a PDF file that has color images of the screenshots/diagrams used in this book. The color images will help you better understand the changes in the output. You can download this file from `http://www.packtpub.com/sites/default/files/downloads/PracticalWindowsForensics_ColorImages.pdf`.

Errata

Although we have taken every care to ensure the accuracy of our content, mistakes do happen. If you find a mistake in one of our books-maybe a mistake in the text or the code- we would be grateful if you could report this to us. By doing so, you can save other readers from frustration and help us improve subsequent versions of this book. If you find any errata, please report them by visiting `http://www.packtpub.com/submit-errata`, selecting your book, clicking on the **Errata Submission Form** link, and entering the details of your errata. Once your errata are verified, your submission will be accepted and the errata will be uploaded to our website or added to any list of existing errata under the Errata section of that title.

To view the previously submitted errata, go to `https://www.packtpub.com/books/content/support` and enter the name of the book in the search field. The required information will appear under the **Errata** section.

Piracy

Piracy of copyrighted material on the Internet is an ongoing problem across all media. At Packt, we take the protection of our copyright and licenses very seriously. If you come across any illegal copies of our works in any form on the Internet, please provide us with the location address or website name immediately so that we can pursue a remedy.

Please contact us at `copyright@packtpub.com` with a link to the suspected pirated material.

We appreciate your help in protecting our authors and our ability to bring you valuable content.

Questions

If you have a problem with any aspect of this book, you can contact us at `questions@packtpub.com`, and we will do our best to address the problem.

1
The Foundations and Principles of Digital Forensics

Everything around us is changing, the way that we communicate, how we do our work, how we store or retrieve data, and even the rate of life is changing. Technology is changing everything. Crime has its share of the change because the nature of targeted valuable assets has changed, it is digital now. The normal users can now perform monetary transactions without leaving their chair, and corporations and businesses of different sizes and types usually exchange their sensitive data using their local network. So in return, instead of breaking into banks or companies, crime has also gone digital. Nowadays, your personal information, bank account details, and your corporate database are some of the targets for digital criminals.

So, how can we investigate these crimes? The investigation concepts haven't changed. This is what we will look at in this introductory chapter.

In this chapter, we will cover the following topics:

- What is digital crime?
- Digital evidence
- Digital forensics goals
- Analysis approaches

What is digital crime?

Let's suppose that a criminal breaks into a bank to steal the money in the safe, and in another case an attacker somehow hacked into the bank's private network and transferred money to his account. Both of these are targeting the monetary assets of the company.

In the first case, if an investigator needs to track a criminal, they would apply their investigation skills to the crime scene. They would track the attacker's fingerprints and activities to finally get a clear idea about what happened and identify the criminal. In the second scenario, the investigator needs to track the criminal's digital traces on the local system, the network, and even through the Internet in order to understand the criminal's activities, and this may uncover their digital identity.

In an ordinary crime, the investigator needs to find the crime's motivation and target. In cybercrime, the investigator needs to know the malicious code—the weapon—that the attacker used in conducting their crime, the vulnerability exploited to compromise the digital system, and the size of the damage. In the same way, we can apply the same investigation mechanisms to digital crime after taking into consideration the different nature of assets and attacks.

There are various targets of digital crime. These start from harassment to stealing credit cards and money online, to espionage between countries or big companies; as we recently saw there were some famous and aggressive malware programs and attacks that were thought to be developed with nation-level support against other nations, targeting some infrastructure or sensitive information. Also, these attacks that were targeted at some famous companies in different fields led to information and data leakage.

For these reasons, investing in securing the assets in their digital form has gained great importance in the last decade in both governmental and private sectors. One branch of the information security process is **digital forensics**.

Digital forensics

Identifying and analyzing information security incidents and the related digital evidence is called **digital forensics**. Generally, forensic science is the scientific method of gathering and examining data about the past to extract useful information related to the case under investigation. Digital forensics is the analysis of digital evidence in order to answer questions related to a digital incident, which takes place at the time of the analysis in case of a live analysis or takes place in the past; this is called **postmortem analysis**.

Postmortem analysis is applied after the incident has occurred, and it usually takes place in all cases. However, some cases require the analysis to be conducted during the incident. Generally, the analysis can confirm or refute a hypothesis about the incident to rebuild a full picture about the activities of both the attacker and the victim during the time of the incident.

One of the definitions of digital forensics is Rodney McKemmish's, which stated the following:

> *"Forensic Computing is the process of identifying, preserving, analyzing, and presenting digital evidence in a manner that is legally acceptable."*

From this, we can divide the digital forensics analysis into four subphases, which also represent the four principles of a successful process:

- **Identification**: The investigator or the analyst must understand the circumstances of the incident and collect the data that is important to the investigation. They need to understand the usual behavior of the systems and the structure of the network, and they need to interview responsible individuals if needed. These are important to totally understand the environment and handle the possible evidence properly so that they do not lose valuable information or miss collecting related evidence.

    During incident handling, the first responder may need to acquire a live system. Each acquisition or analysis step performed on a live system will leave a trace, and in some cases, this overwrites previous data or traces either in the system memory or on the hard drive. The responder must understand the consequences of using the handling tools on the system and try to minimize their tools' traces on the system in order to minimize data loss during incident handling.

- **Acquisition and preservation**: The acquisition methods of digital evidence must ensure integrity preservation of the evidence and justify this when needed.

    Acquiring all the data from the incident scene will help in the analysis phase to build a whole picture of the incident. In a busy working environment, retrieving the status of the incident scene won't be easy. One way to memorize this is to take notes about all the systems in the scene, and in some cases, taking snapshots will be beneficial to remembering how these devices were connected.

- **Analysis**: Different platforms and technologies mean different types of evidence, which need to be examined. Therefore, the analyst or the investigator needs to have the required technical and investigation skills to find and extract the related information to the case under investigation.

  The analyst needs to examine all the data collected even if the case has been solved. Examining all the evidence could provide new clues or state new possibilities.

- **Reporting and presentation of the digital evidence**: This should summarize the first three phases of the process. It should include the steps taken in order to identify, seize, and examine the digital evidence. Besides including the findings of the examination, the conclusion of the findings and the expert opinion must be included in the report.

Digital evidence

As a normal reaction, the change in technology led to a change of possible evidence, as compared to previous traditional evidence. All the components of the computer system could be evidence, such as the following:

- The hard drive of the criminal or the victim
- The operating system artifacts and special files
- The network traffic
- The computer memory
- Mobile phones and tablets
- Cloud storage
- Shared storage
- Network devices
- The systems' logs
- The devices' logs
- GPS devices
- Simply, any device that can store or process data

Due to the wide range of possible evidence, the incident handler or first responder who will handle and process the available devices in the incident scene must have sufficient experience in dealing with whatever types of evidence they may find at the scene.

Handling digital devices is a very significant task, which the whole investigation process relies on. This is considered to be one of the main principal needs that have to be fulfilled in order to conduct successful digital analysis.

Digital forensic goals

The main object in the digital forensic analysis is the digital device related to the security incident under investigation. The digital device was either used to commit a crime, to target an attack, or is a source of information for the analyst. The goals of the analysis phase in the digital forensics process differ from one case to another. It can be used to support or refute assumptions against individuals or entities, or it can be used to investigate information security incidents locally on the system or over a network.

Consider analyzing a compromised system, the goals of the digital forensics, as a whole, are to answer these questions:

- What happened to the system under analysis?
- How was it compromised?

During the analysis too, the analyst could answer some other questions based on their findings, such as the following:

- *Who is the attacker?* This asks whether the analyst could find the attacker IP and/or an IP of the command and control server or in some cases the attacker profile.
- *When did it happen?* This asks whether the analyst could ascertain the time of the infection or compromise.
- *Where did it happen?* This asks whether the analyst could identify the compromised systems in the network and the possibility of other victims.
- *Why did it happen?* This is based on the attacker's activities in the hacked system, the analyst can form an idea of the attacker's motivation, either financial, espionage, or other.

Analysis approaches

During incident handling, each case can be considered as a different scenario. Therefore, different approaches can take place during the first response, based on the circumstances of the individual case. There are two general approaches that can be used to deal with a security incident:

- **Live analysis**: This is usually performed when the analyst has a live system in hand. Shutting the system down is one of the "don'ts" that the responder shouldn't do. Performing some primary analysis of the live system can provide valuable information that can guide the analyst in the future investigation. Also, in some situations, a quick analysis of the incident is highly required when there is no time to go through the normal steps of the analysis.
- **Postmortem analysis**: This is the normal steps of the process, where the responder acquires all the available data from the incident scene, and then conducts postmortem analysis on the evidence.

Mainly, the hybrid approach is considered the best, where the responder conducts the live analysis on the powered on and accessible systems, records their findings, and acquires all the data, including the live ones, for postmortem analysis. Combining both results from live and postmortem analysis can clearly explain the status of the system under investigation. Performing the acquisition first in such a case is the best practice as the evidence will be acquired before any analysis traces are in the system.

Summary

In this introductory chapter, we discussed some definitions that are related to digital forensic science, its goals, and its analysis approaches.

In the next chapter, the live and postmortem analysis approaches will be explained in details with the tools that are recommended for each approach.

2
Incident Response and Live Analysis

The stages of preparation to respond to an incident are a matter which much attention should be paid to. In some cases, the lack of necessary tools during the incident leads to the inability to perform the necessary actions at the right time.

Taking into account that the reaction time of an incident depends on the efficiency of the incident handling process, it becomes clear that in order to prepare the IR team, its technical support should be very careful.

The whole set of requirements can be divided into several categories for the IR team:

- Skills
- Hardware
- Software

Let's consider the main issues that may arise during the preparation of the incident response team in more detail.

If we want to build a computer security incident response team, we need people with a certain set of skills and technical expertise to perform technical tasks and effectively communicate with other external contacts. Now, we will consider the skills of members of the team.

The set of skills that members of the team need to have can be divided into two groups:

- Personal skills
- Technical skills

Personal skills

Personal skills are very important for a successful response team. This is because the interaction with team members who are technical experts but have poor social skills can lead to misunderstanding and misinterpretation of the results, the consequences of which may affect the team's reputation.

A list of key personal skills will be discussed in the following sections.

Written communication

For many IR teams, a large part of their communication occurs through written documents. These communications can take many forms, including e-mails concerning incidents documentation of event or incident reports, vulnerabilities, and other technical information notifications. Incident response team members must be able to write clearly and concisely, describe activities accurately, and provide information that is easy for their readers to understand.

Oral communication

The ability to communicate effectively though spoken communication is also an important skill to ensure that the incident response team members say the right words to the right people.

Presentation skills

Not all technical experts have good presentation skills. They may not be comfortable in front of a large audience. Gaining confidence in presentation skills will take time and effort for the team's members to become more experienced and comfortable in such situations.

Diplomacy

The members of the incident response team interact with people who may have a variety of goals and needs. Skilled incident response team members will be able to anticipate potential points of contention, be able to respond appropriately, maintain good relationships, and avoid offending others. They also will understand that they are representing the IR team and their organization.

Diplomacy and tact are very important.

The ability to follow policies and procedures

Another important skill that members of the team need is the ability to follow and support the established policies and procedures of the organization or team.

Team skills

IR staff must be able to work in the team environment as productive and cordial team players. They need to be aware of their responsibilities, contribute to the goals of the team, and work together to share information, workload, and experiences. They must be flexible and willing to adapt to change. They also need skills to interact with other parties.

Integrity

The nature of IR work means that team members often deal with information that is sensitive and, occasionally, they might have access to information that is newsworthy. The team's members must be trustworthy, discrete, and able to handle information in confidence according to the guidelines, any constituency agreements or regulations, and/or any organizational policies and procedures.

In their efforts to provide technical explanations or responses, the IR staff must be careful to provide appropriate and accurate information while avoiding the dissemination of any confidential information that could detrimentally affect another organization's reputation, result in the loss of the IR team's integrity, or affect other activities that involve other parties.

Knowing one's limits

Another important ability that the IR team's members must have is the ability to be able to readily admit when they have reached the limit of their own knowledge or expertise in a given area. However difficult it is to admit a limitation, individuals must recognize their limitations and actively seek support from their team members, other experts, or their management.

Coping with stress

The IR team's members often could be in stressful situations. They need to be able to recognize when they are becoming stressed, be willing to make their fellow team members aware of the situation, and take (or seek help with) the necessary steps to control and maintain their composure. In particular, they need the ability to remain calm in tense situations—ranging from an excessive workload to an aggressive caller to an incident where human life or a critical infrastructure may be at risk. The team's reputation, and the individual's personal reputation, will be enhanced or will suffer depending on how such situations are handled.

Problem solving

IR team members are confronted with data every day, and sometimes, the volume of information is large. Without good problem-solving skills, staff members could become overwhelmed with the volumes of data that are related to incidents and other tasks that need to be handled. Problem-solving skills also include the ability for the IR team's members to "think outside the box" or look at issues from multiple perspectives to identify relevant information or data.

Time management

Along with problem-solving skills, it is also important for the IR team's members to be able to manage their time effectively. They will be confronted with a multitude of tasks ranging from analyzing, coordinating, and responding to incidents, to performing duties, such as prioritizing their workload, attending and/or preparing for meetings, completing time sheets, collecting statistics, conducting research, giving briefings and presentations, traveling to conferences, and possibly providing on-site technical support.

Technical skills

Another important component of the skills needed for an IR team to be effective is the technical skills of their staff. These skills, which define the depth and breadth of understanding of the technologies that are used by the team, and the constituency it serves, are outlined in the following sections.

In turn, the technical skills, which the IR team members should have, can be divided into two groups: **security fundamentals** and **incident handling skills**.

Security fundamentals

Let's look at some of the security fundamentals in the following subsections.

Security principles

The IR team's membersneed to have a general understanding of the basic security principles, such as the following:

- Confidentiality
- Availability
- Authentication
- Integrity
- Access control
- Privacy
- Nonrepudiation

Security vulnerabilities and weaknesses

To understand how any specific attack is manifested in a given software or hardware technology, the IR team's members need to be able to first understand the fundamental causes of vulnerabilities through which most attacks are exploited. They need to be able to recognize and categorize the most common types of vulnerabilities and associated attacks, such as those that might involve the following:

- Physical security issues
- Protocol design flaws (for example, man-in-the-middle attacks or spoofing)

- Malicious code (for example, viruses, worms, or Trojan horses)
- Implementation flaws (for example, buffer overflow or timing windows/race conditions)
- Configuration weaknesses
- User errors or indifference

The Internet

It is important that the IR team's members also understand the Internet. Without this fundamental background information, they will struggle or fail to understand other technical issues, such as the lack of security in underlying protocols and services that are used on the Internet or to anticipate the threats that might occur in the future.

Risks

The IR team's members need to have a basic understanding of computer security risk analysis. They should understand the effects on their constituency of various types of risks (such as potentially widespread Internet attacks, national security issues as they relate to their team and constituency, physical threats, financial threats, loss of business, reputation, or customer confidence, and damage or loss of data).

Network protocols

Members of the IR team need to have a basic understanding of the common (or core) network protocols that are used by the team and the constituency that they serve. For each protocol, they should have a basic understanding of the protocol, its specifications, and how it is used. In addition to this, they should understand the common types of threats or attacks against the protocol, as well as strategies to mitigate or eliminate such attacks.

For example, at a minimum, the staff should be familiar with protocols, such as IP, TCP, UDP, ICMP, ARP, and RARP. They should understand how these protocols work, what they are used for, the differences between them, some of the common weaknesses, and so on. In addition to this, the staff should have a similar understanding of protocols, such as TFTP, FTP, HTTP, HTTPS, SNMP, SMTP, and any other protocols.

The specialist skills include a more in-depth understanding of security concepts and principles in all the preceding areas in addition to expert knowledge in the mechanisms and technologies that lead to flaws in these protocols, the weaknesses that can be exploited (and why), the types of exploitation methods that would likely be used, and the strategies to mitigate or eliminate these potential problems. They should have expert understanding of additional protocols or Internet technologies (DNSSEC, IPv6, IPSEC, and other telecommunication standards that might be implemented or interface with their constituent's networks, such as ATM, BGP, broadband, voice over IP, wireless technology, other routing protocols, or new emerging technologies, and so on). They could then provide expert technical guidance to other members of the team or constituency.

Network applications and services

The IR team's staff need a basic understanding of the common network applications and services that the team and the constituency use (DNS, NFS, SSH, and so on). For each application or service they should understand the purpose of the application or service, how it works, its common usages, secure configurations, and the common types of threats or attacks against the application or service, as well as mitigation strategies.

Network security issues

The members of the IR team should have a basic understanding of the concepts of network security and be able to recognize vulnerable points in network configurations. They should understand the concepts and basic perimeter security of network firewalls (design, packet filtering, proxy systems, DMZ, bastion hosts, and so on), router security, the potential for information disclosure of data traveling across the network (for example, packet monitoring or "sniffers"), or threats that are related to accepting untrustworthy information.

Host or system security issues

In addition to understanding security issues at a network level, the IR team's members need to understand security issues at a host level for the various types of operating systems (UNIX, Windows, or any other operating systems that are used by the team or constituency). Before understanding the security aspects, the IR team's member must first have the following:

- Experience using the operating system (user security issues)

- Some familiarity with managing and maintaining the operating system (as an administrator)

Then, for each operating system, the IR team member needs to know how to perform the following:

- Configure (harden) the system securely
- Review configuration files for security weaknesses
- Identify common attack methods
- Determine whether a compromise attempt occurred
- Determine whether an attempted system compromise was successful
- Review log files for anomalies
- Analyze the results of attacks
- Manage system privileges
- Secure network daemons
- Recover from a compromise

Malicious code

The IR team's members must understand the different types of malicious code attacks that occur and how these can affect their constituency (system compromises, denial of service, loss of data integrity, and so on). Malicious code can have different types of payloads that can cause a denial of service attack or web defacement, or the code can contain more "dynamic" payloads that can be configured to result in multifaceted attack vectors. Staff should understand not only how malicious code is propagated through some of the obvious methods (disks, e-mail, programs, and so on), but they should also understand how it can propagate through other means, such as PostScript, Word macros, MIME, peer-to-peer file sharing, or boot-sector viruses that affect operating systems running on PC and Macintosh platforms. The IR team's staff must be aware of how such attacks occur and are propagated, the risks and damage associated with such attacks, prevention and mitigation strategies, detection and removal processes, and recovery techniques.

Specialist skills include expertise in performing analysis, black box testing, reverse engineering malicious code that is associated with such attacks, and in providing advice to the team on the best approaches for an effective response.

Programming skills

Some team members need to have system and network programming experience. The team should ensure that a range of programming languages is covered on the operating systems that the team and the constituency use. For example, the team should have experience in the following:

- C
- Python
- Awk
- Java
- Shell (all variations)
- Other scripting tools

These scripts or programming tools can be used to assist in the analysis and handling of incident information (for example, writing different scripts to count and sort through various logs, search databases, look up information, extract information from logs or files, and collect and merge data).

Incident handling skills

- Local team policies and protocols
- Understanding and identifying intruder techniques
- Communication with sites
- Incident analysis
- Maintenance of incident records

The hardware for IR and Jump Bag

Certainly, a set of equipment that may be required during the processing of the incident should be prepared in advance, and this matter should be given much attention. This set is called the **Jump Bag**.

The formation of such a kit is largely due to the budget the organization could afford. Nevertheless, there is a certain necessary minimum, which will allow the team to handle incidents in small quantities.

If the budget allows it, it is possible to buy a turnkey solution, which includes all the necessary equipment and the case for its transportation. As an instance of such a solution, FREDL + Ultra Kit could be recommended. **FREDL** is short for **Forensic Recovery of Evidence Device Laptop**. With Ultra Kit, this solution will cost about 5000 USD.

Ultra Kit contains a set of write-blockers and a set of adapters and connecters to obtain images of hard drives with a different interface:

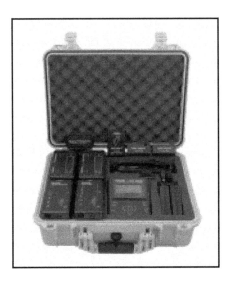

 More details can be found on the manufacturer's website at https://www.digitalintelligence.com/products/ultrakit/.

Certainly, if we ignore the main drawback of such a solution, this decision has a lot of advantages as compared to the cost. Besides this, you get a complete starter kit to handle the incident. Besides, Ultra Kit allows you to safely transport equipment without fear of damage.

 The FRED-L laptop is based on a modern hardware, and the specifications are constantly updated to meet modern requirements. Current specifications can be found on the manufacturer's website at http://www.digitalintelligence.com/products/fredl/.

However, if you want to replace the expensive solution, you could build a cheaper alternative that will save 20-30% of the budget. It is possible to buy the components included in the review of decisions separately.

As a workstation, you can choose a laptop with the following specifications:

- Intel Core i7-6700K Skylake Quad Core Processor, 4.0 GHz, 8MB Intel Smart Cache
- 16 GB PC4-17000 DDR4 2133 Memory
- 256 GB Solid State Internal SATA Drive
- Intel Z170 Express Chipset
- NVIDIA GeForce GTX 970M with 6 GB GDDR5 VRAM

This specification will provide a comfortable workstation to work on the road.

As a case study for the transport of the equipment, we recommend paying attention to Pelican (http://www.pelican.com) cases. In this case, the manufacturer can choose the equipment to meet your needs.

One of the typical tasks in handling of incidents is obtaining images from hard drives. For this task, you can use a duplicator or a bunch of write-blockers and computer.

Duplicators are certainly a more convenient solution; their usage allows you to quickly get the disk image without using additional software. Their main drawback is the price. However, if you often have to extract the image of hard drives and you have a few thousand dollars, the purchase of the duplicator is a good investment.

If the imaging of hard drives is a relatively rare problem and you have a limited budget, you can purchase a write blocker which will cost 300-500 USD. However, it is necessary to use a computer and software, which we will discuss in later chapters.

To pick up the necessary equipment, you can visit http://www.insectraforensics.com, where you can find equipment from different manufacturers.

Also, do not forget about the hard drives themselves. It is worth buying a few hard drives with large volumes for the possibility of good performance.

To summarize, responders need to include the following items in a basic set:

- Several network cables (straight through or loopback)
- A serial cable with a serial USB adapter
- Network serial adapters
- Hard drives (various sizes)
- Flash drives
- A Linux Live DVD
- A portable drive duplicator with a write-blocker
- Various drive interface adapters
- A four port hub
- A digital camera
- Cable ties
- Cable snips
- Assorted screws and hex drivers
- Notebooks and pens
- Chain of Custody forms
- Incident handling procedure

Software

After talking about the hardware, we did not forget about the software that you should always have on hand. The variety of software that can be used in the processing of the incident allows you to select software-based preferences, skills, and budget. Some prefer command-line utilities, and some find that GUI is more convenient to use.

Sometimes, the use of certain tools is dictated by the circumstances under which it's needed to work.

Some utilities will be discussed in further sections and later chapters. However, we strongly recommend that you prepare these in advance and thoroughly test the entire set of required software.

Live versus mortem

The initial reaction to an incident is a very important step in the process of computer incident management. The correct method of carrying out and performing this step depends on the success of the investigation.

Moreover, a correct and timely response is needed to reduce the damage caused by the incident.

The traditional approach to the analysis of the disks is not always practical, and in some cases, it is simply not possible.

In today's world, the development of computer technology has led to many companies having a distribution network in many cities, countries, and continents. Wish this physical disconnection of the computer from the network, following the traditional investigation of each computer is not possible.

In such cases, the incident responder should be able to carry out a prior assessment remotely and as soon as possible, view a list of running processes, open network connections, open files, and get a list of registered users in the system. Then, if necessary, carry out a full investigation.

In this chapter, we will look at some approaches that the responder may apply in a given situation. However, even in these cases when we have physical access to the machine, live response is the only way of incident response.

For example, cases where we are dealing with large disk arrays. In this case, there are several problems at once. The first problem is that the space to store large amounts of data is also difficult to identify. In addition to this, the time that may be required to analyze large amounts of data is unreasonably high.

Typically, such large volumes of data have a highly loaded server serving hundreds of thousands of users, so their trip, or even a reboot, is not acceptable for business.

Another scenario that requires the Live Forensics approach is when an encrypted filesystem is used. In cases where the analyst doesn't have the key to decrypt the disc, Live Forensics is a good alternative to obtain data from a system where encryption of the filesystem is used.

This is not an exhaustive list of cases when the Live Analysis could be applicable.

It is worth noting one very important point. During the Live Analysis, it is not possible to avoid changes in the system.

Connecting external USB devices or network connectivity, user log on, or launching an executable file will be modified in the system in a variety of log files, registry keys, and so on. Therefore, you need to understand what changes were caused by the actions of responders and document them.

Volatile data

Under the principle of "order of Volatility", you must first collect information that is classified as Volatile Data (the list of network connections, the list of running processes, log on sessions, and so on), which will be irretrievably lost in case the computer is powered off.

Then, you can start to collect nonvolatile data, which can also be obtained with the traditional approach in the analysis of the disk image. The main difference in this case is that a Live Forensics set of data is easier to obtain with a working machine.

The process of obtaining a memory dump and a disk image as well as their analysis is described in detail in other chapters. This chapter will focus on the collection of Volatile data.

Typically, this category includes the following data:

- System uptime and the current time
- Network parameters (NetBIOS name cache, active connections, the routing table, and so on).
- NIC configuration settings

- Logged on users and active sessions
- Loaded drivers
- Running services
- Running processes and their related parameters (loaded DLLs, open handles, and ownership)
- Autostart modules
- Shared drives and files opened remotely

Recording the time and date of the data collection allows you to define a time interval in which the investigator will perform an analysis of the system:

```
(date / t) & (time / t)>%COMPUTER_NAME% \ systime.txt
systeminfo | find "Boot Time" >>% COMPUTERNAME% \ systime.txt
```

The last command allows you to show how long the machine worked since the last reboot.

Using the %COMPUTERNAME% environment variable, we can set up separate directories for each machine in case we need to repeat the process of collecting information on different computers in a network.

In some cases, signs of compromise are clearly visible in the analysis of network activity. The next set of commands allows you to get this information:

```
nbtstat -c> %COMPUTERNAME%\NetNameCache.txt
netstat -a -n -o>%COMPUTERNAME%\NetStat.txt
netstat -rn>%COMPUTNAME%\NetRoute.txt
ipconfig / all>%COMPUTERNAME%\NIC.txt
promqry>%COMPUTERNAME%\NSniff.txt
```

The first command uses nbtstat.exe to obtain information from the cache of NetBIOS. You display the NetBIOS names in their corresponding IP address. The second and third commands use netstat.exe to record all of the active compounds, listening ports, and routing tables.

For information about network settings, the ipconfig.exe network interfaces command is used.

The last block command starts the Microsoft promqry utility, which allows you to define the network interfaces on the local machine, which operates in promiscuous mode. This mode is required for network sniffers, so the detection of the regime indicates that the computer can run software that listens to network traffic.

To enumerate all the logged on users on the computer, you can use the Sysinternals tools:

```
psloggedon -x>%COMPUTERNAME% \ LoggedUsers.tx:
logonsessions -p >> %COMPUTERNAME%\LoggedOnUsers.txt
```

The `PsLoggedOn.exe` command lists both types of users, those who are logged on to the computer locally, and those who logged on remotely over the network. Using the `-x` switch, you can get the time at which each user logged on.

With the `-p` key, `logonsessions` will display all of the processes that were started by the user during the session.

It should be noted that `logonsessions` must be run with administrator privileges.

To get a list of all drivers that are loaded into the system, you can use the WDK `drivers.exe` utility:

```
drivers.exe>%COMPUTERNAME%\drivers.txt
```

The next set of commands to obtain a list of running processes and related information is as follows:

```
tasklist / svc>%COMPUTERNAME% \ taskdserv.txt
psservice>%COMPUTERNAME% \ trasklst.txt
tasklist / v>%COMPUTERNAME% \ taskuserinfo.txt
pslist / t>%COMPUTERNAME%\tasktree.txt
listdlls>%COMPUTERNAME%\lstdlls.txt
handle -a>%COMPUTERNAME%\lsthandles.txt
```

The `tasklist.exe` utility that is made with the `/ svc` key enumerates the list of running processes and services in their context. While the previous command displays a list of running services, PsService receives information on services using the information in the registry and SCM database.

Services are a traditional way through which attackers can access a previously compromised system. Services can be configured to run automatically without user intervention, and they can be launched as part of another process, such as `svchost.exe`.

In addition to this, remote access can be provided through completely legitimate services, such as telnet or ftp. To associate users with their running processes, use the `tasklist / v` command key.

To enumerate a list of DLLs loaded in each process and the full path to the DLL, you can use `listsdlls.exe` from SysInternals.

Another `handle.exe` utility can be used to list all the handles, which are open processes. This handles registry keys, files, ports, mutexes, and so on.

Other utilities require run with administrator privileges. These tools can help identify malicious DLLs that were injected into the processes, as well as files, which have not been accessed by these processes.

The next group of commands allows you to get a list of programs that are configured to start automatically:

```
autorunsc.exe -a>%COMPUTERNAME% \ autoruns.txt
at>%COMPUTERNAME% \ at.txt
schtasks / query>%COMPUTERNAME% \ schtask.txt
```

The first command starts the SysInternals utility, autoruns, and displays a list of executables that run at system startup and when users log on. This utility allows you to detect malware that uses the popular and well-known methods for persistent installation into the system.

Two other commands (`at` and `schtasks`) display a list of commands that run in the schedule. To start the `at` command also requires administrator privileges.

To install backdoors mechanisms, services are often used, but services are constantly working in the system and, thus, can be easily detected during live response. Thus, create a backdoor that runs on a schedule to avoid detection. For example, an attacker could create a task that will run the malware just outside working hours.

To get a list of network share drives and disk files that are deleted, you can use the following two commands:

```
psfile>%COMPUTERNAME%\openfileremote.txt
net share>%COMPUTERNAME%\drives.txt
```

Nonvolatile data

After Volatile data has been collected, you can continue to collect Nonvolatile Data. This data can be obtained at the stage of analyzing the disk, but as we mentioned earlier, analysis of the disk is not possible in some cases.

This data includes the following:

- The list of installed software and updates
- User info
- Metadata about a filesystem's timestamps

Registry data

However, upon receipt of this data with the live running of the system, there are difficulties that are associated with the fact that many of these files cannot be copied in the usual way, as they are locked by the operating system. To do this, use one of the utilities. One such utility is the `RawCopy.exe` utility, which is authored by *Joakim Schicht*.

This is a console application that copies files off NTFS volumes using the low-level disk reading method.

The application has two mandatory parameters, target file and output path:

- `-param1`: This is the full path to the target file to extract; it also supports `IndexNumber` instead of file path
- `-param2`: This is a valid path to output directory

This tool will let you copy files that are usually not accessible because the system has locked them. For instance, the registry hives such as `SYSTEM` and `SAM`, files inside `SYSTEM VOLUME INFORMATION`, or any file on the volume.

This supports the input file specified either with the full file path or by its `$MFT` record number (index number).

Here's an example of copying the `SYSTEM` hive off a running system:

```
RawCopy.exe C:\WINDOWS\system32\config\SYSTEM   %COMPUTERNAME%\SYSTEM
```

Here's an example of extracting the `$MFT` by specifying its index number:

```
RawCopy.exe C:0   %COMPUTERNAME%\mft
```

Here's an example of extracting the `MFT` reference number `30224` and all attributes, including `$DATA`, and dumping it into `C:\tmp`:

```
RawCopy.exe C:30224 C:\tmp -AllAttr
```

To download RawCopy, go to `https://github.com/jschicht/RawCopy`.

Knowing what software is installed and what its updates are helps further the investigation because this shows possible ways to compromise a system through a vulnerability in the software. One of the first actions that the attacker makes is to attack during a system scan to detect active services and exploit the vulnerabilities in them.

Thus, services that were not patched can be utilized for remote system penetration.

One way to install a set of software and updates is to use the `systeminfo` utility:

```
systeminfo > %COMPUTERNAME%\sysinfo.txt.
```

Moreover, skilled attackers can themselves perform the same actions and install necessary updates in order to hide the traces of penetration into the system.

After identifying the vulnerable services and their successful exploits, the attacker creates an account for themselves in order to subsequently use legal ways to enter the system. Therefore, the analysis of data about users of the system reveals the following traces of the compromise:

- The `Recent` folder contents, including LNK files and jump lists
- LNK files in the `Office Recent` folder
- The `Network Recent` folder contents
- The entire `temp` folder
- The entire `Temporary Internet Files` folder
- The `PrivacyIE` folder
- The `Cookies` folder
- The `Java Cache` folder contents

Now, let's consider the preceding cases as follows:

1. Collecting the `Recent` folder is done as follows:

```
robocopy.exe  %RECENT% %COMPUTERNAME%\Recent /ZB
/copy:DAT /r:0 /ts /FP /np /E log:%COMPUTERNAME%\Recent
\log.txt
```

Here `%RECENT%` depends on the version of Windows.

- For Windows 5.x (Windows 2000, Windows XP, and Windows 2003), this is as follows:

```
%RECENT% = %systemdrive%\Documents and
Settings\%USERNAME%\Recent
```

- For Windows 6.x (Windows Vista and newer):

```
%RECENT% =%systemdrive%\Users\%USERNAME%\AppData\Roaming
\Microsoft\Windows\Recent
```

2. Collecting the `Office Recent` folder is done as follows:

```
robocopy.exe  %RECENT_OFFICE%
%COMPUTERNAME%\Recent_Office /ZB /copy:DAT /r:0 /ts /FP
/np /E log:%COMPUTERNAME%\Recent_Office\log.txt
```

- Here `%RECENT_OFFICE%` depends on the version of Windows.
- For Windows 5.x (Windows 2000, Windows XP, and Windows 2003), this is as follows:

```
%RECENT_OFFICE% = %systemdrive%\Documents and
Settings\%USERNAME%\Application Data\Microsoft\Office
\Recent
```

- For Windows 6.x (Windows Vista and newer), this is as follows:

```
%RECENT% =%systemdrive%\Users\%USERNAME%\AppData\Roaming
\Microsoft\Windows\Office\Recent
```

3. Collecting the `Network Shares Recent` folder is done as follows:

```
robocopy.exe   %NetShares% %COMPUTERNAME%\NetShares /ZB
/copy:DAT /r:0 /ts /FP /np /E
log:%COMPUTERNAME%\NetShares\log.txt
```

- Here `%NetShares%` depends on the version of Windows.
- For Windows 5.x (Windows 2000, Windows XP, and Windows 2003), this is as follows:

```
%NetShares% = %systemdrive%\Documents and
Settings\%USERNAME%\Nethood
```

- For Windows 6.x (Windows Vista and newer), this is as follows:

```
%NetShares % =''%systemdrive%\Users\%USERNAME%\AppData
\Roaming\Microsoft\Windows\Network Shortcuts''
```

4. Collecting the `Temporary` folder is done as follows:

```
robocopy.exe   %TEMP% %COMPUTERNAME%\TEMP /ZB /copy:DAT
/r:0 /ts /FP /np /E log:%COMPUTERNAME%\TEMP\log.txt
```

- Here `%TEMP%` depends on the version of Windows.

- For Windows 5.x (Windows 2000, Windows XP, and Windows 2003), this is as follows:

```
%TEMP% = %systemdrive%\Documents and Settings\%USERNAME%
\Local Settings\Temp
```

- For Windows 6.x (Windows Vista and newer), this is as follows:

```
%TEMP% =''%systemdrive%\Users\%USERNAME%\AppData
\Local\Temp ''
```

5. Collecting the `Temporary Internet Files` folder is done as follows:

```
robocopy.exe   %TEMP_INTERNET_FILES%
%COMPUTERNAME%\TEMP_INTERNET_FILES /ZB /copy:DAT /r:0
/ts /FP /np /E log:%COMPUTERNAME%\TEMP\log.txt
```

- Here `%TEMP_INTERNET_FILE%` depends on the version of Windows.

- For Windows 5.x (Windows 2000, Windows XP, and Windows 2003), this is as follows:

```
%TEMP_INTERNET_FILE% = ''%systemdrive%\Documents and
Settings\%USERNAME%\Local Settings\Temporary Internet
Files''
```

- For Windows 6.x (Windows Vista and newer), this is as follows:

```
%TEMP_INTERNET_FILE% =''%systemdrive%\Users\%USERNAME%\
AppData\Local\Microsoft\Windows\Temporary Internet
Files"
```

6. Collecting the `PrivacIE` folder is done as follows:

```
robocopy.exe  %PRIVACYIE % %COMPUTERNAME%\PrivacyIE /ZB
/copy:DAT /r:0 /ts /FP /np /E
log:%COMPUTERNAME%/PrivacyIE/log.txt
```

- Here `%PRIVACYIE%` depends on the version of Windows.
- For Windows 5.x (Windows 2000, Windows XP, and Windows 2003), this is as follows:

```
%PRIVACYIE% = ''%systemdrive%\Documents and
Settings\%USERNAME%\ PrivacIE''
```

- For Windows 6.x (Windows Vista and newer), this is as follows:

```
%PRIVACYIE% =''%systemdrive%\Users\%USERNAME%\
AppData\Roaming\Microsoft\Windows\PrivacIE "
```

7. Collecting the `Cookies` folder is done as follows:

```
robocopy.exe  %COOKIES% %COMPUTERNAME%\Cookies /ZB
/copy:DAT /r:0 /ts /FP /np /E log:%COMPUTERNAME%\Cookies
\.txt
```

- Here `%COOKIES%` depends on the version of Windows.
- For Windows 5.x (Windows 2000, Windows XP, and Windows 2003), this is as follows:

```
%COOKIES% = ''%systemdrive%\Documents and
Settings\%USERNAME%\Cookies''
```

- For Windows 6.x (Windows Vista and newer), this is as follows:

```
%COOKIES% =''%systemdrive%\Users\%USERNAME%\
AppData\Roaming\Microsoft\Windows\Cookies"
```

8. Collecting the `Java Cache` folder is done as follows:

```
robocopy.exe   %JAVACACHE%  %COMPUTERNAME%\JAVACACHE /ZB
/copy:DAT /r:0 /ts /FP /np /E
log:%COMPUTERNAME%\JAVACAHE\log.txt
```

- Here `%JAVACACHE%` depends on the version of Windows.
- For Windows 5.x (Windows 2000, Windows XP, and Windows 2003), this is as follows:

```
%JAVACACHE% = ''%systemdrive%\Documents and
Settings\%USERNAME%\Application Data\Sun\Java\Deployment
\cache''
```

- For Windows 6.x (Windows Vista and newer), this is as follows:

```
%JAVACACHE% =''%systemdrive%\Users\%USERNAME%\AppData
\LocalLow\Sun\Java\Deployment\cache"
```

Remote live response

However, as mentioned earlier, it is often necessary to carry out the collection of information remotely. On Windows systems, this is often done using the SysInternals PsExec utility. PsExec lets you execute commands on remote computers and does not require the installation of the system.

How the program works is a `psexec.exe` resource executable is another PsExecs executable. This file runs the Windows service on a particular target machine. Before executing the command, PsExec unpacks this hidden resource in the administrative sphere of the remote computer at `Admin$` (`C:\Windows`) file `Admin$\system32\psexecsvc.exe`.

After copying this, PsExec installs and runs the service using the API functions of the Windows management services. Then, after starting psexesvc, a data connection (input commands and getting results) between psexesvc and psexec is established. Upon completion of the work, psexec stops the service and removes it from the target computer.

If the remote collection of information is necessary, a working machine running UNIX OS can use the Winexe utility.

Winexe is a GNU/Linux-based application that allows users to execute commands remotely on WindowsNT/2000/XP/2003/Vista/7/8 systems. It installs a service on the remote system, executes the command, and uninstalls the service. Winexe allows execution of most of the Windows shell commands:

```
winexe -U [Domain/]User%Password //host command
```

To launch a Windows shell from inside your Linux system, use the following command:

```
winexe -U HOME/Administrator%Pass123 //192.168.0.1 "cmd.exe"
```

Summary

In this chapter, we discussed what we should have in the Jump Bag to handle a computer incident, and what kind of skills the members of the IR team require.

Also, we took a look at live response and collected Volatile and Nonvolatile information from a live system. We also discussed different tools to collect information. We also discussed when we should to use a live response approach as an alternative to traditional forensics.

In the following chapter, we will consider the issues related to Volatile data collection.

3
Volatile Data Collection

This chapter is dedicated to some issues that are related to the acquisition of data, which has changed very fast. Due to its nature, it reflects the state of the system at a certain time because the collection of data takes place on a live system.

The **Request for Comments RFC** 3227 document provides a list of digital evidence and the order in which it should be collected. The main principle that should guide this is that the most rapidly changing data should be collected first.

The list of evidence from RFC comprises the following:

- Registers and cache CPU
- Routing table, ARP cache, process table, kernel statistics, and memory
- Temporary filesystems
- Disk
- Remote logging and monitoring data that is relevant to the system's media
- Physical configuration and network topology
- Archival media

According to this list, the volatile data which should be collected first are memory and network related data.

Memory acquisition

For many years, the main technique for conducting digital forensics was analysis of hard disk images. Certainly, if a hard disk image is available, we have a good chance of getting a lot of data to resolve the incident. However, this approach has some disadvantages.

Modern hard drives have a huge size, or sometimes we have to deal with RAID arrays, so analysis of such large amounts of data will require a long time. Also, Full Disk Encryption technology could be implemented and without encryption keys it will be not possible to get access to the files on the disk. Moreover, analysis of hard disk content does not always give the whole picture of what was happened at a particular point in time. Also, today there is a lot of bodiless malware; in this case, malicious code is not presented in the filesystem as a file.

All these listed facts force a forensics specialist to seek new alternative ways to solve forensics tasks. So, researchers look at the RAM as an alternative source of information.

As well-known and modern PCs are built on the von Neumann architecture, any piece of code which is executed on the computer should appear somewhere in the memory. The memory could be a useful source of evidence. Another advantage of using memory is its small size. Despite the fact that nowadays a user's workstation has more and more RAM, it still has a far smaller size than modern hard drives. However, for a long time analysis of memory was not widely used. The process of memory analysis was just scanning dump memory to search some strings. This situation changed when tools such as Volatility Framework appeared.

So today, memory forensics is no longer optional but is a compulsory step for a professional investigation. However, before memory analysis, we should first get to the dump of the memory, and we should do it in the right way. Otherwise, even with powerful tools, such as Volatility, the analysis of memory will be unsuccessful.

There are a lot of tools which allow creating memory dumps for any operating system—MS Windows, Linux, or Mac OS X. Some of them are very simple, and all you need to do is just push the button. However, the professional should understand how it works and be ready to fix problems in case they happen.

Issues related to memory access

Now, let's discuss some of the issues that are related to memory access on MS Windows. In MS Windows, there is a `\Device\PhysicalMemory` kernel object, which presents direct access to the physical memory of the system. To get the contents of the memory, we should read this file. Before Windows Server 2003 SP2, a given file was accessible from the user's space. However, starting from this update and in all later versions of MS Windows, this object is accessible from kernel space only. User space applications can read this file, but to open and edit it, the kernel space code or driver is required. Moreover, any manipulation of this object is a dangerous operation. The device memory is part of the physical memory, which is mapped to other devices in the system. This is the area of memory for devices, such as graphics cards, mapped to this part of physical memory in such way that the operating system could send data to such devices. Some particular blocks of memory are reserved for these devices and data that is written to these addresses are sent to the device. Thus, the writing or the request for access to this area of memory that is reserved for the device is translated into a request, which is sent to a real device.

How the request will be handled by a device depends on the device. Also, it could cause the system to hang or crash and destroy evidence. So, the software and the hardware that are used to dump memory should exclude these areas of memory from the process. We suggest testing all tools before using them. Besides the problem just described, there are malware which could change the behavior of tools and change the result of memory dumps.

Although we have never faced such malware in real life, there are a few PoC written by some researchers which could prove this threat. So, if the process of memory acquisition fails, this could make the system crash and cause a loss of data as well.

Choosing a tool

To choose a tool we need to answer the following questions:

- What is the supported OS version?
- What is the supported hardware architecture (x32, x64)?
- What is the required privilege level?
- Where are the results stored?

Volatile Data Collection

Today, there are a lot free and commercial tools on the market that support all versions of MS Windows that we could use to dump memory:

Free tools	Commercial tools
DumpIt	F-Response
WinPMEM (rekall)	Guidance Winen
FTKImager	HBGary Fastdump PRO
BelkaSoft Live RAM Capturer	

We need to note that the commercial tools are not always better. Which tool we should use depends on the case of usage, experience, and qualification of responder, and on other factors.

Despite all the possible options, the principles that we suggest for you to follow are the same:

1. Minimize impact to the system.
2. Run the tool from a safe environment.
3. Store results outside the system.

We will divide all use cases into three groups with two approaches, hardware and software:

- Locally
- Remotely
- Post mortem

Each of them has their own advantages and disadvantages. For example, let's take a look at the hardware approach. In this case, administrator privileges are not required, but you should have local physical access to the PC under investigation. The given approach is based on **Direct Memory Access (DMA)** and some technologies, such as Fireware, Thunderbolt, ExpressCard, or PCI. The disadvantage of this approach is that you need to install some hardware and software into the system before you can use it. Also, this action requires a reboot of the system. So, doing this could destroy some evidence. Another disadvantage is the limitation of the 4 GB memory size, which we can dump using the FireWare technology. However, solutions based on PCI are rare and expensive.

As we mentioned earlier, there are a lot of variants of use cases. Therefore, it is impossible to observe every one of them in a single chapter.

The most simple and prevalent case is the local software approach. In this approach, we can use a number of utilities, and we will look at some of them now.

DumpIt

In cases where the system has no more than 4 GB of RAM, the DumpIt utility is a good choice. DumpIt has a very simple command-line interface, and it is easy to use even for an inexperienced person. To dump the whole system memory, you should copy it to some removable device with enough space to store the memory dump. Then, plug this device in to the system and run it from the drive. After running this, DumpIt will create a file that contains the memory dump of the system in the same path from where DumpIt was executed:

```
C:\Users\Alina\Desktop\DumpIt>C:\Users\Alina\Desktop\DumpIt\DumpIt.exe
   DumpIt - v1.3.2.20110401 - One click memory memory dumper
   Copyright (c) 2007 - 2011, Matthieu Suiche <http://www.msuiche.net>
   Copyright (c) 2010 - 2011, MoonSols <http://www.moonsols.com>

     Address space size:    1073741824 bytes (  1024 Mb)
     Free space size:      50747002880 bytes ( 48396 Mb)

     * Destination = \??\C:\Users\Alina\Desktop\DumpIt\WS-015-20140321-083858.raw

     --> Are you sure you want to continue? [y/n] y
     + Processing...
```

Unfortunately, the free version of DumpIt doesn't work correctly with memory more than 4 GB.

Volatile Data Collection

If you have 8 GB of memory or more, we suggest using Belkasoft Live RAM Capturer. This software also has a simple graphical interface. It works on both architectures: x32 and x64 bits:

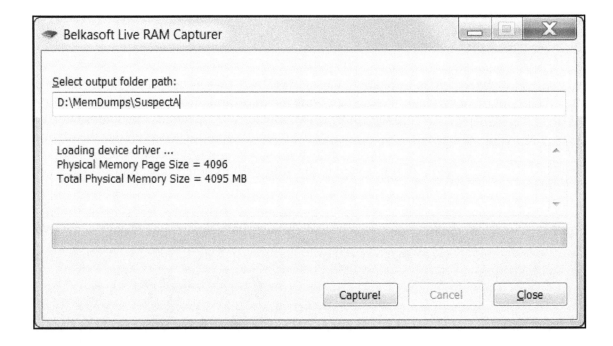

FTK Imager

One more popular utility for memory dump is FTK Imager. It is also free. There are two versions of it. We suggest using the FTK Imager Lite version. It does not require installation, has an easy-to-use interface, and has a lot of useful features:

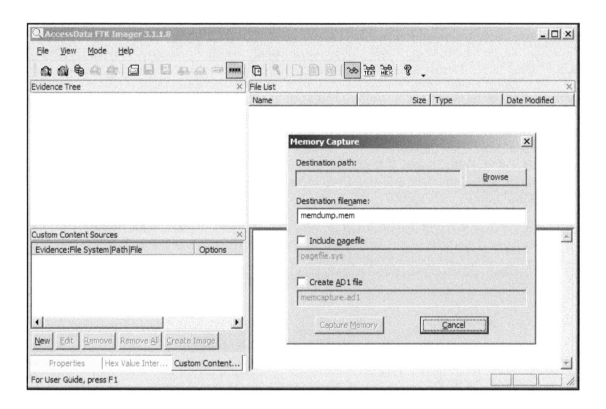

Acquiring memory from a remote computer using iSCSI

Another common scenario is the acquisition of memory from a remote computer. Consider the case when we need to dump memory from a remote Windows workstation using different operating systems including MS Windows, Mac OS X, and Linux. To do this, we can use the **iSCSI** protocol. Internet Small Computer System Interface protocol was developed in 1998 by IBM and CISCO. This protocol allows clients (named initiator) to send SCSI (CDBs) to SCSI storage devices (named target), which are located on remote servers.

Initiator is an iSCSI client and it works as an SCSI adapter except that it uses the IP network rather than physical bus. The iSCSI target is a server that provides a network interface to a storage device. Thus, we should install the iSCSI target on workstation of investigator where we will store the memory dump. There are a few free implementations of iSCSI for Microsoft and StarWind. Also, F-Response provides features to access a remote PC by iSCSI. Most operating systems have a free built-in initiator client software, including MS Windows 2000 SP4 and higher.

So, in our use case, we will use our own written iSCSI target software, **KFA** (**Kaspersky Forensics Agent**), and the `iscsiadm` utility as initiator on a Linux station.

To dump memory using Kaspersky Forensics Agent, run the utility on the target system with the `-mountphysmem` option:

To provide access with authorization, we can use the `chaplogin` and `chapsecret` options:

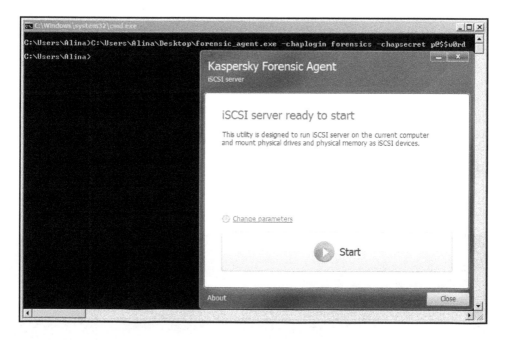

It is now possible to connect to the selected media using any iSCSI initiator:

1. Now, we test the connection:

   `sudo iscsiadm -m discovery -t st -p TargetAddress`

2. Having verified that the iSCSI connection is in working order, we establish a full connection:

   `sudo iscsiadm -m node --login`

3. Make sure that the memory is visible in the Ubuntu environment as a new device.
4. Now, you can dump it with the `dd` utility as usual.

Now, you have a memory dump, and you are ready to analyze it!

Using the Sleuth Kit

We want to discuss one more use case. It is possible that an investigator has only a hard disk image and no opportunity to dump memory from the system of interest. In this case, we still have the ability to receive some kind of system memory information. MS Windows saves the contents of memory in the `hiberfil.sys` file when the system goes to hibernate. So, if we have a disk image, we can extract `hiberfil.sys` from the disk.

To do this, we need to use the Sleuth Kit. Let's take a look at how we can do this:

1. To obtain information about partitions on the disk, use the following command:

    `mmls image`

    The output will be as follows:

```
forensics@forensics:~/evidences$ mmls image.dd
DOS Partition Table
Offset Sector: 0
Units are in 512-byte sectors

     Slot    Start        End          Length       Description
00:  Meta    0000000000   0000000000   0000000001   Primary Table (#0)
01:  -----   0000000000   0000002047   0000002048   Unallocated
02:  00:00   0000002048   0000206847   0000204800   NTFS (0x07)
03:  00:01   0000206848   0016775167   0016568320   NTFS (0x07)
04:  -----   0016775168   0016777215   0000002048   Unallocated
```

2. Then, use `fls` to list files on the root directory of the NTFS partition:

    `fls -o 2048 image.dd | grep hiberfil.sys`
    `r/r 32342-128-1: hiberfil.sys`

3. Finally, extract `hiberfil.sys`:

    `icat -o 2048 image.dd 32342 > hiberfil.sys`

Now, you can analyze `hiberfil.sys` with an analysis tool, such as Volatility.

Network-based data collection

Nowadays, it is difficult enough to find computers that don't have any network connections. This is almost impossible in the enterprise environment. Network connections reflect the interaction of computers with the outer world. Also, the network is the main source of threats. Today, the Internet is a very aggressive environment. Threats of various levels from spam to APT often penetrate computers via networks.

So, in almost every incident, computers have network activities that are related to the incident. There are a lot of examples of such events from receiving e-mails with malicious attachments and visits of a malicious URL. However, sometimes to have only host-based evidence to get a whole picture about an incident is not enough. In such cases, network-based evidence can help a lot.

Network forensics is a vast topic. We won't cover all the issues. In this chapter, we just want to look at this as an additional source of evidence. There is a lot of network-based evidence, but we will focus on network traffic acquisition.

Forensics investigators can capture the network traffic from physical media, such as cables or air and network devices, such as switches or hubs.

Now, we will give a short introduction to this topic to understand how we can collect network traffic.

Hubs

These are a simple network devices that allow connecting all devices from a local subnet. Hubs don't have any functionality beside the physical connection of all devices.

When such a device receives the network frame, it transfers packets on other ports. Thus, every device that is connected to the hub will receive all traffic that is dedicated for other devices. In the case of a hub-based network, it is simple enough to capture traffic from a given segment of a network. We should note that sometimes some manufactures designate some devices which are in reality switches as hubs.

The most reliable way to figure out what kind of device you are dealing with is to connect the station to the device, turn the network interface to promiscuous mode, and capture the traffic using the tcpdump utility or a similar utility. If you only have a broadcast and packets are dedicated to this station, this means that you have a **switch device**. If the traffic contains packets for other stations, you have a **hub**.

Investigators should be careful when they use hubs to capture traffic. In this case, investigators could see all traffic, but it could also be everybody from a local network. A compromised system could work as a passive sniffer and eavesdrop on all transferred data. Any investigator activities and data in the network could be intercepted. So, it's a good idea to use an already installed hub, but the installation of a new one to capture the network traffic will bring new risks.

Switches

Switches are the most prevalent network devices used to build local networks. They also serve as hubs serve to connect network devices into the network. However, unlike hubs, they use software to keep track of the stations connected to the ports of the switch. This information will be kept in the CAM table. When the switch receives a new packet, it will forward this packet only to a certain port according to the CAM table. So, each station receives only its traffic.

Investigators can often capture the network traffic on switch devices because most of them have the functionality of replicating traffic from one or a few ports to other ports for aggregation and analysis. Various vendors use different terms for this, the most widely used is **SPAN** (**Switched Port Analyzer**) or **RSPAN** (**Remote SPAN**). Sometimes, the term port mirroring is used. Also, switches have various hardware capacities. Port mirroring is limited by the physical capacity of a device. Consider this example, we have a 100 Mbps switch, and we want to mirror four ports to another one. With an average load of 50 Mbps for every port, the load for mirror ports will be 200 Mbps, which is far from the capacity of every port. Thus, some packets will be dropped in the process.

We should note that the approach with the SPAN port can change the collected traffic. However, there is one more method to capture the traffic. This is a network tap.

Network taps are placed between stations and switches and can look at and capture all traffic for this host. Network taps duplicate all traffic, including corrupted and any other packets. So, this approach is more suitable for forensics.

After we finally choose the method that we will use to capture the traffic, we need some software. A common solution for this is the `libpcap` library and software based on it, including `tcpdump`, Wireshark, and so on.

There are two main approaches to using such software to capture the traffic. They are filtering in capturing, and capturing all data and filtering it later.

In some cases, filtering during collection is a good idea if you have limited storage space to keep the traffic. From other side, libpcap has a very powerful filtering capability called **Berkley Packet Filter** (**BPF**). Using BPF filters, we can control what traffic we will capture and what we will drop. If you know exactly what you want to capture, this approach can save a lot of time and resources for you. BPF can filter traffic based on a comparison of fields in the protocols at second, third, and fourth levels. Also, the BPF language has some built-in primitives: `host id`, `dst host id`, `src host id`, `net id`, `dst net id`, `src net id`, `ether id`, `dst ether id`, `src ether id`, `port id`, `dst port id`, `src port id`, `gateway id`, `ip proto id`, `ether proto id`, `tcp`, `udp`, `icmp`, and `arp`. You could find more in manual documentation on `pcap-filter`.

Tcpdump

`tcpdump` is a tool to capture, filter, and analyze network traffic. The main purpose of this tool is to capture the traffic and print it out or store it in a file. `tcpdump` captures the traffic in bit-to-bit as it is transferred via media. We can use `tcpdump` to analyze traffic for troubleshooting in the network. In this case, you will use BPF to prefilter. However, usually this approach is a good fit for the initial triage only:

```
Archivo  Editar  Ver  Terminal  Ayuda
root@calipso:~# tcpdump -i eth0 host 74.125.47.103 -nnnnn
tcpdump: verbose output suppressed, use -v or -vv for full protocol decode
listening on eth0, link-type EN10MB (Ethernet), capture size 96 bytes
07:14:30.592075 IP 192.168.5.214 > 74.125.47.103: ICMP echo request, id 22795, seq 1, length 64
07:14:30.703180 IP 74.125.47.103 > 192.168.5.214: ICMP echo reply, id 22795, seq 1, length 64
07:14:31.593332 IP 192.168.5.214 > 74.125.47.103: ICMP echo request, id 22795, seq 2, length 64
07:14:31.705012 IP 74.125.47.103 > 192.168.5.214: ICMP echo reply, id 22795, seq 2, length 64
07:14:32.595115 IP 192.168.5.214 > 74.125.47.103: ICMP echo request, id 22795, seq 3, length 64
07:14:32.705317 IP 74.125.47.103 > 192.168.5.214: ICMP echo reply, id 22795, seq 3, length 64
07:14:33.596426 IP 192.168.5.214 > 74.125.47.103: ICMP echo request, id 22795, seq 4, length 64
07:14:33.708091 IP 74.125.47.103 > 192.168.5.214: ICMP echo reply, id 22795, seq 4, length 64
07:14:34.598190 IP 192.168.5.214 > 74.125.47.103: ICMP echo request, id 22795, seq 5, length 64
07:14:34.709148 IP 74.125.47.103 > 192.168.5.214: ICMP echo reply, id 22795, seq 5, length 64
07:14:35.599248 IP 192.168.5.214 > 74.125.47.103: ICMP echo request, id 22795, seq 6, length 64
07:14:35.709447 IP 74.125.47.103 > 192.168.5.214: ICMP echo reply, id 22795, seq 6, length 64
^C
12 packets captured
12 packets received by filter
0 packets dropped by kernel
```

In forensics practice, other approaches are more prevalent. Tcpdump is used to capture traffic during long periods of time and to store it in a file on disk with further analysis and correlation with other data.

Volatile Data Collection

The `tcpdump` is a high-fidelity tool, but the quality of captured traffic depends on resources available on the host where `tcpdump` is running. For instance, the performance of `tcpdump` will depend on the power of the CPU. The capturing of packets is a CPU-intensive activity, and if CPU is overloaded, `tcpdump` will fail and drop packets. In forensics cases, we want to capture all packets and this issue could be critical. In the case of high-loaded networks, the storage space for traffic is also an important question. As we mentioned earlier, you can use filtration of traffic and keep only useful information.

Despite the fact that filtration will save resources, such as CPU, disk space, and capacity, it should be implemented carefully because excessive filtration could cause a loss of evidence.

Wireshark

One more popular utility for capture and traffic analysis is Wireshark:

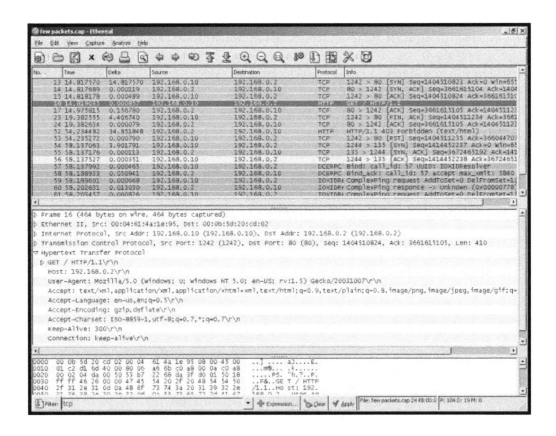

Wireshark is a tool with an easy to use graphical user interface. So it can be a good tool for beginners in network forensics. It also has a lot of features for filtration, decryption, and analysis of network traffic. Therefore, this makes Wireshark a must-have tool for any network investigator. Wireshark allows capturing traffic from any interface on the system if you have the necessary permissions, displaying it in real time, and storing it in a file on disk.

Moreover, there are a few useful command-line tools, which are distributed together with Wireshark.

Tshark

Tshark is the CLI version of Wireshark. It has almost the same functionality and works with the same file formats:

```
sansforensics@SIFT-Workstation:~$ tshark -r cap -R 'tcp port 80 and (((ip[2:2] - ((ip[0]&0xf)<<2)) - ((tcp[12]&0xf0)>>2)) != 0)' -R 'http.request.method == "GET" || http.request.method == "HEAD"'
  39    3.445956 192.168.1.112 -> 180.71.56.227 HTTP GET /install.asp?version=1.0.0.1&id=IE65&mac=000C29D1083C&iever=8 HTTP/1.0
  52    4.375852 192.168.1.112 -> 180.71.56.227 HTTP GET /update/IE65/IETab.ini HTTP/1.1
  61    4.406935 192.168.1.112 -> 180.71.56.227 HTTP GET /update/IE65/IEU1002.exe HTTP/1.1
 339    4.873198 192.168.1.112 -> 180.71.56.227 HTTP GET /ex.dat HTTP/1.1
 350    5.385375 192.168.1.112 -> 180.71.56.227 HTTP GET /exh.dat HTTP/1.1
 390   20.469865 192.168.1.112 -> 180.71.56.227 HTTP GET /update/IE65/IETab.ini HTTP/1.0
 400   26.218939 192.168.1.112 -> 180.71.56.227 HTTP GET /update/IE65/IETab.ini HTTP/1.1
 408   26.234793 192.168.1.112 -> 180.71.56.227 HTTP GET /ex.dat HTTP/1.1
 416   26.746695 192.168.1.112 -> 180.71.56.227 HTTP GET /exh.dat HTTP/1.1
 425   32.199564 192.168.1.107 -> 61.111.58.147 HTTP GET /connectiontest.html HTTP/1.1
 436   37.445997 192.168.1.112 -> 180.71.56.227 HTTP GET /update.asp?version=1.0.0.2&id=IE65&mac=000C29D1083C&oldversion=1.0.0.1&iever=8 HTTP/1.0
 447   92.207612 192.168.1.107 -> 61.111.58.147 HTTP GET /connectiontest.html HTTP/1.1
sansforensics@SIFT-Workstation:~$
```

Dumpcap

One more useful tool from the Wireshark kit is Dumpcap. It is dedicated to capturing network packets. Therefore, it is optimized for good performance in capture and will spend less system resources. If you plan to capture the traffic and analyze it with Wireshark, then the Dumpcap utility will be a good tool to capture the network traffic:

```
sansforensics@SIFT-Workstation:~$ tshark -r cap -R 'tcp port 80 and (((ip[2:2] - ((ip[0]&0xf)<<2)) - ((tcp[12]&0xf0)>>2)) != 0)' -R 'http.request.method == "GET" || http.request.method == "HEAD"'
 39    3.445956 192.168.1.112 -> 180.71.56.227 HTTP GET /install.asp?version=1.0.0.1&id=IE65&mac=000C29D1083C&iever=8 HTTP/1.0
 52    4.375852 192.168.1.112 -> 180.71.56.227 HTTP GET /update/IE65/IETab.ini HTTP/1.1
 61    4.406935 192.168.1.112 -> 180.71.56.227 HTTP GET /update/IE65/IEU1002.exe HTTP/1.1
339    4.873198 192.168.1.112 -> 180.71.56.227 HTTP GET /ex.dat HTTP/1.1
350    5.385375 192.168.1.112 -> 180.71.56.227 HTTP GET /exh.dat HTTP/1.1
390   20.469865 192.168.1.112 -> 180.71.56.227 HTTP GET /update/IE65/IETab.ini HTTP/1.0
400   26.218939 192.168.1.112 -> 180.71.56.227 HTTP GET /update/IE65/IETab.ini HTTP/1.1
408   26.234793 192.168.1.112 -> 180.71.56.227 HTTP GET /ex.dat HTTP/1.1
416   26.746695 192.168.1.112 -> 180.71.56.227 HTTP GET /exh.dat HTTP/1.1
425   32.199564 192.168.1.107 -> 61.111.58.147 HTTP GET /connectiontest.html HTTP/1.1
436   37.445997 192.168.1.112 -> 180.71.56.227 HTTP GET /update.asp?version=1.0.0.2&id=IE65&mac=000C29D1083C&oldversion=1.0.0.1&iever=8 HTTP/1.0
447   92.207612 192.168.1.107 -> 61.111.58.147 HTTP GET /connectiontest.html HTTP/1.1
sansforensics@SIFT-Workstation:~$
```

Summary

In this chapter, we covered issues that are related to volatile data collection. We discussed different tools and approaches to how to collect memory and network traffic.

In the next chapter, we will discuss issues that are related to non-volatile data collection. We will discuss how to duplicate hard drives and how to use standalone tools such as IR CD for this.

4
Nonvolatile Data Acquisition

In this chapter, we will discuss the acquisition of **Hard Disk Drives** or **HDD**. Data acquisition is critical because performing analysis on the original hard drive may cause failure on the only hard drive that contains the data or you may write to that original hard drive by mistake.

So, creating a forensics image from the hard drive must be performed prior to the analysis. The acquisition of the HDD can be either conducted at the incident scene or in the analysis lab, on a live or a powered off system, and over network or locally, as we will see in this chapter.

In a nutshell, we will cover the following topics:

- Forensic image
- Incident response CDs
- Live imaging of a hard drive
- Linux for the imaging of a hard drive
- Virtualization in data acquisition
- Evidence integrity
- Disk wiping in Linux

Forensic image

Imaging of a hard drive is the process of creating an exact forensic image of the victim or the suspect hard drive in order to conduct the analysis on the imaged hard drive instead of the original one. To create an exact copy of the hard drive, there are two options that can be followed:

- **Duplication**: This is where the destination of this process is the whole hard drive. In some references, this step can be addressed as cloning when the destination hard drive has the same brand, model, and size of the source hard drive. Duplication can be conducted using what are called **forensic hardware duplicators**. These are hardware devices, which basically have two interfaces for the source and the destination hard drives. Once they start operating, they will just copy blocks of data from the source to the destination regardless of the structure of the filesystem that is used in the source hard drive.

   > Usually, hardware duplication is faster than other software tools as it operates in wire speed. Some duplicators have special capabilities, such as performing some search operations during acquisition, or they can create up to eight duplicates in the same period of time. Duplication can also be performed with software tools, such as dd if the destination of the tool is a complete hard drive, not a file. This will be discussed later in this chapter.

- **Imaging**: This is where the destination of the hard drive is a container file or image file. This image may have different formats, which will also be discussed later in this chapter.

In the following section, some techniques and tools—which include both software duplication and imaging—will be illustrated.

Incident Response CDs

Due to the needed speed in the **Incident Response** (**IR**) process, the usage of incident response CDs can save precious time. IR CDs usually are Linux distributions. These distributions contain many incident response and digital forensic tools, which aim to boot mainly from the target system to acquire different types of possible evidence without the need to disconnect the hard drive.

This is designed to leave the least traces on the target system, so it boots with write protection enabled by default to all the connected hard drives. This gives the user the ability to grant the write access to the destination hard drive only. It is better to not connect to the destination hard drive until the system boots from the incident response CD. Of course, booting from the IR CD means that the system under investigation is down, and you will start the machine and boot from the CD. No running system memory is available in this case.

IR CDs also have the ability to acquire the memory and the hard drive of a live system. You need to insert the CD and run the imaging program to acquire the memory and the hard drive.

In the following sections, we will discuss some examples of the available IR CDs.

DEFT

Digital Evidence and Forensics Toolkit (DEFT) contains many acquisition and analysis tools that can be used in the on-scene analysis approach when the investigator boots the machine from it:

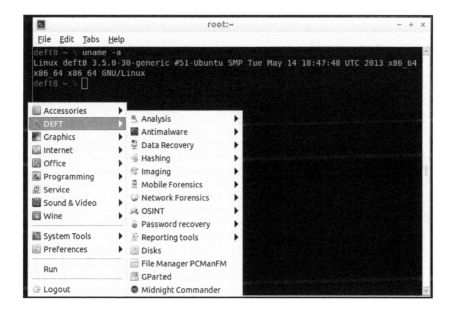

A booted DEFT CD

Nonvolatile Data Acquisition

DEFT also comes with **Digital Advanced Response Toolkit (DART)**. DART can run in the Windows live system, and it has a good and different collection of tools in each part of the incident response steps. Using DART you can perform the following actions:

- Acquire the Windows memory and hard drive
- Perform live data recovery when needed
- Conduct some forensics analysis on some Windows artifacts
- Collect information about the running system
- Monitor the system networking

You can view the DART interface in the following screenshot:

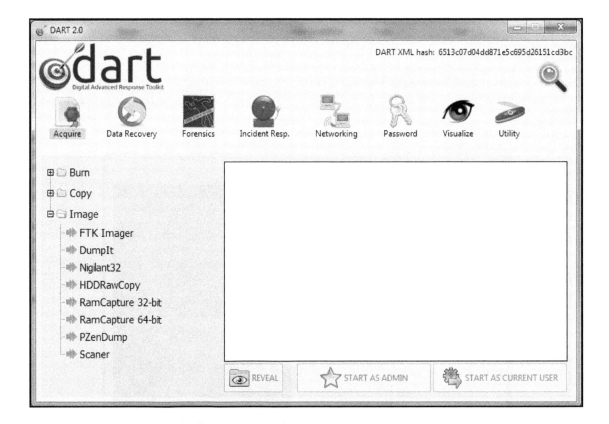

Incident response tool DART

[56]

Chapter 4

Helix

Helix is an IR CD that has both free and commercial versions. It can work with three operating systems: **Windows**, **Linux**, and **Mac** in live acquisition. This is displayed in the following screenshot:

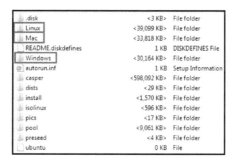

Figure A: Different OS support in Helix in live acquisition

Like DEFT, you can boot from the Helix CD in case of a powered off system. In this case, you can clone the hard drive to another hard drive and perform the same function of the hard drive duplicators. Go to **Applications** | **Acquisition and Analysis** | **Helix pro**. In the opened window, you can duplicate the hard drive or image up to four images either from the system memory or the system hard drive. Helix can also calculate the images' hash functions: MD5, SHA1, SHA256, or SHA512, or altogether:

Booting from the Helix IR CD

[57]

Live imaging of a hard drive

In case of a live system, you will need to do the following:

- Image the volatile data, such as system memory first as discussed earlier
- Power the system down
- Disconnect the hard drive
- Image the hard drive separately

However, in some situations, you will also need to image the hard drive without switching the system off. An example is in case the system is a server that is hosting a critical service that cannot be taken down, or there is an encryption present in the system, which will be reactivated if the system is powered off. This is why live acquisition is the preferred choice all the time.

FTK imager in live hard drive acquisition

In this section, we will use the FTK imager in imaging the hard drive of the live target machine. We will use the FTK image lite (`http://accessdata.com/product-download/digital-forensics/ftk-imager-lite-version-3.1.1`), which doesn't require any installation, to leave least traces in the live system. Navigate to **File** | **Create Disk Image**.

From the pop-up window, select one of the following source evidence types:

- **Physical disk**: This is the whole hard drive, starting from the MBR to the last sector of the hard drive
- **Logical disk**: This is one partition from the hard drive.
- **Image file**: This is if you need to convert an image from one format to another, that is, from the E01 format to a raw format

In our case, we will select the whole physical hard drive. You now need to select the source hard drive, and make sure that you select the right hard drive of the target machine. After this, you will have the option of selecting the type of image that you want. The three most important options are as follows:

- **Raw image format**: This is simply a bit-to-bit copy of the hard drive without leaving or adding any single bit. This image format is usually accompanied by a separate file, containing meta information about the image file.
- **E01**: This is the **EnCase evidence file**. It contains information that is related to the acquisition process, such as the investigator name, the timestamp, and the typed notes during the acquisition. It calculates the checksum for every 32 KB of data, and at the end of the image file, it adds the MD5 hash for the whole bit stream.
- **AFF**: This is the **Advanced Forensics Format**, and it is used to store disk images and forensics images' metadata. This is not a proprietary but open format, which can be used with any tool for analysis and won't exclusively work with a single tool.

You can still transfer the image from one format to another after the original imaging process. So, we can always select the raw format and then convert to any other format that we will need during the analysis phase. You now need to add the destination information, taking in to consideration that you are working on a live system and have no write protection enabled. Be careful and select the destination folder in the externally attached storage or shared folder over the network.

There is an option to divide the image into multifiles. You can provide the size of the single file. This option will be very helpful in case you don't have enough storage on a single hard drive and need to divide the image between different hard drives. This will also be useful in case you have a FAT32 formatted volume that can't handle files more than 4 GB in size.

Nonvolatile Data Acquisition

Also, you can create more than one image in the same process, which will save some time if you have a case with more than one investigator working on it.

You may choose to verify the image after its creation by calculating the hash function to the image and comparing the result to the hash function's result of the hard drive. In case of a match, the image hasn't been altered. The hash function will be discussed later in this chapter:

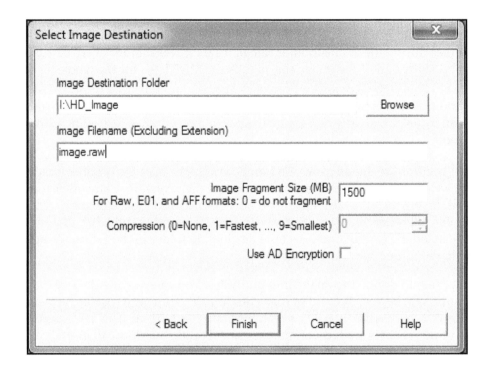

FTK—selection of the image destination

 FTK Imager images the hard drive bit-to-bit to a single file image. You can't image the hard drive to another one like you can do with duplicators.

Imaging over the network with FTK imager

In some situations, you can't connect to the target system with a USB to run your tools and connect your storage. In this case, you can acquire the system over the network.

What you need to do is connect your machine to the same network with the target system and make sure the target system can reach your machine using the ping command. From your machine, verify that enough space is available. Now, create a new folder and share this folder with suitable read/write privileges.

In our example, the shared folder name is Share and this is located in C:\. The handler's machine and has been assigned an IP of 192.168.57.128 and the source/target machine is Windows 7:

1. To test the shared folder availability, run the \\192.168.57.128 command from the source machine in the **Run** window shown as follows:

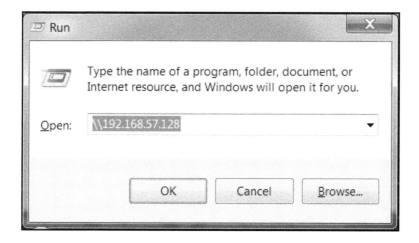

Opening the shared folder

Nonvolatile Data Acquisition

2. An authentication window must pop up. Enter the machine IP, the username, and the user password:

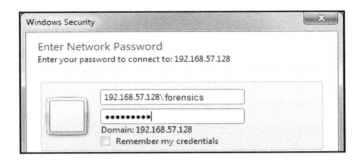

Shared folder authentication

3. If everything went well, you will see a folder named **Share**. Right-click on this folder and select **Map Network Drive**. You can select any drive letter, in our case, we selected the letter Z:

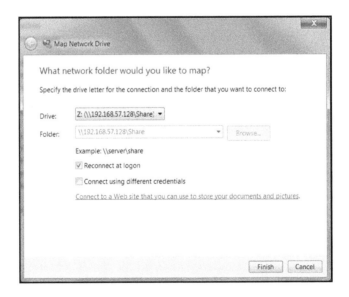

Mapping the shared folder

4. Now from the source machine, run the FTK Lite program, and then open **Create Disk image** from **File**. Follow the same steps and for the location of the image, browse to the mapped network drive; it may ask you to authenticate again:

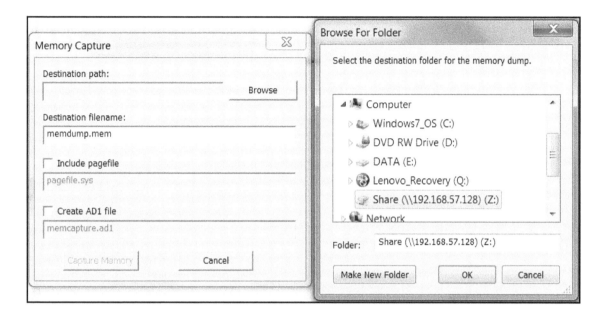

Saving the image to the shared folder

5. After clicking on the **Finish** button, you will notice a progress status bar that represents the already captured data from the overall hard drive size.

On the handler's machine, you will find a file named `image.raw`, which is created under the Share shared folder, and you can notice the increase of the file size until it reaches the maximum size of the target machine's hard drive.

Incident response CDs in live acquisition

As discussed earlier, the incident response CDs come with built-in and easy-to-access tools to perform different jobs. One of these jobs is the imaging of the hard drive of the live system, as in the DART tool set and Helix.

Nonvolatile Data Acquisition

With Helix, if it didn't start automatically in the live system, you can open the program from the suitable operating system folder (*Figure A* in the *Helix* section). The program will work with the same interface, but in case of working from a live system, you won't be able to duplicate the hard drive. The clone option won't be available in the list because the hard drive isn't in a steady state and is constantly changing as a result of the operating system's actions. A verification process takes place after the imaging process. It calculates the hash of the resulting image and compares the value to the hash of the bit stream during the imaging process. If there is a match, it means that there are no errors in the image.

To acquire the image over the network, Helix has a built-in capability to do so with the same server/client concept. In the destination machine, which is the handler machine, you need to run the network listener from the same `receiver.exe` folder:

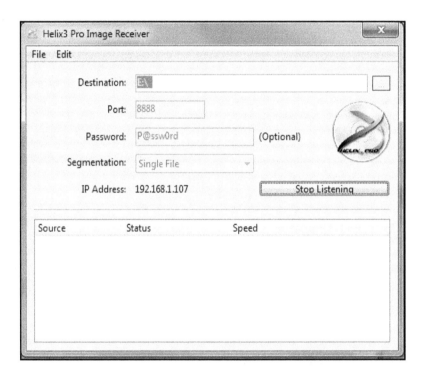

Helix network listener

After providing full information to the listener, start listening to any network connection requests.

In the source machine, select the destination as the Helix receiver. Then to set up the connection, enter the listener IP, the same port, and the password if any:

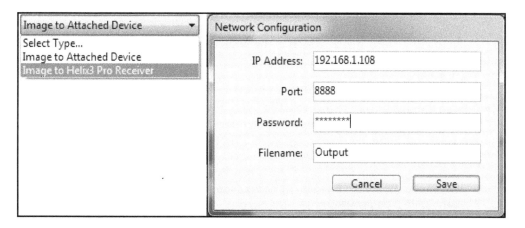

After starting the acquisition process, a new connection will start in the listener, and a new image file can be found at the specified location on the destination machine.

Linux for the imaging of a hard drive

Suppose that you already have a dead system and you need to take the machine's hard drive out in order to image it. What you need to do first is make sure that you are connecting the hard drive to your preferred Linux machine via write blocker to prevent any accidental writing to the hard drive, which could change the evidence and make it inadmissible.

The dd tool

In the Linux operating system, there is a built-in tool called dd. The dd tool is considered to be a forensically sound tool, as it copies blocks of data, regardless of its structure. There are a lot of suggestions of what dd stands for, but we can say that dd stands for **duplicate disk** or **duplicate data**, and if someone used it in wrong way it can be **disk destroyer** or **delete data**. This tool can convert and copy files and hard drives.

Suppose the suspicious hard drive, which is the source and is connected by a write blocker, is mounted as /dev/sda and the destination hard drive is mounted as sdb. We have the following two options:

- Image the hard drive to a single file, which is useful in space management, transferring the image file between different investigators in the same case, and for case archiving, as mentioned earlier. In this case, you will use the dd tool with the following using root privileges:

```
dd conv=sync,noerror bs=64K if=/dev/sda of=/media
/Elements/HD_image/image.dd
```

From here, we can see the following:

- `conv = sync, noerror`: This pads the block with nulls to the left if, for some reason, the block couldn't be read; dd will continue to execute and won't step due to some error.
- `bs`: This is each block size of the transferred data. Considering a big block size may be faster, but choosing the smaller block size is more efficient. Suppose you select bs to be 4 MB, so if an error occurred in the first sector of 4 MB, it will ignore all the rest of the block which may cause you some important data loss during the imaging process.
- `if`: This is an input file, either a whole hard disk or single partition.

- `Of`: This is an output file.
- `/media/Elements`: This is the mount point of the destination hard drive.
- In this case, the cursor will be silent until the imaging ends.
- Now, there is a way to see the progress of the imaging process, which will help in troubleshooting and detecting any problems that occurred during the acquisition, by pipelining the `dd` command with the `pv` as the following:

```
dd conv=sync, noerror bs=64K if=/dev/sda | pv | dd
of=/media/Elements/HD_image/image.dd
```

Here, you will see the moving progress bar, which means that the process is still running the imaged size and the imaging speed:

dd with the progress status

dd over the network

You also can use `dd` over the network using the `nc` netcat. To perform this action, on the destination machine with IP `192.168.57.128`, open a listener on port 3333 and pipeline the received data to `dd` with the desired location and output file name:

```
nc -l -p 3333 | dd of=/media/root/elements/HD_image/image.raw
```

Otherwise, you can just direct the output to the desired file:

```
nc -l -p 3333 >  /media/root/elements/HD_image/image.raw
```

Nonvolatile Data Acquisition

You can see this in the following screenshot:

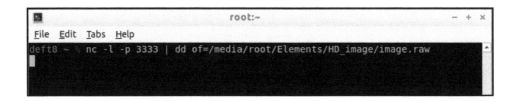

dd over the network using netcat (at destination)

On the target machine, start the dd by pipelining the output to the nc client, as follows:

```
dd conv=sync,noerror bs=64K if=/dev/sda | pv | nc
192.168.57.128 3333
```

The output is as follows:

dd over the network using netcat (at source)

Duplicate the whole hard drive to another hard drive. In this case, you can use all the previous steps, but instead of mentioning the destination file path, you need to mention the hard drive's driver assigned location under /dev.
So,/media/Elements/HD_image/image.dd will be replaced with/dev/sdb in the first example.

Using the dd tool, you can restore an image to a hard drive. You just need to change the input file to the image and the output file to the hard drive, such as/dev/sda:

```
dd if=/media/Elements/HD_image/image.dd of=/dev/sda
```

Virtualization in data acquisition

Virtualization offers great benefits to digital forensics science. In virtualization, everything is a file, including the guest memory and the guest hard drive. What the handler needs to do is to identify the right file of the source that they need to acquire and copy this file to the external storage.

The snapshot concept that can be found in most of the virtualization programs offers the investigator more images of the machine at different times. This can, if acquired and analyzed, view the timeline behavior of the machine, that is, before and after the malware infection:

Windows XP Professional.vmem	03-Oct-10 9:53 AM	VMEM File	524,288 KB
Windows XP Professional-Snapshot1.vmem	29-Sep-10 8:44 AM	VMEM File	524,288 KB
Windows XP Professional-Snapshot2.vmem	03-Oct-10 11:50 AM	VMEM File	524,288 KB

Windows memory files in the virtual machine

In the previous image, we can see the vmem files of the VMware program. VMware is one of the virtualization programs. This image contains the current memory file and two vmem files for two snapshots taken on two different dates. The size of the files are all the same because this is like the memory dump process, it copies the entire machine's memory.

Evidence integrity (the hash function)

What can we do to prove that the evidence hasn't been altered or changed? This step is very important to prove in court, if required, that you didn't add, remove, or edit the evidence during imaging or analysis. Most of the imaging tools come with many hash function implementations, such as MD5, SHA1, and SHA256. The hash function is a mathematical implementation, which is an irreversible or one-way function. This means that if you have input data A and hash function F, you will get $F(A) = H$. However, it's been proved that $F'(H) \mathrel{!}= A$, where F is the hash function and F' is any mathematical function. We can't get A, the original data, from H, the hash digest.

For example, if we have different strings applied to the same hash function, the hash function must map each string to different hashes:

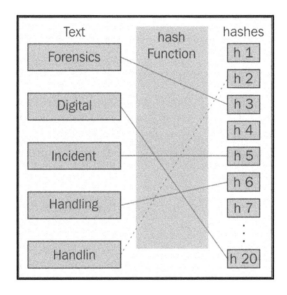

The hash function

As shown in the preceding diagram, each text resulted in a different hash after applying all the texts to the same hash function. Even if the change is a single character, such as **Handling** and **Handlin** in the preceding figure, the output must be very different. If slight changes in the input bring out slight changes in the hashes, the hash function is considered less perfect.

Hash collision occurs when two different inputs create the same hash when applied to the same hash function. So, it is better to use more than one hash function, such as MD5 and SHA512.

The length of the hash digest doesn't depend on the input length. Whatever the input length, the hash length will be the same. This is a matter of time and the available processing power and resources. The following table contains some of the famous hash functions with their digest length:

Hash algorithm	Digest length
MD5	128 bit
SHA-1	160 bit
SHA-256	256 bit
SHA-512	512 bit

The hash length for different hash algorithms

Nonvolatile Data Acquisition

With FTK Imager, you can select and image to verify them after they are created. This will run the created image against various hash functions and compare the results with the digests created during the imaging process of the source. This will create a small report showing the digest values and whether this is a match or not:

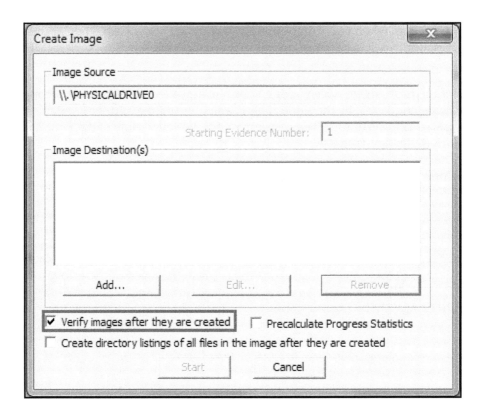

The hash verification in FTK Imager

You can prove that you didn't alter the evidence by writing the digest of the received evidence in the chain of custody records.

 In the Linux operating system, there is a built-in function called **md5sum** where you can apply your image to it, and it will calculate the MD5 hash for you.

It is worth mentioning that the content of the file is the only factor that affects the hash function, neither the metadata nor the filename affect the hash digest.

During live disk acquisition, the imaging is running in a specific point of time. No integrity can be preserved in the original disk as the operating system uses it and changes it all the time. However, the evidence integrity can be preserved starting from the first created image of the system disk.

Disk wiping in Linux

The investigator can't use the same hard drive for two different hard drives if they are using the duplication way to image the hard drive. This could overlap different files from different cases and will result in unreliable and untrue findings. After completing work on the duplicate hard drive, you must wipe it and prepare it for another case or hard drive. Don't wait until another case is assigned to you; wiping takes a long time.

This process is equivalent to the imaging process but the source file is a file full of zeros. In the Linux operating system there is a /dev/zero file. You need to use this file as your input file to the dd tool, and your output file will be the hard drive that needs to be wiped. Another file that can be used in this process as well is /dev/null:

```
dd if=/dev/zero of=/dev/sda bs=2K conv=noerror,sync
```

Summary

In this chapter, we covered some IRCDs and discussed the live acquisition using IRCDs and FTK Imager and imaging over the network using IRCDs and the dd tool. We also viewed how to preserve evidence integrity and how to wipe a disk for forensic usage.

In the next chapter, we will discuss how to create a timeline of the system activities and why it is important from a digital forensics prospective.

5
Timeline

In this chapter, we will look at timeline analysis. We will learn a few different approaches to perform a timeline analysis with The Sleuth Kit and Plaso Framework. We will also cover some theoretical issues that are specific to some filesystems and how they work with file time-related attributions. Also, we will demonstrate how we can use Plaso in practice.

In a nutshell, we will cover the following topics:

- Timeline
- **The Sleuth Kit** (TSK)
- Plaso architecture
- Plaso in practice

Timeline introduction

One question, which is very prominent in forensics is, "When?"

In other words, time is a very important factor at which analytics is based in the process of forensics. There are many artifacts that we use in an investigation which have temporal characteristics. These characteristics allow us to build the whole picture of an incident.

Moreover, timeline analysis could help when we analyze different types of evidence. Timeline analysis may be built on the base of any source that has timestamps. This could be the metadata of the filesystem, registry, event log files, log files of applications, memory, network traffic, and so on.

Timeline

Certainly, the timeline is one of the most useful techniques that is applied in digital forensics. However, this is based on the analysis of particular artifacts, so it is very important to understand how to analyze the artifacts that are suppliers of timeline events.

Despite the apparent simplicity of the idea underlying the timeline, in practice, it is not so easy. One of the difficulties is the large amount of data that has to be analyzed. The issue with a running system is that there are a few users and many system services, which produce a lot of events. We need to filter out such activities from normal users.

The idea of a timeline is not very new. It has been around since the year 2000, when Rob Lee and some other forensic people started applying it in digital forensics. Originally, filesystems served as a source of data for the timeline. We will consider the NTFS filesystem as the most prevalent filesystem in our review.

The timeline of the NTFS filesystem is based on the timestamps in some attributes of the filesystem objects.

Every object of the filesystem has the following timestamps:

- M: This is the date of data modification
- A: This is the date of data access
- C: This is the date of metadata change
- B: This is the date of metadata creation

Based on the analysis of this data, we can determine when a file was created, copied, moved, and so on. The NTFS filesystem uses `FILETIME` as its time format in UTC. **UTC** is **Coordinated Universal Time**. `FILETIME` contains a 64-bit value representing the number of 100-nanosecond intervals since January 1, 1601 (UTC). MS Windows also uses other time formats. They are the UNIX time format, DOS Date format, and `SYSTEMTIME` format.

Also, we should highlight some cases when the file is moved across different filesystems, for example, a file is copied to a USB key. In most cases, USB uses the FAT32 filesystem, so files on the FAT32 system have different attributes, and timestamps are on the NTFS and FAT32 filesystems.

Let's consider case when a file is created on the NTFS filesystem and then is copied to USB with the FAT32 filesystem. In this case, the modification date remains unchanged, but the C date on the USB drive changes and will fit to the date of file creation on the USB. Microsoft has an explanation on how attributes are changed in different situations at http://support.microsoft.com/kb/299648. The following are the file properties with regards to the date and time stamps:

- In the case that a file is copied from `C:\fatfolder` to `C:\fatfolder\subfolder`, it keeps the same date and time of modification but changes the date and time of creation to the current date and time
- In the case that a file is moved from `C:\fatfolder` to `C:\fatfolder\subfolder`, it keeps the same date and time of modification and keeps the same date and time of creation
- In the case that a file is copied from `C:\fatfolder` to `D:\NTFSfolder`, it keeps the same date and time of modification but changes the date and time of creation to the current date and time
- In the case that a file is moved from `C:\fatfolder` to `D:\NTFSfolder`, it keeps the same date and time of modification and keeps the same date and time of creation
- In the case that a file is copied from `D:\NTFSfolder` to `D:\NTFSfolder\SUBfolder`, it keeps the same date and time of modification but changes the date and time of creation to the current date and time
- In the case that a file is moved from `D:\NTFSfolder` to `D:\NTFSfolder\SUBfolder`, it keeps the same date and time of modification and keeps the same date and time of creation

In all cases, the date and time of modification of a file does not change unless a property of the file has changed. The date and time of creation of the file changes, depending on whether the file was copied or moved.

The following are the folder properties with regards to the date and time stamps:

- In the case that two new folders on an NTFS partition called `D:\NTFSfolder1` and `D:\NTFSfolder2` are created, both the date and time of creation and modification are the same

Timeline

- In the case that the `D:\NTFSfolder2` folder is moved into the `D:\NTFSfolder1` folder, creating `D:\NTFSfolder1\NTFSfolder2`, then the following occurs:
    - `D:\NTFSfolder1`: This is when the created folder is the same and the modified stamp changes.
    - `D:\NTFSfolder1\NTFSfolder2`: This is when both the created folder changes and the modified folder stay the same.

  This behavior occurs because even though you moved the folder, a new folder is seen as being created within the `D:\NTFSfolder1` folder by the Master File Table (MFT).

- In the case that the `D:\NTFSfolder2` folder is copied into the `D:\NTFSfolder1` folder, creating the `D:\NTFSfolder1\NTFSfolder2` folder, and the `D:\NTFSfolder2` folder still exists (after having copied it):
    - `D:\NTFSfolder1`: This is when the created folder is the same and the modified folder time and date stamp changes.
    - `D:\NTFSfolder2`: This is when no changes occur because it is the original folder.
    - `D:\NTFSfolder1\NTFSfolder2`: This is when both the created folder and the modified folder change to the same stamp, which is that of the time of the move.

  This behavior occurs because even though you copied the folder, the new folder is seen as being created by the MFT and is given a new created and modified time stamp.

The FAT filesystem has different behavior with regards to the modified time stamp. On a FAT filesystem, the modified date of a folder does not change if the contents of the folder change. For example, if `D:\FATfolder2` is copied or moved into `D:\FATfolder1`, the created date and modified date of `D:\FATfolder1` remain unchanged. The following table reflects the changes of attributes in accordance with operations on the file:

Operations	Attribute
Renaming	..C.
Displacement inside a volume	..C.
Displacement between volumes	.AC.
Copying	.ACB
Access	.AC.

[78]

Modification	M.C.
Creation	MACB
Deletion	....

> **TIP**
> When we talk about a moving action, we mean moving of the file with Windows Explorer and the cut and paste procedure, not the `move` command in the command line.

One more thing what we want to mention is that some investigators make the mistake of assuming that disabling the last accessed time will stop any updates to the file's last access time (default on Vista+). This is incorrect. The last accessed time will be changed in the case of the copy or move commands; it remains unchanged only if the files are opening.

Also, the moving of a file by cutting and pasting in Windows Explorer in the border of the filesystem doesn't change the creation time. However, it will be changed if a file is moved on the command line with the `move` command.

The Sleuth Kit

Let's considers the stages of the creation of a timeline for a filesystem.

The first step for creation of the timeline is building of body file.

There are three types of data to collect:

- Existing on filesystem files, which we could list with the `dir` or `ls` command.
- Deleted files, which are deleted but structures of them still exist. This allows for recovering the full path and other attributes of the file. However, this depends on the filesystem, as not all filesystems allow this.
- Unallocated inodes (`$Orphan` files), which are file structures which do not exist anymore.

To build a bodyfile, we will use the `fls` tool from TSK. The `fls` tool allows interacting with a forensics image as with the filesystem and extracting timeline data from the filesystem level.

Timeline

This gets the value of the inode directory, processes its content, and displays the names of files in the directory (including deleted files). If the value of inode is not present, it will display the content of the root directory:

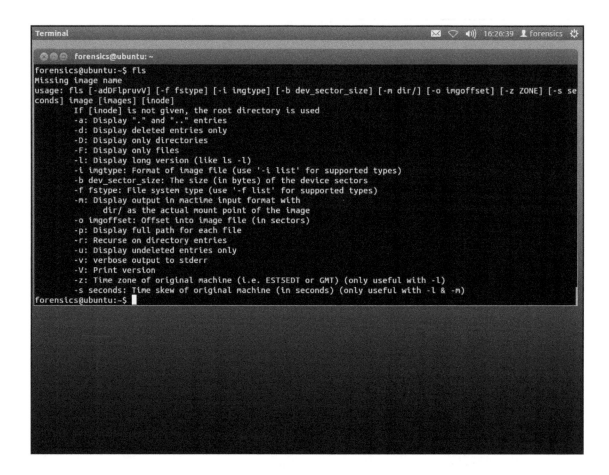

In our case, one of the most important options is -m, which allows output in a format for use with the mactime tool:

```
forensics@ubuntu:~$ mactime
mactime [-b body_file] [-p password_file] [-g group_file] [-i day|hour idx_file] [-d] [-h] [-V] [-y] [-z TIME_ZONE] [DATE]
            -b: Specifies the body file location, else STDIN is used
            -d: Output in comma delimited format
            -h: Display a header with session information
            -i [day | hour] file: Specifies the index file with a summary of results
            -y: Dates are displayed in ISO 8601 format
            -m: Dates have month as number instead of word (does not work with -y)
            -z: Specify the timezone the data came from (in the local system format) (does not work with -y)
            -g: Specifies the group file location, else GIDs are used
            -p: Specifies the password file location, else UIDs are used
            -V: Prints the version to STDOUT
            [DATE]: starting date (yyyy-mm-dd) or range (yyyy-mm-dd..yyyy-mm-dd)
forensics@ubuntu:~$
```

So if you have an `image.dd` and you want to create a timeline, you should enter the following three commands:

```
mmls image.dd
fls -m  -o <offset of fs partition> -r images.dd > body.txt
mactime -b body.txt -z TZ > timeline.txt
```

Super timeline – Plaso

The filesystem is not the only source of data that contains timestamps of events in the system. When computers work, even when users do not do anything, a lot of events occur in the system. For example, Windows XP creates a System Restore Point every 24 hours, runs disk defragmentation every three days so that sectors of deleted files will be rewritten. Windows 7 has a Volume Shadow Copy mechanism, which also creates backup files and so on. All these actions occur automatically without any user activity. So, even in idle mode, Windows has a lot of events. In the case that the system has active users, we would see many more events. The information about these events will reflect in different places: in the registry, event log files, log files of applications, browser history, and so on.

If we could use all of these sources in the timeline, we could make a whole picture of what happened in the system and link different events in logical chain. This approach is called **Super Timeline**.

To build a super timeline from different sources separately and then merge results could be a complicated and longtime process. However, thanks to cool tools, such as the Plaso framework, this task became much easier.

Kristinn Gudjonsson created the `log2timeline` tool, which allows the creation of a super timeline in an automatic way. Originally, it was written in Perl, but later rewritten in Python. The Python version is now called **Plaso**. It has a lot of features and flexible architecture. It allows the addition of new parsers and plugins to process new types of data.

Plaso architecture

Let's take a look at Plaso architecture. Plaso has a few core components which perform independent roles:

- Preprocessing
- Collection
- Worker
- Storage

Let's look at them in more detail.

Preprocessing

At this stage, some preprocessing tasks should be done prior to all other processing. For example, before mounting the image and determining which OS is installed on the disk, collect some information which will be used in the next stage.

The preprocessing process should collect the following:

- The version of the OS
- The hostname
- Time zone information
- Default applications, such as the default browser, and so on
- Enumerate all users and their paths

Collection

In the collection stage, the process goes over the image, directory, or mount point, and finds all the files that the tool can process.

The collection could be divided into three different scenarios:

- In the simplest case, the collection process recursively goes through either a mount point or an image file and collects every file discovered.
- During the recursive scan, if VSS are to be parsed, a hash is calculated, based on the four timestamps of every file. During the collection phase, from the VSS image, the hash value is compared to already existing hashes for that file. If the file has not previously been collected, it is included; otherwise, it is skipped.
- In the case of a targeted collection, a set of file paths is defined and only the files that fit that pattern are collected.

Worker

The worker is the main part of Plaso. The worker should be monitoring the process queue, and process each file that gets in there. During processing files, the worker will perform the following actions:

- Determining the type of file
- Determining which parsers should be applied to it
- Parsing the file and extract all events from it

- Applying some defined filters to the file
- Sending extracted events to the storage queue
- Determining if this file contains other files within it that can be processed/extracted, and process them as well

Storage

In the storage stage, events from the storage queue are written to a disk.

Now, let's consider the main tools from the Plaso framework:

- **log2timeline**: This is the main command line frontend to the Plaso backend. This is the tool that can be used to extract events from an image, mount point, or a file, and save it in a Plaso storage file for future processing and analysis.
- **Pinfo**: This tool allows the extraction of the information, which is contained in the Plaso storage. It is simple tool, which prints out information from the storage file.
- **pprof**: This is small tool, which could be useful for developers and those that are interested in trying to optimize certain parsers.
- **preg**: This tool provides a different frontend to the registry parser. It parses an image or a registry hive and provides the user with a console or shell to work with the registry.
- **pshell**: This is an iPython console to the Plaso backend. This shell provides the user with access to all the libraries of Plaso and provides an access to more advanced analysis of the output, debugging, and experimentation.
- **psort**:The storage format of Plaso is not a human-readable format and psort allows the convertion of it to a more convenient form. It is used as a postprocessing tool to filter, sort, and process the Plaso storage file.

Plaso in practice

Let's take a look how we can use Plaso in practice.

Let's assume that we have an image of the hard drive from the infected PC, and now we need to investigate this case to figure out how the infection occurred.

First, we need observe the image and determine partitions, which we need to analyze. To do this, we need to use the mmls tool from TSK.

Then, we can build bodyfile with log2timeline:

```
forensics@forensics:~/timeline$ mmls /mnt/hgfs/evidence/image.dd
DOS Partition Table
Offset Sector: 0
Units are in 512-byte sectors

     Slot    Start        End          Length       Description
00:  Meta    0000000000   0000000000   0000000001   Primary Table (#0)
01:  -----   0000000000   0000002047   0000002048   Unallocated
02:  00:00   0000002048   0000206847   0000204800   NTFS (0x07)
03:  00:01   0000206848   0016775167   0016568320   NTFS (0x07)
04:  -----   0016775168   0016777215   0000002048   Unallocated
forensics@forensics:~/timeline$ log2timeline.py -p --parsers win7 -z UTC -o 206848 timeline.body /mnt/hgfs/evidence/image.dd
```

Now, we will use a dynamic format for output. The dynamic output format allows the setting of filtering rules as SQL-SELECT-like requests. We will build our rules based on the following attributes of events:

Attribute	Description
Date	This is the date of the event
Time	This is the time of the event
Timezone	This is the time zone of the event
Source	This is the source of the event (`FILE`,`REG`, ...)
Message, Description	This is the description of the event
User	This is the user associated to the event
Host	This is the ID of the computer associated to the event
inode	This is the ID of the file inside the filesystem
Filename	This is the name of the file linked to the event
Macb	This is the MACB timestamp notation
Timestamp_desc	This is the description of the timestamp (`LastWritten`,...)
Parser	This is the Module that collects and processes data (`WinRegistryParser`, ...)

[85]

Timeline

When we browse a list of executed files, we found a file with a suspicious name, `ZkPECED.exe`. We could use it now as a pivotal point of a timeline investigation.

So, we can filter all files, which contain the `ZkPECED` string in the name of the file.

The following figure displays the results of searching for events associated with files containing the `ZkPECED` keyword in their name, from which it is clear that on April 8, 2014, at 12:39:08 UTC (16:39:08 UTC+4), two files named `ZkPECED.tmp` and `ZkPECED.exe` were created in `\Users\Alina\AppData\Local\Temp` directory:

```
forensics@forensics:~/timeline$ psort.py -q -o dynamic timeline.body "select date,time,timezone,macb,filename,inode where parser is 'PfileStatParser' and filename contains 'ZkPECED'"
date,time,timezone,macb,filename,inode
2014-04-08,12:39:08,UTC,...B,/Users/Alina/AppData/Local/Temp/ZkPECED.tmp,45415
2014-04-08,12:39:08,UTC,.A..,/Users/Alina/AppData/Local/Temp/ZkPECED.tmp,45415
2014-04-08,12:39:08,UTC,..C.,/Users/Alina/AppData/Local/Temp/ZkPECED.tmp,45415
2014-04-08,12:39:08,UTC,M...,/Users/Alina/AppData/Local/Temp/ZkPECED.tmp,45415
2014-04-08,12:39:08,UTC,...B,/Users/Alina/AppData/Local/Temp/ZkPECED.exe,47418
2014-04-08,12:39:08,UTC,..C.,/Users/Alina/AppData/Local/Temp/ZkPECED.exe,47418
2014-04-08,12:39:08,UTC,.A..,/Users/Alina/AppData/Local/Temp/ZkPECED.exe,47418
2014-04-08,12:39:08,UTC,M...,/Users/Alina/AppData/Local/Temp/ZkPECED.exe,47418
2014-04-08,12:39:20,UTC,M...,/Windows/Prefetch/ZKPECED.EXE-9AAFDBB8.pf,47951
2014-04-08,12:39:20,UTC,.A..,/Windows/Prefetch/ZKPECED.EXE-9AAFDBB8.pf,47951
2014-04-08,12:39:20,UTC,...B,/Windows/Prefetch/ZKPECED.EXE-9AAFDBB8.pf,47951
2014-04-08,12:59:16,UTC,..C.,/Windows/Prefetch/ZKPECED.EXE-9AAFDBB8.pf,47951
[INFO] Output processing is done.
forensics@forensics:~/timeline$
```

Using the `--sliceDateTime` and `--slice_sizeMinutes` parameters and the `psort.py` utility, we can restrict the sample data from the file storage (`timeline.body`) to events that occurred in the time range *[DateTime-Minutes, DateTime + Minutes]*.

As we do not know where the `ZkPECED.exe` file executable came from, we perform a search for all executables created or modified within 10 minutes of 12:39:08 UTC:

```
forensics@forensics:~/timeline$ psort.py -q -o dynamic --slice "2014-04-08 12:39:08" --slice_size 10 timeline.body "select date,time,timezone,macb,inode,filename where parser is 'PfileStatParser'" | grep -iE "\.exe$"
[WARNING] You are trying to use both a "slice" and a date filter, the end results might not be what you want it to be... a small delay is introduced to allow you to read this message
2014-04-08,12:31:49,UTC,..C.,46912,/systemhost/24FC2AE3CB0.exe
2014-04-08,12:39:08,UTC,...B,47418,/Users/Alina/AppData/Local/Temp/ZkPECED.exe
2014-04-08,12:39:08,UTC,..C.,47418,/Users/Alina/AppData/Local/Temp/ZkPECED.exe
2014-04-08,12:39:08,UTC,.A..,47418,/Users/Alina/AppData/Local/Temp/ZkPECED.exe
2014-04-08,12:39:08,UTC,M...,47418,/Users/Alina/AppData/Local/Temp/ZkPECED.exe
[INFO] Output processing is done.
forensics@forensics:~/timeline$
```

Note that just before the appearance of the `ZkPECED.exe` file, the metadata of a file in the `systemhost` directory with the suspicious name `24FC2AE3CB0.exe` (inode 46912) changed (meaning that the file was renamed or moved locally), although its other timestamps (`creation`, `last modified`, and `last accessed`) refer back to 2010:

```
forensics@forensics:~/timeline$ psort.py -q -o dynamic timeline.body "select date,time,timezone,macb,inode,filename where parser is 'PfileStatParser' and inode==46912"
date,time,timezone,macb,inode,filename
2010-11-20,21:29:10,UTC,.A..,46912,/systemhost/24FC2AE3CB0.exe
2010-11-20,21:29:10,UTC,...B,46912,/systemhost/24FC2AE3CB0.exe
2010-11-20,21:29:10,UTC,.M..,46912,/systemhost/24FC2AE3CB0.exe
2014-04-08,12:31:49,UTC,..C.,46912,/systemhost/24FC2AE3CB0.exe
[INFO] Output processing is done.
forensics@forensics:~/timeline$
```

Using the `istat` utility in TSK suite, we obtain information about the attributes of the `24FC2AE3CB0.exe` file (inode 46912):

```
forensics@forensics:~/timeline$ istat -o 206848 /mnt/hgfs/evidence/image.dd 46912
MFT Entry Header Values:
Entry: 46912        Sequence: 3
$LogFile Sequence Number: 138242553
Allocated File
Links: 2

$STANDARD_INFORMATION Attribute Values:
Flags: Archive
Owner ID: 0
Security ID: 767   (S-1-5-21-3144881766-2721458579-604590793-1000)
Last User Journal Update Sequence Number: 23530968
Created:         2010-11-20 16:29:08 (EST)
File Modified:   2010-11-20 16:29:08 (EST)
MFT Modified:    2014-04-08 08:31:44 (EDT)
Accessed:        2010-11-20 16:29:08 (EST)

$FILE_NAME Attribute Values:
Flags: Archive
Name: 24FC2AE3CB0.exe
Parent MFT Entry: 48072         Sequence: 2
Allocated Size: 0       Actual Size: 0
Created:         2014-04-08 08:31:44 (EDT)
File Modified:   2014-04-08 08:31:44 (EDT)
MFT Modified:    2014-04-08 08:31:44 (EDT)
Accessed:        2014-04-08 08:31:44 (EDT)

Attributes:
Type: $STANDARD_INFORMATION (16-0)   Name: N/A   Resident   size: 72
Type: $FILE_NAME (48-3)    Name: N/A   Resident   size: 90
Type: $FILE_NAME (48-2)    Name: N/A   Resident   size: 96
Type: $DATA (128-4)    Name: N/A   Non-Resident   size: 411648   init_size: 411648
1850979 1850980 1850981 1850982 1850983 1850984 1850985 1850986
1850987 1850988 1850989 1850990 1850991 1850992 1850993 1850994
1850995 1850996 1850997 1850998 1850999 1851000 1851001 1851002
1851003 1851004 1851005 1851006 1851007 1851008 1851009 1851010
1851011 1851012 1851013 1851014 1851015 1851016 1851017 1851018
1851019 1851020 1851021 1851022 1851023 1851024 1851025 1851026
1851027 1851028 1851029 1851030 1851031 1851032 1851033 1851034
1851035 1851036 1851037 1851038 1851039 1851040 1851041 1851042
1851043 1851044 1851045 1851046 1851047 1851048 1851049 1851050
1851051 1851052 1851053 1851054 1851055 1851056 1851057 1851058
1851059 1851060 1851061 1851062 1851063 1851064 1851065 1851066
1851067 1851068 1851069 1851070 1851071 1851072 1851073 1851074
1851075 1851076 1851077 1851078 1851079
forensics@forensics:~/timeline$
```

Timeline

The preceding screenshot shows that the timestamps contained in the $STANDARD_INFORMATION and $FILENAME attributes do not match, which probably indicates that the timestamps of the 24FC2AE3CB0.exe file (inode 46912) were changed manually.

Hence, it can be assumed that the 24FC2AE3CB0.exe file (inode 46912) was created on April 8 at 12:31:44 UTC (16:31:44 UTC+4), and that its timestamps (created, last modified, and last accessed) were changed "manually", which is one of the signs of malware.

Analyzing the results

Analysis of the results of the WinRegistryParser processing module establishes that links to both suspicious executable files are stored in the Windows registry keys that are responsible for auto-running programs at system startup:

```
forensics@forensics:~/timeline$ psort.py -q -o dynamic timeline.body "select date,time,timezone,type,description where parser is 'WinRegistryParser' and description contains 'ZkPECED'"
date,time,timezone,type,description
2014-04-08,12:45:00,UTC,Last Written,[\Software\Microsoft\Windows\CurrentVersion\Policies\Explorer\Run] kl: [REG_SZ] c:\Users\Alina\AppData\Local\Temp\ZkPECED.exe
[INFO] Output processing is done.
forensics@forensics:~/timeline$ psort.py -q -o dynamic timeline.body "select date,time,timezone,type,description where parser is 'WinRegistryParser' and description contains '24FC2AE3CB0'"
date,time,timezone,type,description
2014-04-08,12:31:44,UTC,Last Written,[\Software\Microsoft\Windows\CurrentVersion\Run] YI9B2F0F6EXG1Y1ZLMA: C:\systemhost\24FC2AE3CB0.exe
[INFO] Output processing is done.
forensics@forensics:~/timeline$
```

The screenshot also shows the time of the last modification of each of the registry keys.

As the source of the 24FC2AE3CB0.exe file is also unknown, we perform a search for files created before 12:31:49 UTC, excluding files with safe extensions from the search results:

```
forensics@forensics:~/timeline$ psort.py -q -o dynamic timeline.body "select date,time,timezone,macb,inode,filename where parser is 'PfileStatParser' and date < '2014-04-08 12:32:00' and date > '2014-04-08 12:29:08' and timestamp_desc == 'crtime'" | grep -ivE "\.(jpg|png|txt|css|xml|gif|evtx)$"
```

[88]

The result of this command will be as follows:

```
2014-04-08,12:31:24,UTC,...B,48067,/Users/Alina/AppData/LocalLow/Sun/Java/Deployment/cache/6.0/11/7d088b-2be562b3.idx
2014-04-08,12:31:24,UTC,...B,48068,/Users/Alina/AppData/LocalLow/Sun/Java/Deployment/cache/6.0/11/7d088b-2be562b3
2014-04-08,12:31:25,UTC,...B,48063,/Users/Alina/AppData/Local/Microsoft/Windows/Temporary Internet Files/Content.IE5/TB0B4ALG/Capture[1].aspx
2014-04-08,12:31:25,UTC,...B,46627,/Users/Alina/AppData/Local/Microsoft/Windows/Temporary Internet Files/Content.IE5/TB0B4ALG/CA6Z8V1C.HTM
2014-04-08,12:31:25,UTC,...B,47978,/Users/Alina/AppData/Local/Microsoft/Windows/Temporary Internet Files/Content.IE5/1THZQXYD/events;sz=300x250;page=front
;tile=4;ord=5343ec1136d8e[1]
2014-04-08,12:31:25,UTC,...B,46674,/Users/Alina/AppData/Local/Microsoft/Windows/Temporary Internet Files/Content.IE5/1BY86ZOW/events;sz=300x70;page=front;
tile=5;pos=1;ord=5343ec1136d8e[1]
2014-04-08,12:31:25,UTC,...B,48069,/Users/Alina/AppData/LocalLow/Sun/Java/Deployment/cache/6.0/lastAccessed
2014-04-08,12:31:25,UTC,...B,46628,/Users/Alina/AppData/Local/Microsoft/Windows/Temporary Internet Files/Content.IE5/1BY86ZOW/events;sz=300x70;page=front;
tile=7;pos=3;ord=5343ec1136d8e[1]
2014-04-08,12:31:26,UTC,...B,47981,/Users/Alina/AppData/Local/Microsoft/Windows/Temporary Internet Files/Content.IE5/1BY86ZOW/events;sz=300x70;page=front;
tile=6;pos=2;ord=5343ec1136d8e[1]
2014-04-08,12:31:26,UTC,...B,47992,/Users/Alina/AppData/Local/Microsoft/Windows/Temporary Internet Files/Content.IE5/TB0B4ALG/chartbeat[2].js
[INFO] Output processing is done.
2014-04-08,12:31:29,UTC,...B,48070,/Windows/Prefetch/JP2LAUNCHER.EXE-DFC71DBB.pf
2014-04-08,12:31:32,UTC,...B,48075,/Users/Alina/AppData/LocalLow/Sun/Java/Deployment/cache/6.0/47/57ebc62f-6dfa622f
2014-04-08,12:31:32,UTC,...B,48074,/Users/Alina/AppData/LocalLow/Sun/Java/Deployment/cache/6.0/47/57ebc62f-6dfa622f.idx
2014-04-08,12:31:39,UTC,...B,48071,/Users/Alina/AppData/LocalLow/Sun/Java/Deployment/cache/6.0/35/1ed2c623-6.0.lap
2014-04-08,12:31:46,UTC,...B,48077,/Windows/Prefetch/1DSVE2WEFD.EXE-D783D579.pf
2014-04-08,12:31:49,UTC,...B,47964,/systemhost/946CA974F286A64
2014-04-08,12:31:49,UTC,...B,48079,/Windows/Prefetch/24FC2AE3CB0.EXE-DC17388D.pf
```

The screenshot shows that, a few seconds before the appearance of the `24FC2AE3CB0.exe` file, the `jp2launcher.exe` file process has been started. It starts the Java virtual machine for Java applets and `.jnlp` files. So after this, two `Java.idx` files named `7d088b-2be562b3.idx` (inode 48067) and `57ebc62f-6dfa622f.idx` (inode 48074) were created.

The results of the `JavaIDXParser` processing module gives us some information about objects loaded in the Java virtual machine:

```
forensics@forensics:~/timeline$ psort.py -q -o dynamic timeline.body "select date,time,timezone,description,filename where parser is 'JavaIDXParser' and
date < '2014-04-08 12:32:00' and date > '2014-04-08 12:29:08'"
date,time,timezone,description,filename
2014-04-08,12:31:31,UTC,IDX Version: 605 Host IP address: (85.17.137.151) Download URL: http://finansial.gov/utis1.jar,/Users/Alina/AppData/LocalLow/Sun/
Java/Deployment/cache/6.0/11/7d088b-2be562b3.idx
2014-04-08,12:31:31,UTC,IDX Version: 605 Host IP address: (85.17.137.151) Download URL: http://w282d1wb.athleticsdrycleaner.pw/f/1389931620/4067114524/2,
/Users/Alina/AppData/LocalLow/Sun/Java/Deployment/cache/6.0/47/57ebc62f-6dfa622f.idx
[INFO] Output processing is done.
forensics@forensics:~/timeline$
```

The information displayed in the screenshot shows that a Java archive named `utis1.jar` was downloaded from the URL `http://finansial.gov` (IP 85.17.137.151), and an unknown object named 2 was downloaded from the URL `http://w282d1wb.athleticsdrycleaner.pw/f/1389931620/4067114524/`.

The `utis1.jar` Java archive is saved in the `/Users/Alina/AppData/LocalLow/Sun/Java/Deployment/cache/6.0/11/7d088b-2be562b3` file (inode 48068), and the unknown object named 2 in `/Users/Alina/AppData/LocalLow/Sun/Java/Deployment/cache/6.0/47/57ebc62f-6dfa622f` (inode 48075).

Timeline

With the help of the `icat` utility in The Sleuth Kit suite, we can obtain the contents of both Java IDX files, from which we extract the size of the objects that were downloaded by the Java virtual machine:

```
forensics@forensics:~/timeline$ icat -o 206848 /mnt/hgfs/evidence/image.dd 48067 | hexdump -vC
00000000  00 00 00 00 02 5d 00 00  00 36 e4 00 00 01 44 91  |.....]...6....D.|
00000010  56 9b 00 00 00 00 00 00  00 00 00 00 00 00 00 00  |V...............|
00000020  00 00 00 00 00 00 01 3b  00 00 00 55 00 00 00 0f  |.......;...U....|
00000030  00 00 00 00 00 00 01 45  41 52 4a 94 00 00 00 00  |.......EARJ.....|
00000040  00 00 00 00 00 00 00 00  00 00 00 0a 00 00 00 00  |................|
00000050  00 00 0a 00 00 00 05 00  00 00 01 45 41 52 4a 94  |...........EARJ.|
00000060  00 00 00 00 00 00 00 00  00 00 00 00 00 00 00 00  |................|
00000070  00 00 00 00 00 00 00 00  00 00 00 00 00 00 00 00  |................|
00000080  00 00 00 1e 68 74 74 70  3a 2f 2f 66 69 6e 61 6e  |....http://finan|
00000090  73 69 61 6c 2e 67 6f 76  2f 75 74 69 73 6c 2e 6a  |sial.gov/utisl.j|
000000a0  61 72 00 00 00 0d 38 35  2e 31 37 2e 31 33 37 2e  |ar....85.17.137.|
000000b0  31 35 31 00 00 00 07 00  06 3c 6e 75 6c 6c 3e 00  |151......<null>.|
000000c0  0f 48 54 54 50 2f 31 2e  31 20 32 30 30 20 4f 4b  |.HTTP/1.1 200 OK|
000000d0  00 0e 63 6f 6e 74 65 6e  74 2d 6c 65 6e 67 74 68  |..content-length|
000000e0  00 05 31 34 30 35 32 00  0d 6c 61 73 74 2d 6d 6f  |..14052..last-mo|
000000f0  64 69 66 69 65 64 00 1d  57 65 64 2c 20 30 35 20  |dified..Wed, 05 |
00000100  4d 61 72 20 32 30 31 34  20 30 38 3a 32 32 3a 35  |Mar 2014 08:22:5|
00000110  36 20 47 4d 54 00 0c 63  6f 6e 74 65 6e 74 2d 74  |6 GMT..content-t|
00000120  79 70 65 00 18 61 70 70  6c 69 63 61 74 69 6f 6e  |ype..application|
00000130  2f 6a 61 76 61 2d 61 72  63 68 69 76 65 00 00 04  |/java-archive..d|
00000140  61 74 65 00 1d 54 75 65  2c 20 30 38 20 41 70 72  |ate..Tue, 08 Apr|
00000150  20 32 30 31 34 20 31 32  3a 33 31 3a 32 32 20 47  | 2014 12:31:22 G|
00000160  4d 54 00 06 73 65 72 76  65 72 00 16 41 70 61 63  |MT..server..Apac|
00000170  68 65 2f 32 2e 32 2e 32  32 20 28 55 62 75 6e 74  |he/2.2.22 (Ubunt|
00000180  75 29 00 1b 64 65 70 6c  6f 79 2d 72 65 71 75 65  |u)..deploy-reque|
00000190  73 74 2d 63 6f 6e 74 65  6e 74 2d 74 79 70 65 00  |st-content-type.|
000001a0  1a 61 70 70 6c 69 63 61  74 69 6f 6e 2f 78 2d 6a  |.application/x-j|
000001b0  61 76 61 2d 61 72 63 68  69 76 65 1f 8b 08 00 00  |ava-archive.....|
000001c0  00 00 00 00 00 f3 4d cc  cb 4c 4b 2d 2e d1 0d 4b  |......M..LK-...K|
000001d0  2d 2a ce cc cf b3 52 30  d4 33 e0 e5 72 2e 4a 4d  |-*....R0.3..r.JM|
000001e0  2c 49 4d d1 75 aa 04 09  98 eb 19 c4 1b 98 2b 68  |,IM.u.........+h|
000001f0  f8 17 25 26 e7 a4 2a 38  e7 17 15 e4 17 25 96 00  |..%&..*8.....%..|
00000200  95 6b f2 72 f1 72 01 00  3c 3a 53 31 44 00 00 00  |.k.r.r..<:S1D...|
00000210  ac ed 00 05 77 04 00 00  00 00 77 03 30 0d 0a     |....w.....w.0..|
0000021f
forensics@forensics:~/timeline$
```

The output presented in the screenshot indicates that the `utisl.jar` file («7d088b-2be562b3») is 14,052 bytes in size:

```
forensics@forensics:~/timeline$ icat -o 206848 /mnt/hgfs/evidence/image.dd 48074 | hexdump -vC
00000000  00 00 00 00 02 5d 00 00  06 48 00 00 00 01 44 91  |.....]...H....D.|
00000010  fd 18 18 00 00 00 00 00  00 00 00 00 00 00 00 00  |................|
00000020  00 00 00 00 00 00 00 fd  00 00 00 00 00 00 00 00  |................|
00000030  00 00 00 00 00 00 01 45  41 52 69 5a 00 00 00 00  |.......EARiZ....|
00000040  00 00 00 00 00 00 00 00  00 00 00 00 00 00 00 00  |................|
00000050  00 00 00 00 00 00 00 00  00 00 01 45 41 52 69 5a  |...........EARiZ|
00000060  00 00 00 00 00 00 00 00  00 00 00 00 00 00 00 00  |................|
00000070  00 00 00 00 00 00 00 00  00 00 00 00 00 00 00 00  |................|
00000080  00 00 00 40 68 74 74 70  3a 2f 2f 77 32 38 32 64  |...@http://w282d|
00000090  31 77 62 2e 61 74 68 6c  65 74 69 63 73 64 72 79  |1wb.athleticsdry|
000000a0  63 6c 65 61 6e 65 72 2e  70 77 2f 66 2f 31 33 38  |cleaner.pw/f/138|
000000b0  39 39 33 31 36 32 30 2f  34 30 36 37 31 31 34 35  |9931620/40671145|
000000c0  32 34 2f 32 00 00 00 0d  38 35 2e 31 37 2e 31 33  |24/2....85.17.13|
000000d0  37 2e 31 35 31 00 00 00  05 00 06 3c 6e 75 6c 6c  |7.151......<null|
000000e0  3e 00 0f 48 54 54 50 2f  31 2e 31 20 32 30 30 20  |>..HTTP/1.1 200 |
000000f0  4f 4b 00 0e 63 6f 6e 74  65 6e 74 2d 6c 65 6e 67  |OK..content-leng|
00000100  74 68 00 06 34 31 31 36  34 38 00 0d 6c 61 73 74  |th..411648..last|
00000110  2d 6d 6f 64 69 66 69 65  64 00 1d 57 65 64 2c 20  |-modified..Wed, |
00000120  30 35 20 4d 61 72 20 32  30 31 34 20 31 31 3a 32  |05 Mar 2014 11:2|
00000130  34 3a 34 37 20 47 4d 54  00 04 64 61 74 65 00 1d  |4:47 GMT..date..|
00000140  54 75 65 2c 20 30 38 20  41 70 72 20 32 30 31 34  |Tue, 08 Apr 2014|
00000150  20 31 32 3a 33 31 3a 33  31 20 47 4d 54 00 06 73  | 12:31:31 GMT..s|
00000160  65 72 76 65 72 00 16 41  70 61 63 68 65 2f 32 2e  |erver..Apache/2.|
00000170  32 2e 32 32 20 28 55 62  75 6e 74 75 29           |2.22 (Ubuntu)|
0000017d
forensics@forensics:~/timeline$
```

The output presented in the figures indicates that the object **2** (`57ebc62f-6dfa622f`) is 411,648 bytes.

This is because, according to the output of the `istat` and `icat` utilities, the size and contents of the `/systemhost/24FC2AE3CB0.exe` (inode 46912) and `/Users/Alina/AppData/LocalLow/Sun/Java/Deployment/cache/6.0/47/57ebc62f-6dfa622f` **(inode 48075) files match**:

```
forensics@forensics:~/timeline$ icat -o 206848 /mnt/hgfs/evidence/image.dd 48075 | md5sum
1f1365b223e20aa69549b35409a7701f  -
forensics@forensics:~/timeline$ icat -o 206848 /mnt/hgfs/evidence/image.dd 46912 | md5sum
1f1365b223e20aa69549b35409a7701f  -
forensics@forensics:~/timeline$
```

It can be assumed that on March 13, 2014, a Java applet was downloaded from the URL `http://finansial.gov` (IP 85.17.137.151), which, when started, downloaded an executable file of size 411,648 bytes. The body of the file was saved in the `/systemhost/24FC2AE3CB0.exe` file. A link to the specified executable file was added as the `YI9B2F0F6EXG1Y1ZLMA` parameter in the `HKCU\Software\Microsoft\CurrentVersion\Run` registry key, which is responsible for auto-running programs when the operating system starts.

The results of the `MsiecfParser` parser, indicate that while working with Internet Explorer on April 8, 2014, at 12:31:13 UTC, the user accessed, perhaps unknowingly, the resource `http://finansial.gov`, from which the `utisl.jar` Java applet was subsequently downloaded and executed:

```
forensics@forensics:~/timeline$ psort.py -q -o dynamic timeline.body "select date,time,timezone,type,description_short where parser is 'MsiecfParser'" | grep -i "finansial.gov"
2014-03-05,08:54:13,UTC,Content Modification Time,Location: http://finansial.gov/
2014-04-08,12:31:13,UTC,Last Access Time,Location: http://finansial.gov/
2014-04-08,12:31:14,UTC,Last Checked Time,Location: http://finansial.gov/
[INFO] Output processing is done.
forensics@forensics:~/timeline$
```

Next, on analyzing the results of the `WinEvtxParser` processing module, we select from the Windows security log (`Security.evtx`) successful authentication events in the system (`EventId` 4624) after the appearance of the Java `.idx` files on April 8, 2014, at 12:31:13 UTC:

```
forensics@forensics:~/timeline$ psort.py -q -o dynamic timeline.body "select date,time,timezone,description where parser is 'WinEvtxParser' and filename contains 'security' and date > '2014-04-08 12:31:32' and description contains '[4624]'"
date,time,timezone,description
2014-04-08,12:33:28,UTC,[4624 / 0x00001210] Record Number: 570 Event Level: 0 Source Name: Microsoft-Windows-Security-Auditing Computer Name: ws-016 Strings: [u'S-1-5-18'  u'WS-016$'  u'WORKGROUP'  u'0x00000000000003e7'  u'S-1-5-18'  u'SYSTEM'  u'NT AUTHORITY'  u'0x00000000000003e7'  u'5'  u'Advapi  '  u'Negotiate'  None  u'{00000000-0000-0000-0000-000000000000}'  u'-'  u'-'  u'0'  u'0x000001f0'  u'C:\\Windows\\System32\\services.exe'  u'-'  u'-']
2014-04-08,12:33:55,UTC,[4624 / 0x00001210] Record Number: 574 Event Level: 0 Source Name: Microsoft-Windows-Security-Auditing Computer Name: ws-016 Strings: [u'S-1-0-0'  u'-'  u'-'  u'0x0000000000000000'  u'S-1-5-18'  u'SYSTEM'  u'NT AUTHORITY'  u'0x00000000000003e7'  u'0'  u'-'  u'-'  u'{00000000-0000-0000-0000-000000000000}'  u'-'  u'-'  u'0'  u'0x00000004'  u'-'  u'-'  u'-']
2014-04-08,12:33:55,UTC,[4624 / 0x00001210] Record Number: 576 Event Level: 0 Source Name: Microsoft-Windows-Security-Auditing Computer Name: ws-016 Strings: [u'S-1-5-18'  u'WS-016$'  u'WORKGROUP'  u'0x00000000000003e7'  u'S-1-5-18'  u'SYSTEM'  u'NT AUTHORITY'  u'0x00000000000003e7'  u'5'  u'Advapi  '  u'Negotiate'  u''  u'{00000000-0000-0000-0000-000000000000}'  u'-'  u'-'  u'0'  u'0x000001f4'  u'C:\\Windows\\System32\\services.exe'  u'-'  u'-']
2014-04-08,12:33:55,UTC,[4624 / 0x00001210] Record Number: 578 Event Level: 0 Source Name: Microsoft-Windows-Security-Auditing Computer Name: ws-016 Strings: [u'S-1-5-18'  u'WS-016$'  u'WORKGROUP'  u'0x00000000000003e7'  u'S-1-5-20'  u'NETWORK SERVICE'  u'NT AUTHORITY'  u'0x00000000000003e4'  u'5'  u'Advapi  '  u'Negotiate'  u''  u'{00000000-0000-0000-0000-000000000000}'  u'-'  u'-'  u'0'  u'0x000001f4'  u'C:\\Windows\\System32\\services.exe'  u'-'  u'-']
2014-04-08,12:33:55,UTC,[4624 / 0x00001210] Record Number: 580 Event Level: 0 Source Name: Microsoft-Windows-Security-Auditing Computer Name: ws-016 Strings: [u'S-1-5-18'  u'WS-016$'  u'WORKGROUP'  u'0x00000000000003e7'  u'S-1-5-19'  u'LOCAL SERVICE'  u'NT AUTHORITY'  u'0x00000000000003e5'  u'5'  u'Advapi  '  u'Negotiate'  u''  u'{00000000-0000-0000-0000-000000000000}'  u'-'  u'-'  u'0'  u'0x000001f4'  u'C:\\Windows\\System32\\services.exe'  u'-'  u'-']
2014-04-08,12:33:55,UTC,[4624 / 0x00001210] Record Number: 584 Event Level: 0 Source Name: Microsoft-Windows-Security-Auditing Computer Name: ws-016 Strings: [u'S-1-5-18'  u'WS-016$'  u'WORKGROUP'  u'0x00000000000003e7'  u'S-1-5-18'  u'SYSTEM'  u'NT AUTHORITY'  u'0x00000000000003e7'  u'5'  u'Advapi  '  u'Negotiate'  u''  u'{00000000-0000-0000-0000-000000000000}'  u'-'  u'-'  u'0'  u'0x000001f4'  u'C:\\Windows\\System32\\services.exe'  u'-'  u'-']
2014-04-08,12:33:55,UTC,[4624 / 0x00001210] Record Number: 582 Event Level: 0 Source Name: Microsoft-Windows-Security-Auditing Computer Name: ws-016 Strings: [u'S-1-5-18'  u'WS-016$'  u'WORKGROUP'  u'0x00000000000003e7'  u'S-1-5-18'  u'SYSTEM'  u'NT AUTHORITY'  u'0x00000000000003e7'  u'5'  u'Advapi  '  u'Negotiate'  u''  u'{00000000-0000-0000-0000-000000000000}'  u'-'  u'-'  u'0'  u'0x000001f4'  u'C:\\Windows\\System32\\services.exe'  u'-'  u'-']
2014-04-08,12:33:57,UTC,[4624 / 0x00001210] Record Number: 586 Event Level: 0 Source Name: Microsoft-Windows-Security-Auditing Computer Name: ws-016 Strings: [u'S-1-5-18'  u'WS-016$'  u'WORKGROUP'  u'0x00000000000003e7'  u'S-1-5-18'  u'SYSTEM'  u'NT AUTHORITY'  u'0x00000000000003e7'  u'5'  u'Advapi  '  u'Negotiate'  u''  u'{00000000-0000-0000-0000-000000000000}'  u'-'  u'-'  u'0'  u'0x000001f4'  u'C:\\Windows\\System32\\services.exe'  u'-'  u'-']
```

To present the result in a more convenient form, we can convert it with the following commands:

```
sed -r "s/^([^\[]+),.+Strings: \[(.+)\]$/\1\  \2/" |
sed -r "s/\s*u'([^']+)'\s*/\|\1\|/g" |
sed -r "s/\|+/\|/g" |
awk 'BEGIN {FS="\\|"; OFS=", "}; {print $1, $7, $8, $6,
$10, $20, $21}'
```

You can see them in the following screenshot:

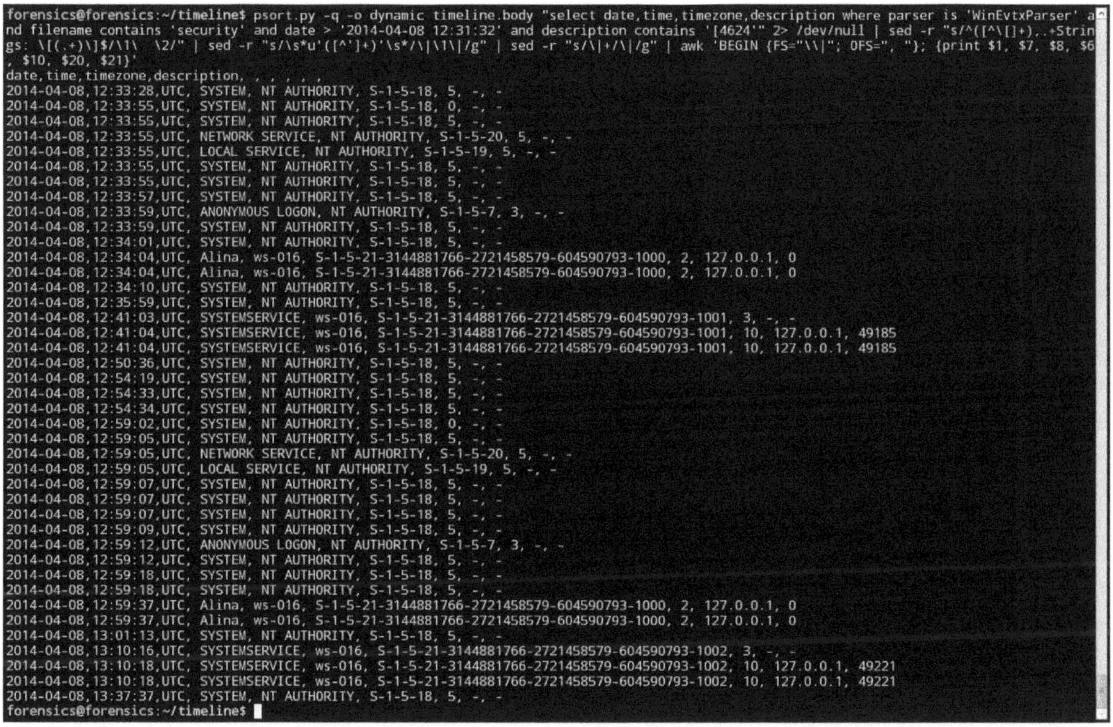

forensics@forensics:~/timeline$ psort.py -q -o dynamic timeline.body "select date,time,timezone,description where parser is 'WinEvtxParser' a
nd filename contains 'security' and date > '2014-04-08 12:31:32' and description contains '[4624'" 2> /dev/null | sed -r "s/^([^\[]+),.+Strin
gs: \[(.+)\]$/\1\ \2/" | sed -r "s/\s*u'([^']+)'\s*/\|\1\|/g" | sed -r "s/\|+/\|/g" | awk 'BEGIN {FS="\\|"; OFS=", "}; {print $1, $7, $8, $6
, $10, $20, $21}'
date,time,timezone,description, , , , , ,
2014-04-08,12:33:28,UTC, SYSTEM, NT AUTHORITY, S-1-5-18, 5, -, -
2014-04-08,12:33:55,UTC, SYSTEM, NT AUTHORITY, S-1-5-18, 0, -, -
2014-04-08,12:33:55,UTC, SYSTEM, NT AUTHORITY, S-1-5-18, 5, -, -
2014-04-08,12:33:55,UTC, NETWORK SERVICE, NT AUTHORITY, S-1-5-20, 5, -, -
2014-04-08,12:33:55,UTC, LOCAL SERVICE, NT AUTHORITY, S-1-5-19, 5, -, -
2014-04-08,12:33:55,UTC, SYSTEM, NT AUTHORITY, S-1-5-18, 5, -, -
2014-04-08,12:33:55,UTC, SYSTEM, NT AUTHORITY, S-1-5-18, 5, -, -
2014-04-08,12:33:57,UTC, SYSTEM, NT AUTHORITY, S-1-5-18, 5, -, -
2014-04-08,12:33:59,UTC, ANONYMOUS LOGON, NT AUTHORITY, S-1-5-7, 3, -, -
2014-04-08,12:33:59,UTC, SYSTEM, NT AUTHORITY, S-1-5-18, 5, -, -
2014-04-08,12:34:01,UTC, SYSTEM, NT AUTHORITY, S-1-5-18, 5, -, -
2014-04-08,12:34:04,UTC, Alina, ws-016, S-1-5-21-3144881766-2721458579-604590793-1000, 2, 127.0.0.1, 0
2014-04-08,12:34:04,UTC, Alina, ws-016, S-1-5-21-3144881766-2721458579-604590793-1000, 2, 127.0.0.1, 0
2014-04-08,12:34:10,UTC, SYSTEM, NT AUTHORITY, S-1-5-18, 5, -, -
2014-04-08,12:35:59,UTC, SYSTEM, NT AUTHORITY, S-1-5-18, 5, -, -
2014-04-08,12:41:03,UTC, SYSTEMSERVICE, ws-016, S-1-5-21-3144881766-2721458579-604590793-1001, 3, -, -
2014-04-08,12:41:04,UTC, SYSTEMSERVICE, ws-016, S-1-5-21-3144881766-2721458579-604590793-1001, 10, 127.0.0.1, 49185
2014-04-08,12:41:04,UTC, SYSTEMSERVICE, ws-016, S-1-5-21-3144881766-2721458579-604590793-1001, 10, 127.0.0.1, 49185
2014-04-08,12:50:36,UTC, SYSTEM, NT AUTHORITY, S-1-5-18, 5, -, -
2014-04-08,12:54:19,UTC, SYSTEM, NT AUTHORITY, S-1-5-18, 5, -, -
2014-04-08,12:54:33,UTC, SYSTEM, NT AUTHORITY, S-1-5-18, 5, -, -
2014-04-08,12:54:34,UTC, SYSTEM, NT AUTHORITY, S-1-5-18, 5, -, -
2014-04-08,12:59:02,UTC, SYSTEM, NT AUTHORITY, S-1-5-18, 0, -, -
2014-04-08,12:59:05,UTC, SYSTEM, NT AUTHORITY, S-1-5-18, 5, -, -
2014-04-08,12:59:05,UTC, NETWORK SERVICE, NT AUTHORITY, S-1-5-20, 5, -, -
2014-04-08,12:59:05,UTC, LOCAL SERVICE, NT AUTHORITY, S-1-5-19, 5, -, -
2014-04-08,12:59:07,UTC, SYSTEM, NT AUTHORITY, S-1-5-18, 5, -, -
2014-04-08,12:59:07,UTC, SYSTEM, NT AUTHORITY, S-1-5-18, 5, -, -
2014-04-08,12:59:07,UTC, SYSTEM, NT AUTHORITY, S-1-5-18, 5, -, -
2014-04-08,12:59:09,UTC, SYSTEM, NT AUTHORITY, S-1-5-18, 5, -, -
2014-04-08,12:59:12,UTC, ANONYMOUS LOGON, NT AUTHORITY, S-1-5-7, 3, -, -
2014-04-08,12:59:12,UTC, SYSTEM, NT AUTHORITY, S-1-5-18, 5, -, -
2014-04-08,12:59:18,UTC, SYSTEM, NT AUTHORITY, S-1-5-18, 5, -, -
2014-04-08,12:59:18,UTC, SYSTEM, NT AUTHORITY, S-1-5-18, 5, -, -
2014-04-08,12:59:37,UTC, Alina, ws-016, S-1-5-21-3144881766-2721458579-604590793-1000, 2, 127.0.0.1, 0
2014-04-08,12:59:37,UTC, Alina, ws-016, S-1-5-21-3144881766-2721458579-604590793-1000, 2, 127.0.0.1, 0
2014-04-08,13:01:13,UTC, SYSTEM, NT AUTHORITY, S-1-5-18, 5, -, -
2014-04-08,13:10:16,UTC, SYSTEMSERVICE, ws-016, S-1-5-21-3144881766-2721458579-604590793-1002, 3, -, -
2014-04-08,13:10:18,UTC, SYSTEMSERVICE, ws-016, S-1-5-21-3144881766-2721458579-604590793-1002, 10, 127.0.0.1, 49221
2014-04-08,13:10:18,UTC, SYSTEMSERVICE, ws-016, S-1-5-21-3144881766-2721458579-604590793-1002, 10, 127.0.0.1, 49221
2014-04-08,13:37:37,UTC, SYSTEM, NT AUTHORITY, S-1-5-18, 5, -, -
forensics@forensics:~/timeline$

Note that the authentication type, `(LogonType),10`, indicates that the target system made a connection via the RDP protocol.

Timeline

The screenshot shows that on April 8, several RDP protocol connections were made by the user, SYSTEMSERVICE. Pay attention to two features: the connection was made using IP address 127.0.0.1 (loopback), that is, effectively from the computer under investigation to itself; and the **security identifiers** (**SIDs**) of the user SYSTEMSERVICE are different, that is, the user was recreated several times in the specified time interval.

By filtering the results of the WinEvtxParser module for EventId 4720 (user creation) and the user name SYSTEMSERVICE, we come to the conclusion that the specified user was first created on April 8 at 12:40:52 UTC, and three attempts were later made to recreate it:

```
forensics@forensics:~/timeline$ psort.py -q -o dynamic timeline.body "select date,time,timezone,description where parser is 'WinEvtxParser' and filename contains 'security' and date > '2014-04-08 12:31:32' and description contains '[4720' and description contains 'u\'SYSTEMSERVICE\''"
date,time,timezone,description
2014-04-08,12:40:52,UTC,[4720 / 0x00001270] Record Number: 605 Event Level: 0 Source Name: Microsoft-Windows-Security-Auditing Computer Name: ws-016 Strings: [u'SYSTEMSERVICE'  u'ws-016'  u'S-1-5-21-3144881766-2721458579-604590793-1001'  u'S-1-5-18'  u'WS-016$'  u'WORKGROUP'  u'0x00000000000003e7'  u'-'  u'SYSTEMSERVICE'  u'%%1793'  u'-'  u'%%1793'  u'%%1793'  u'%%1793'  u'%%1793'  u'%%1793'  u'%%1794'  u'%%1794'  u'513'  u'-'  u'0x0'  u'0x15'  u'\r\n\t\t%%2080\r\n\t\t%%2082\r\n\t\t%%2084'  u'%%1793'  u'-'  u'%%1797']
2014-04-08,13:10:14,UTC,[4720 / 0x00001270] Record Number: 1058 Event Level: 0 Source Name: Microsoft-Windows-Security-Auditing Computer Name: ws-016 Strings: [u'SYSTEMSERVICE'  u'ws-016'  u'S-1-5-21-3144881766-2721458579-604590793-1002'  u'S-1-5-18'  u'WS-016$'  u'WORKGROUP'  u'0x00000000000003e7'  u'-'  u'SYSTEMSERVICE'  u'%%1793'  u'-'  u'%%1793'  u'%%1793'  u'%%1793'  u'%%1793'  u'%%1793'  u'%%1794'  u'%%1794'  u'513'  u'-'  u'0x0'  u'0x15'  u'\r\n\t\t%%2080\r\n\t\t%%2082\r\n\t\t%%2084'  u'%%1793'  u'-'  u'%%1797']
[INFO] Output processing is done.
forensics@forensics:~/timeline$
```

So, now we can establish a likely scenario for the incident: on April 8, 2014, the user Alina accessed, perhaps unknowingly, the resource http://finansial.gov, as a result of which the utisl.jar Java applet was downloaded and executed.

Next, an unknown object of size 411,648 bytes was downloaded from the URL, http://w282d1wb.athleticsdrycleaner.pw/f/1389931620/4067114524/, the body of which was saved in the /systemhost/24FC2AE3CB0.exe file. A link to the specified executable file was added as the YI9B2F0F6EXG1Y1ZLMA parameter in the HKCU\Software\Microsoft\CurrentVersion\Run registry key, which is responsible for auto-running programs at system startup.

Thereafter, the system repeatedly created a suspicious user named SYSTEMSERVICE, under which local connections were made to the system via the RDP protocol.

Summary

In this chapter, we looked at time-related attributions on different filesystems, how to build a timeline with TSK and with the Plaso framework.

In the next chapter, we will cover how to analyze dates on the NTFS and FAT filesystems. We will continue to work with TSK and study other utilities from TSK.

6
Filesystem Analysis and Data Recovery

Although there are many automated and commercial tools available nowadays, understanding how these tools perform can distinguish one from another, and this can provide great support during expert testimony in the courtroom. Filesystem analysis and data recovery are considered as the main categories in the digital forensics process. Extracting files from a storage device or recovering deleted ones with evidential related data can solve a case.

In this chapter, we will go through two different filesystems: the FAT and the NTFS. We will basically explain how the files are structured in each one and how the recovery process of deleted files actually works. We will start with the famous TSK or The Sleuth Kit and how its command line tools are categorized, as they are based on each layer in the hard drive or the forensic image. After this, we will discuss Autopsy, the TSK graphical user interface. At the end of this chapter, we will show you Foremost of these, which is the Linux-based file carving tool that is used to recover files based on their signature.

Hard drive structure

Before we start explaining the different filesystem structures, we need to illustrate the different parts in a partitioned hard drive in Windows OS. The following figure illustrates simply the structure of a whole partitioned hard drive:

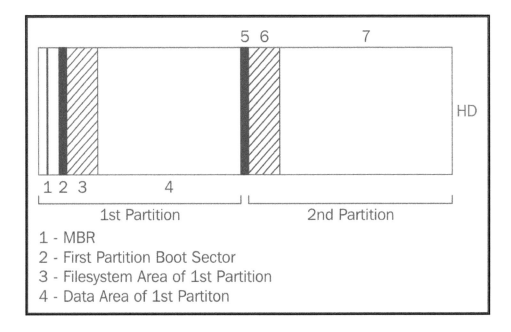

Simple hard drive logical parts

Master boot record

The master boot record is the first sector (512 bytes) of the hard drive. It contains, besides the boot code, all the information about the hard drive. One of the important pieces of information that can be found in the MBR is the partition table, which contains information about the partition structure in the hard drive, and for each partition, it can tell where it starts, its size, and type.

The investigator can check the existing partition with the information in the MBR and the printed size of the hard drive for a match. If there is some missing space, the handler may assume the presence of an intended action to hide some space contains usually some related important information.

Partition boot sector

The first sector (512 bytes) of each partition contains information, such as the type of the filesystem, the booting code location, the sector size, and the cluster size in reference to sector.

The filesystem area in partition

If the user formatted the partition, for example, in the NTFS filesystem, some sectors at the beginning of the partition will be reserved for the **Master File Table** or **MFT**. MFT is the location that contains the metadata about the files in the system. Each entry is 1KB in size, and when a user deletes a file, the file's entry in the MFT is marked as unallocated. However, the file's information still exists until another file uses this MFT entry and overwrites the previous file's information.

Normal backups usually store the allocated entries only and ignore the unallocated areas in the MFT. This won't be helpful in recovering deleted files during the analysis step.

Data area

After reserving the filesystem's area, the rest of the partition space will be available for the file's data, which contains the actual data of the file. Each unit of the data area is called **cluster** or **block**. In the same way, if a user deletes a file from the hard drive, the clusters that contain data that is related to this file will be marked as unallocated, and the data will exist until new data that is related to a new file overwrites it.

These clusters are considered either allocated or unallocated:

- **Allocated cluster**: This is a cluster that contains data that is related to a file that exists and has an entry in the filesystem MFT area
- **Unallocated cluster**: This is a cluster that isn't connected to an existing file and it may be any of the following:
    - **Empty**: This means that it has no data of a deleted file or its content has been wiped
    - **Not empty**: This contains data that is related to a deleted file and still hasn't been overwritten with a new file's data.

While running a backup tool to the system, it backs up only the files that exist in the current filesystem MFT area and identifies its related cluster in the data area as allocated. This is NOT a forensically sound image which needs to acquire all the hard drive areas even if it was deleted by the user. That is why, when you backup your system using no compression, the size of the backup will be the size of the used space in the partition.

However, when using forensic imaging techniques, the size of the resulting image will be equal to exactly the size of the source; it will either comprise the whole hard drive or a single partition.

In the following section, we will quickly overview how FAT and NTFS work.

The FAT filesystem

FAT or File Allocation Table became famous with the announcement of the DOS operating system from Microsoft in 1980. After this, FAT went through many improvements trying to make it adapt with the rapidly improving technology. So, we can see FAT12, FAT16, FAT32, and exFAT. Each version overcame some of the limitations of the filesystem until the announcement of NTFS filesystem.

FAT components

FAT partition contains five main areas. They comprise the following:

- **Boot sector**: This is the first sector of the partition that is loaded in memory. If this partition is the active partition, it contains information such as, but not limited to, the following:
    - **Jump code**: This is the location of the bootstrap and OS initialization code
    - **Sector size**: This is almost fixed (512 bytes)
    - **Cluster size**: This is in sectors (sectors/clusters)
    - **Number of sectors**: The total number of sectors in the partition
    - **Number of root entries**: This value is used with FAT12 and FAT16 only

- **FAT table**: This is the filesystem, which is named after this area. Starting from the first cluster of the file, which can be found in the root directory entry of a file, the FAT area tracks the rest of the file in the data area. Each data cluster, for example, cluster X is the first cluster that contains the data of file Y, has an entry in the FAT area. This entry can have four values:
    - 0: This indicates that cluster X is an unallocated cluster
    - **Number**: This indicates the number of the next cluster following cluster X, and it contains the next part of file Y
    - **EOF**: This is end of the file, and it indicates that cluster X is the last cluster that contains the data of file Y, End of File Y
    - **BAD**: This indicates that cluster X is a bad cluster, and it cannot be used or accessed by the operating system. This data tracking schema is called the FAT chain, and it must exist for each file.

- **Another copy of the FAT table**: This is used if the first FAT got corrupted.
- **Root directory entries**: This is when each entry describes either directory or file in the filesystem, and its location from the root directory. Each entry contains information, such as the following:
    - Short File name with an 8.3 naming schema; eight characters for the name and three characters for the extension
    - Long file name if the file name exceeds the 8.3 schema, it will reserve another complete entry to store the file name
    - Entry's status such as directory, file, or deleted
    - Some file properties, such as read only, hidden and archive
    - File size, which is not important in the case of a directory
    - Timestamps of the file
    - The address of the first cluster, which contains the file's data

    As we can see no modern properties can be added to the file, such as compression, permissions, and encryption, which was one of the FAT filesystem limitations.

- **Data area**: This is the rest of the partition. It contains the actual contents of the files in the partition, and it is divided in clusters with a size mentioned in the boot sector. Cluster numbering starts with cluster 2, so cluster 0 and cluster 1 don't exist.

For an example of how this works, we have created table 1. Each major column represents one of the FAT areas, excluding the boot sector. Now, let's suppose that the first file, F1.txt, has a size of 1KB and starts at cluster 2:

- Cluster 2 contains the first part of the F1.txt file
- In the FAT entry that describes cluster 2, we will find the next cluster in the chain which, in our case, is cluster 3
- At cluster 3, we can find the next part of the F1.txt file
- In the FAT entry that describes cluster 3, we can find EoF because no more data in the F1.txt file needs to be stored

The same can be applied to the other files:

FAT TABLE (Each entry describes one cluster)					Root directory entries			DATA Area (Cluster is 512 bytes)				
					Name	Size	First Cluster					
3	EoF	BAD	6	7	F1.txt	1024	2	F11	F12		F21	F22
9	BAD	EoF			F2.txt	2048	5	F23		F24		

The FAT filesystem

FAT limitations

FAT had some serious limitations, which raised the need for a more advanced filesystem:

- The number after each FAT, such as FAT12, FAT16, or FAT32, represents the number of bits that are assigned to address clusters in the FAT table:
    - **FAT12**: This is 2^12 = 4,096 clusters at the maximum.
    - **FAT16**: This is 2^16 = 65,536 clusters at the maximum.
    - **FAT32**: This is 2^32 = 4,294,967,296 clusters, but it has 4 reserved bits, so it is actually 28 bits. So, 2^28 = 268,435,456 at the maximum.
    - **exFAT**: This uses the whole 32 bits for addressing.

- The maximum partition size in FAT32 = the maximum number of clusters, which is 268,435,456, multiplied by the maximum cluster size, which is 23 KB = 8,589,934,592 KB = 8 TB.

- For the maximum file size in FAT32, as an example, the bit file used to store the file size in bytes is 32 bit long. The maximum number this can store is 2^32= 4,294,967,296 bytes = 4 GB. So, the maximum file size that FAT32 can handle is 4 GB. That is why we can't store files whose size exceeds 4 GB in the FAT32 filesystem.
- Properties such as access control and encryption weren't available in the FAT filesystem.

The NTFS filesystem

NTFS or **New Technology Filesystem** is the default filesystem in Windows NT as a result of the storage capacity increasing and the need for a more secure, scalable, and advanced filesystem. NTFS overcame the FAT limitations and was more suitable for high storage capacity. In NTFS, everything is a file including the filesystem area itself, as we will see in the following section.

NTFS components

Like FAT and any other filesystem, NTFS has its components as follows:

The boot sector is the first sector in the partition, and it contains some information about the filesystem itself, such as start code, sector size, cluster size in sectors, and the number of reserved sectors. The filesystem area contains many files, including the MFT or Master File Table, which contains the metadata of the files and directories in the partition. It will be discussed later.

- The data area holds the actual contents of the files, and it is divided in clusters with a size determined during formatting and mentioned in the boot sector.

Master File Table (MFT)

As everything in NTFS is a file, the filesystem area is also a single file called $MFT. In this file, there is an entry for each file in the partition. This entry is 1,024 bytes in size. Actually, $MFT file has an entry for itself. Each entry has a header of 42 bytes at the beginning and has a signature of 0xEB52904E, which is equivalent to FILE as ASCII.

The signature also can be BAD, in this case, it indicates an error that occurred in this entry. After the header, there will be another 982 bytes left to store the file metadata. If there is space left to store the file contents, typically in small size files, the file's data is stored in the entry itself and no space in the data area is used by this file.

Each MFT entry has another substructure called **attributes**. MFT uses attributes to store the metadata of the file. Different attribute types can be used in single MFT entry. Each attribute is assigned to store different information. For example, the Standard Information Attribute contains the timestamp and the size of the file, whereas the Data Attribute holds the actual contents of the file.

The attribute can be either of the following:

- **Resident**: This contains all its data within the MFT entry.
- **Non-resident**: Because of the limitation of the MFT size, some attributes may need to store their data in the data area. A clear example of this kind of attribute is the data attribute.

Storing the file metadata in attributes creates flexibility for NTFS to add more types of attributes that are recognized by the operating system in the future. If one file has many attributes and needs more than one MFT entry to store its metadata, it can use another entry and link both entries with a sequence number.

The Sleuth Kit (TSK)

The Sleuth Kit or TSK is a collection of open source digital forensic tools developed by *Brian Carrier* and *Wieste Venema*. TSK can read and parse different types of filesystems, such as FAT, NTFS, and EXT. Each area of the hard drive in the figure in the *Hard drive structure* section has a set of tools in The Sleuth Kit that parses that area and extracts forensically important information for the investigator. Usually, each step leads to the next while using TSK in analysis.

In the upcoming sections, we will go through the different tool sets of The Sleuth Kit. We will use an image of the hard drive with Windows 7 installed, which shows the results from each part in the hard drive. The image was acquired using the FTK Imager lite from a Windows 7 virtual machine with a size of only 15 GB and a single NTFS partition.

As we will see, TSK tool names are easy to understand as they consist of two parts. The first part represents the area or the layer under investigation, such as mm for media management, fs for filesystem, i for metadata, and f for filename layer. The second part is the normal Linux command that reflects the effect of this tool, such as ls to list and cat to display the contents, for example, the mmls tool.

Volume layer (media management)

In this area of the hard drive, TSK parses information about the structure of the whole hard drive from the **MBR** or **Master Boot Record**, which is the first sector of the hard drive. We can parse this area with TSK using different tools.

The information about each partition is in the hard drive, and it can be determined from the partition table at the end of the MBR sector. The offset of each partition will be used as an input to the upcoming TSK tools to specify the partition of interest. The mmls tool is used to list information, such as in the following screenshot:

```
digforensics@forensics:/mnt/hgfs/windows7$ mmls sampleimage.dd
DOS Partition Table
Offset Sector: 0
Units are in 512-byte sectors

     Slot    Start        End          Length       Description
00:  Meta    0000000000   0000000000   0000000001   Primary Table (#0)
01:  -----   0000000000   0000002047   0000002048   Unallocated
02:  00:00   0000002048   0031453183   0031451136   NTFS (0x07)
03:  -----   0031453184   0031457279   0000004096   Unallocated
digforensics@forensics:/mnt/hgfs/windows7$
```

The mmls tool

Filesystem Analysis and Data Recovery

From the result of running `mmls` against the image, we can see that there is only one NTFS partition that starts at sector (2,048). This is the partition of interest, so we will use the start sector as the offset with the rest of the tools when needed. This also provides the partition table type, which is normal DOS in our case here. To display only the allocated volumes, we can use the `-a` option:

```
digforensics@forensics:/mnt/hgfs/windows7$ mmls -a sampleimage.dd
DOS Partition Table
Offset Sector: 0
Units are in 512-byte sectors

     Slot    Start       End         Length      Description
02:  00:00   0000002048  0031453183  0031451136  NTFS (0x07)
digforensics@forensics:/mnt/hgfs/windows7$
```

A list allocated volumes only

The next command is `mmcat`, which displays the partition contents as shown in the following screenshot:

```
digforensics@forensics:/mnt/hgfs/windows7$ mmcat sampleimage.dd 02 | hexdump -C -v | more
00000000  eb 52 90 4e 54 46 53 20  20 20 20 00 02 08 00 00  |.R.NTFS    .....|
00000010  00 00 00 00 00 f8 00 00  3f 00 ff 00 00 08 00 00  |........?.......|
00000020  00 00 00 00 80 00 80 00  ff ef 1f 01 00 00 00 00  |................|
00000030  00 00 0c 00 00 00 00 00  02 00 00 00 00 00 00 00  |................|
00000040  f6 00 00 00 01 00 00 00  e6 be d8 fa e4 d8 fa 18  |................|
00000050  00 00 00 00 fa 33 c0 8e  d0 bc 00 7c fb 68 c0 07  |.....3.....|.h..|
00000060  1f 1e 68 66 00 cb 88 16  0e 00 66 81 3e 03 00 4e  |..hf......f.>..N|
00000070  54 46 53 75 15 b4 41 bb  aa 55 cd 13 72 0c 81 fb  |TFSu..A..U..r...|
00000080  55 aa 75 06 f7 c1 01 00  75 03 e9 dd 00 1e 83 ec  |U.u.....u.......|
00000090  18 68 1a 00 b4 48 8a 16  0e 00 8b f4 16 1f cd 13  |.h...H..........|
000000a0  9f 83 c4 18 9e 58 1f 72  e1 3b 06 0b 00 75 db a3  |.....X.r.;...u..|
000000b0  0f 00 c1 2e 0f 00 04 1e  5a 33 db b9 00 20 2b c8  |........Z3... +.|
000000c0  66 ff 06 11 00 03 16 0f  00 8e c2 ff 06 16 00 e8  |f...............|
000000d0  4b 00 2b c8 77 ef b8 00  bb cd 1a 66 23 c0 75 2d  |K.+.w......f#.u-|
000000e0  66 81 fb 54 43 50 41 75  24 81 f9 02 01 72 1e 16  |f..TCPAu$....r..|
000000f0  68 07 bb 16 68 70 0e 16  68 09 00 66 53 66 53 66  |h...hp..h..fSfSf|
00000100  55 16 16 16 68 b8 01 66  61 0e 07 cd 1a 33 c0 bf  |U...h..fa....3..|
00000110  28 10 b9 d8 0f fc f3 aa  e9 5f 01 90 90 66 60 1e  |(........_...f`.|
00000120  06 66 a1 11 00 66 03 06  1c 00 1e 66 68 00 00 00  |.f...f.....fh...|
00000130  00 66 50 06 53 68 01 00  68 10 00 b4 42 8a 16 0e  |.fP.Sh..h...B...|
00000140  00 16 1f 8b f4 cd 13 66  59 5b 5a 66 59 66 59 1f  |.......fY[ZfYfY.|
00000150  0f 82 16 00 66 ff 06 11  00 03 16 0f 00 8e c2 ff  |....f...........|
00000160  0e 16 00 75 bc 07 1f 66  61 c3 a0 f8 01 e8 09 00  |...u...fa.......|
00000170  a0 fb 01 e8 03 00 f4 eb  fd b4 01 8b f0 ac 3c 00  |..............<.|
00000180  74 09 b4 0e bb 07 00 cd  10 eb f2 c3 0d 0a 41 20  |t.............A |
00000190  64 69 73 6b 20 72 65 61  64 20 65 72 72 6f 72 20  |disk read error |
--More--
```

The mmcat tool

[106]

In the previous figure, we used `mmcat` with the image name `sampleimage.dd` and the number of the target partition as in the `mmls` output 02. Then, we pipelined the output to the `hexdump` tool. You can see in the beginning of the partition, the volume boot record starts with the NTFS partition signature at offset 0x03 with a value of (NTFS) or 0x(4E54465320202020).

Filesystem layer

The TSK tool for this layer parses the filesystem used in the provided partition and displays some information about it to the investigator. With this tool, we must provide the offset of the target partition from the output of the mmls tool, which in our case is (2,048):

The fsstat tool

We can find the MFT location within the partition, cluster size, and information about the NTFS attributes, which may be used later in further analysis.

The metadata layer

The metadata layer (or inode) parses and describes the information or the metadata record of the file as described in the filesystem. Also, the output of this tool can be used with other tools to narrow the results for a specific file in the image.

The `i` character in the commands in this layer stands for inode—the metadata unique number of a file in the EXT filesystem.

The `ils` command is used to list the inode numbers of the deleted files in the image until told to list all the inode information for all the files in the image. All the results of the `ils` are information about the file, including the inode of the file, the timestamps (MACB) in Unix time, and size of the file. We can use `ils` with the `-m` option to create a compatible output for the `mactime` tool in case we need to create a timeline for the file activity in the image.

Also, using `--m` will allow us to read the filename as well, as shown in the following screenshot:

ils to list the deleted files

The result only shows the deleted files as we can notice the 'dead' status of all the files in the results.

istat

This is used to parse the MFT or the inode record by its unique metadata number and view all the information in the provided record. The resulting information is only metadata, so we can find the timestamps, file attributes, and so on, not the data itself even if the data is short enough to fit in the 1,024 KB length of one MFT record, which is called resident.

Displaying the data contents of the file can be determined by another tool in TSK, which will be discussed next. Each file in the NTFS filesystem has an entry of this kind, even the MFT file itself. In the following figure, we will list information about the first record number 0, which is the $MFT itself:

```
digforensics@forensics:/mnt/hgfs/windows7$ istat -o 2048 sampleimage.dd 0 | more
MFT Entry Header Values:
Entry: 0        Sequence: 1
$LogFile Sequence Number: 110521486
Allocated File
Links: 1

$STANDARD_INFORMATION Attribute Values:
Flags: Hidden, System
Owner ID: 0
Security ID: 256  (S-1-5-18)
Created:        2014-10-10 03:43:12 (EDT)
File Modified:  2014-10-10 03:43:12 (EDT)
MFT Modified:   2014-10-10 03:43:12 (EDT)
Accessed:       2014-10-10 03:43:12 (EDT)

$FILE_NAME Attribute Values:
Flags: Hidden, System
Name: $MFT
Parent MFT Entry: 5     Sequence: 5
Allocated Size: 16384           Actual Size: 16384
Created:        2014-10-10 03:43:12 (EDT)
File Modified:  2014-10-10 03:43:12 (EDT)
MFT Modified:   2014-10-10 03:43:12 (EDT)
Accessed:       2014-10-10 03:43:12 (EDT)

Attributes:
Type: $STANDARD_INFORMATION (16-0)   Name: N/A    Resident    size: 72
Type: $FILE_NAME (48-3)    Name: N/A    Resident    size: 74
Type: $DATA (128-1)    Name: N/A    Non-Resident    size: 59506688    init_size: 59506688
786432 786433 786434 786435 786436 786437 786438 786439
786440 786441 786442 786443 786444 786445 786446 786447
786448 786449 786450 786451 786452 786453 786454 786455
```

The istat tool to view the metadata of a file

icat

This is used to view the contents of a specific data unit. It uses the inode number as a reference to view the data blocks that are related to this file. In the forensic image under investigation, we will view the contents of the $MFT file with inode 0:

```
digforensics@forensics:/mnt/hgfs/windows7$ icat -o 2048 sampleimage.dd 0 | hexdump -Cv | more
00000000  46 49 4c 45 30 00 03 00  8e 6c 96 06 00 00 00 00  |FILE0....l......|
00000010  01 00 01 00 38 00 01 00  a8 01 00 00 00 04 00 00  |....8...........|
00000020  00 00 00 00 00 00 00 00  06 00 00 00 00 00 00 00  |................|
00000030  29 00 ff ff 00 00 00 00  10 00 00 00 60 00 00 00  |)...........`...|
00000040  00 00 18 00 00 00 00 00  48 00 00 00 18 00 00 00  |........H.......|
00000050  43 24 1f d8 5d e4 cf 01  43 24 1f d8 5d e4 cf 01  |C$..]...C$..]...|
00000060  43 24 1f d8 5d e4 cf 01  43 24 1f d8 5d e4 cf 01  |C$..]...C$..]...|
00000070  06 00 00 00 00 00 00 00  00 00 00 00 00 00 00 00  |................|
00000080  00 00 00 00 00 01 00 00  00 00 00 00 00 00 00 00  |................|
00000090  00 00 00 00 00 00 00 00  30 00 00 00 68 00 00 00  |........0...h...|
000000a0  00 00 18 00 00 00 03 00  4a 00 00 00 18 00 01 00  |........J.......|
000000b0  05 00 00 00 00 00 05 00  43 24 1f d8 5d e4 cf 01  |........C$..]...|
000000c0  43 24 1f d8 5d e4 cf 01  43 24 1f d8 5d e4 cf 01  |C$..]...C$..]...|
000000d0  43 24 1f d8 5d e4 cf 01  00 40 00 00 00 00 00 00  |C$..]....@......|
000000e0  00 40 00 00 00 00 00 00  06 00 00 00 00 00 00 00  |.@..............|
000000f0  04 03 24 00 4d 00 46 00  54 00 00 00 00 00 00 00  |..$.M.F.T.......|
00000100  80 00 00 00 50 00 00 00  01 00 40 00 00 00 01 00  |....P.....@.....|
00000110  00 00 00 00 00 00 00 00  bf 38 00 00 00 00 00 00  |.........8......|
00000120  40 00 00 00 00 00 00 00  00 00 8c 03 00 00 00 00  |@...............|
00000130  00 00 8c 03 00 00 00 00  00 00 8c 03 00 00 00 00  |................|
00000140  32 40 38 00 00 0c 21 60  05 7d 31 20 6c a2 11 00  |2@8...!`.}1 l...|
00000150  b0 00 00 00 50 00 00 00  01 00 40 00 00 00 05 00  |....P.....@.....|
00000160  00 00 00 00 00 00 00 00  02 00 00 00 00 00 00 00  |................|
00000170  40 00 00 00 00 00 00 00  00 30 00 00 00 00 00 00  |@........0......|
00000180  08 20 00 00 00 00 00 00  08 20 00 00 00 00 00 00  |. ....... ......|
00000190  31 01 ff ff 0b 11 01 ff  31 01 ca 29 0a 00 ff ff  |1.......1..)....|
000001a0  ff ff ff ff 00 00 00 00  31 40 00 00 0c 00 ff ff  |........1@......|
000001b0  b0 00 00 00 50 00 00 00  01 00 40 00 00 00 05 00  |....P.....@.....|
000001c0  00 00 00 00 00 00 00 00  01 00 00 00 00 00 00 00  |................|
000001d0  40 00 00 00 00 00 00 00  00 20 00 00 00 00 00 00  |@........ ......|
000001e0  08 10 00 00 00 00 00 00  08 10 00 00 00 00 00 00  |................|
000001f0  31 01 ff ff 0b 11 01 ff  00 76 80 02 80 fa 29 00  |1........v....).|
```

Contents of the $MFT file

In some cases, recovery of deleted files will be useful to the case under investigation. We can use the icat tool to copy the contents of any deleted file to another file in the investigator machine for further analysis. For the $MFT file, there are some other tools, which can parse the MFT file individually and list the contents of the filesystem in tree view:

```
digforensics@forensics:/mnt/hgfs/windows7$ icat -o 2048 sampleimage.dd 0 > mft
```

Using icat to copy contents of a deleted file

ifind

During the analysis, if the investigator, for instance, conducted a word search and got a hit in one of the data units in the partition, they would now need to link this data unit to an entry in the filesystem, and `ifind` is what they need. Unlike the previous tools, `ifind` can take a data unit number or filename as an input and map this input to the equivalent entry in the filesystem to collect other information about this file. In our case, we will try to find the `hiberfile.sys`.

To search with the name, we need to use the `--n` option:

ifind to search by filename

The result shows that the inode number related to the file named `hiberfil.sys` is `563`. Using `istat` again to view the information related to this file will reveal information about this file:

```
digforensics@forensics:/mnt/hgfs/windows7$ istat -o 2048 sampleimage.dd 563 | more
MFT Entry Header Values:
Entry: 563        Sequence: 21
$LogFile Sequence Number: 110612579
Allocated File
Links: 1

$STANDARD_INFORMATION Attribute Values:
Flags: Hidden, System, Archive
Owner ID: 0
Security ID: 582   (S-1-5-32-544)
Last User Journal Update Sequence Number: 5600000
Created:           2014-10-10 02:52:23 (EDT)
File Modified:     2014-10-14 20:25:25 (EDT)
MFT Modified:      2014-10-14 20:25:25 (EDT)
Accessed:          2014-10-14 20:25:25 (EDT)

$FILE_NAME Attribute Values:
Flags: Hidden, System, Archive
Name: hiberfil.sys
Parent MFT Entry: 5    Sequence: 5
Allocated Size: 1610211328    Actual Size: 0
Created:           2014-10-10 02:52:23 (EDT)
File Modified:     2014-10-14 20:25:25 (EDT)
MFT Modified:      2014-10-14 20:25:25 (EDT)
Accessed:          2014-10-14 20:25:25 (EDT)

Attributes:
Type: $STANDARD_INFORMATION (16-0)   Name: N/A   Resident    size: 72
Type: $FILE_NAME (48-2)   Name: N/A   Resident    size: 90
Type: $DATA (128-1)   Name: N/A   Non-Resident   size: 1610211328   init_size: 1610211328
3269280 3269281 3269282 3269283 3269284 3269285 3269286 3269287
3269288 3269289 3269290 3269291 3269292 3269293 3269294 3269295
```

Full information about the file with inode 563

The `hiberfil.sys` file is the copy of memory stored to the hard drive when the user elects to use the hibernate option of the machine in case of a dead system analysis. This file can provide a great benefit to the investigator as it provides them with a snapshot of the memory during the last usage of hibernation that can be provided from the timestamp of this file. As we can see, this file is an allocated file, and it can be extracted from the image like we did earlier with the $MFT file, and then used in memory analysis.

In case we need to use the ifind tool with the data unit number, we need to use the -d option. We will get another unique ID, describing the location of the file in the image. This unique ID will be discussed in the next part, the filename layer. In this example, we used the data unit ID of 3269280, which is one of the data units of the `hiberfil.sys` file:

```
digforensics@forensics:/mnt/hgfs/windows7$ ifind -o 2048 sampleimage.dd -d 3269280
563-128-1
digforensics@forensics:/mnt/hgfs/windows7$
```

A data block address with ifind

The filename layer

Tools work in this layer to list the file structure in the hard drive image. Each file will be assigned a unique ID, which can be used with other tools to especially target this file.

To list the files under the partition, we only need to provide the partition offset to the tool:

```
digforensics@forensics:/mnt/hgfs/windows7$ fls -o 2048 sampleimage.dd
r/r 4-128-4:     $AttrDef
r/r 8-128-2:     $BadClus
r/r 8-128-1:     $BadClus:$Bad
r/r 6-128-4:     $Bitmap
r/r 7-128-1:     $Boot
d/d 11-144-4:    $Extend
r/r 2-128-1:     $LogFile
r/r 0-128-1:     $MFT
r/r 1-128-1:     $MFTMirr
d/d 57-144-1:    $Recycle.Bin
r/r 9-128-8:     $Secure:$SDS
r/r 9-144-16:    $Secure:$SII
r/r 9-144-17:    $Secure:$SDH
r/r 10-128-1:    $UpCase
r/r 3-128-3:     $Volume
d/d 35-144-1:    $WINDOWS.~BT
d/d 45-144-1:    $WINDOWS.~LS
d/d 57508-144-5:         Boot
r/r 57561-128-1:         bootmgr
r/r 57572-128-3:         BOOTSECT.BAK
d/d 13688-144-1:         Documents and Settings
r/r 563-128-1:   hiberfil.sys
r/r 57592-128-1:         pagefile.sys
d/d 58-144-1:    PerfLogs
d/d 60-144-6:    Program Files
d/d 247-144-6:   Program Files (x86)
d/d 363-144-6:   ProgramData
d/d 16389-144-6:         System Volume Information
d/d 457-144-5:   Users
d/d 619-144-5:   Windows
r/r 54-128-1:    WinPEpge.sys
-/r * 57745-128-1:       hiberfil.sys
d/d 57856:       $OrphanFiles
digforensics@forensics:/mnt/hgfs/windows7$
```

The fls tools to browse the partition contents

In the preceding figure, we can see the deleted `hiberfil.sys` with a metadata address of 57745 and the allocated one with a metadata address of 563.

In case we need to browse another directory (for example, the Users directory), we can provide the tool with the Users directory's unique ID (457-144-5):

```
digforensics@forensics:/mnt/hgfs/windows7$ fls -o 2048 sampleimage.dd 457-144-5
d/d 16057-144-1:    All Users
d/d 569-144-5:      Default
d/d 16058-144-1:    Default User
r/r 16056-128-1:    desktop.ini
d/d 459-144-6:      Forensics
d/d 605-144-5:      Public
-/d * 57767-144-1:  TEMP
digforensics@forensics:/mnt/hgfs/windows7$
```

Using the directory ID for content listing with the fls tool

As we can see here, we are browsing through the contents of the image without mounting any partition or filesystem to the running OS.

The ffind tool is only used to map the metadata address to the filename, either its related file was deleted or allocated:

```
digforensics@forensics:/mnt/hgfs/windows7$ ffind -o 2048 sampleimage.dd 563
//hiberfil.sys
```

Mapping metadata address to its filename

Data unit layer (Block)

In this layer, the actual contents of the file are stored. The metadata of the file must point to the location of the file contents in this area, as we discussed before with the `ifind` tool.

blkcat

This is used to display the contents of the specific data unit in the image. Let's say we need to display the first data unit of the `ntdll.dll` file in a Windows directory. First, we can find the metadata address for this file using the `ils` tool and grep with the `ntdll.dll` filename:

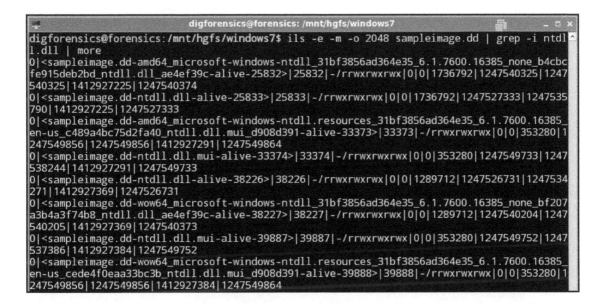

The metadata address for the ntdll.dll file

Filesystem Analysis and Data Recovery

From the results, one of the `ntdll.dll` files has the metadata address of `25833`. The second step is to use the `istat` tool to find the allocated data units to this file using its metadata address:

```
digforensics@forensics:/mnt/hgfs/windows7$ istat -o 2048 sampleimage.dd 25833 | more
MFT Entry Header Values:
Entry: 25833          Sequence: 1
$LogFile Sequence Number: 43093130
Allocated File
Links: 2

$STANDARD_INFORMATION Attribute Values:
Flags: Archive
Owner ID: 0
Security ID: 450   (S-1-5-80-956008885-3418522649-1831038044-1853292631-2271478464)
Created:         2009-07-13 19:22:13 (EDT)
File Modified:   2009-07-13 21:43:10 (EDT)
MFT Modified:    2014-10-10 03:47:05 (EDT)
Accessed:        2009-07-13 19:22:13 (EDT)

$FILE_NAME Attribute Values:
Flags: Archive
Name: ntdll.dll, ntdll.dll
Parent MFT Entry: 6894    Sequence: 1
Allocated Size: 0        Actual Size: 0
Created:         2014-10-10 03:47:05 (EDT)
File Modified:   2014-10-10 03:47:05 (EDT)
MFT Modified:    2014-10-10 03:47:05 (EDT)
Accessed:        2014-10-10 03:47:05 (EDT)

Attributes:
Type: $STANDARD_INFORMATION (16-0)   Name: N/A   Resident    size: 72
Type: $FILE_NAME (48-4)    Name: N/A   Resident   size: 84
Type: $FILE_NAME (48-2)    Name: N/A   Resident   size: 84
Type: $DATA (128-3)    Name: N/A   Non-Resident   size: 1736792   init_size: 1736792
1118226 1118227 1118228 1118229 1118230 1118231 1118232 1118233
1118234 1118235 1118236 1118237 1118238 1118239 1118240 1118241
1118242 1118243 1118244 1118245 1118246 1118247 1118248 1118249
--More--
```

Full information about the ntdll.dll file from the istat tool

The result shows that the first data unit of the file has the number of `1118226`. What we need to do now is use the `blkcat` tool to view the contents of this data unit. We will use the `--h` option to view the contents in hex view:

Using blkcat to display the contents of one data unit

blkls

The default of this tool is to display the unallocated clusters in an image file for further analysis, such as file carving and recovery. If we used this tool with the -e option, it will collect all the blocks of one filesystem, which is useful if we need to extract one partition from a multi-partitions larger image. Here, we need to only collect all the unallocated space in the image and direct the output to a file called `unallocated.blkls` on to the screen.

The resulting file will be in the same size of free space in the partition. Then, further analysis can be done on this file:

```
digforensics@forensics:/mnt/hgfs/windows7$ blkls -o 2048 sampleimage.dd > unallocated.blkls
digforensics@forensics:/mnt/hgfs/windows7$ ls -la unallocated.blkls
-rwxrwxrwx 1 root root 4307230720 Oct 14 13:03 unallocated.blkls
```

blkls to collect all unallocated space in a single file

Blkcalc

To understand the purpose of this tool, let's suppose some analysis on the unallocated space has been conducted, such as a keyword search, and a match that is related to the case under investigation is found. To map the founded location to the full image, we need to use the `blkcalc` tool.

Autopsy

Autopsy is a web-based interface for TSK, which uses the same tools in TSK and presents the results in a graphical interface. To conduct analysis with TSK, the investigator needs to start the server first from the command line. After starting the autopsy, it will give the investigator the URL to access it from the Internet, which in this case is `http://localhost:9999/autopsy`. Don't shut down the process of the autopsy during the analysis; otherwise, the analysis won't be active:

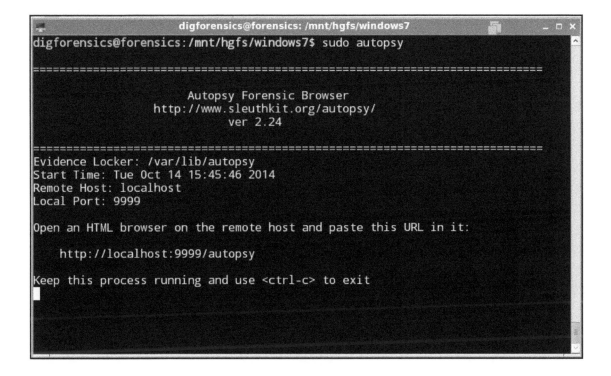

Starting Autopsy

Filesystem Analysis and Data Recovery

Then, from the browser, open that URL to start creating the case:

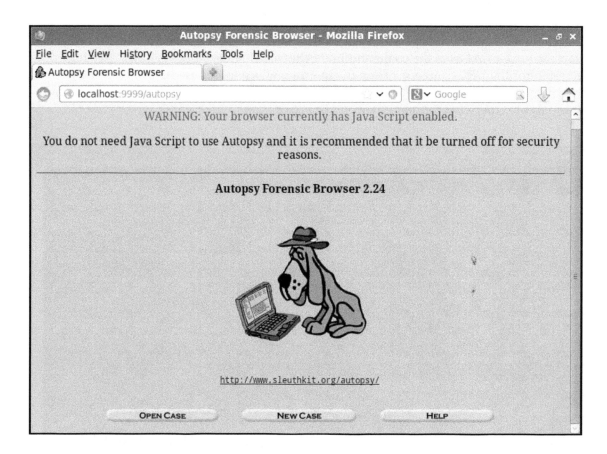

Autopsy interface

We need to create a new case, and then enter some information about the case to make it easy for the investigator to follow up about the cases and who is working on each case:

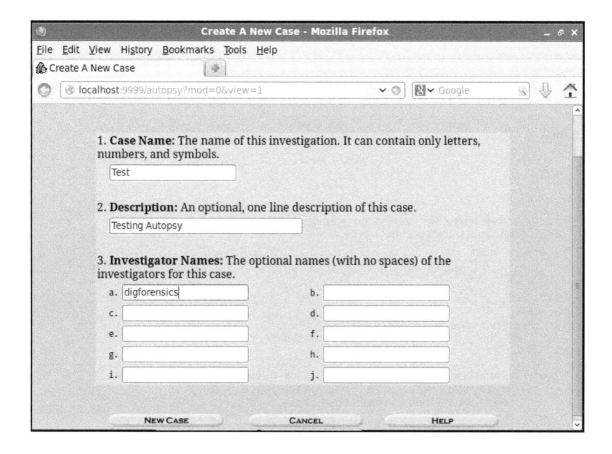

Creating a new case

After creating the case, a directory for this case will be created by default at /var/lib/autopsy (which is named after the case name), including all the files of the case. What we did is just create the case; now, we need to add all the hosts related to the case and add the image that we previously acquired from each host. We need to do this to follow up with the results of the analysis and to be able to differentiate between the sources of the results.

Filesystem Analysis and Data Recovery

If the case under investigation took place in different time zones, that is, it includes hard drives which were running under different time zones, it is a very good idea to adjust the time zone of each host to get normalized results:

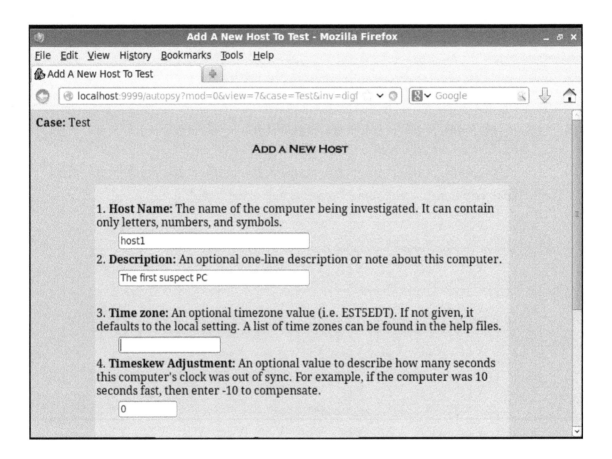

Adding a host to the case

After adding a host, we need to map the host to an image:

Mapping the host to a forensic image

After this, you need to map each host to its corresponding image. You need to enter the path to the image and specify whether it is a disk image or partition image. In our case, it is a complete disk image. We have the option to work with the same image and use only a symbolic link to it, or just copy or move this image:

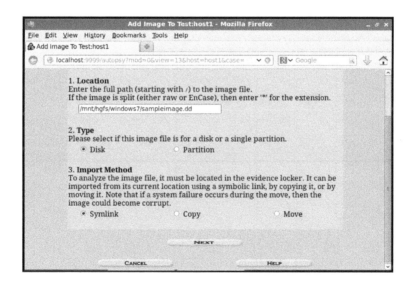

Adding an image to the host

Then, automatically, this will list all the allocated partitions in this image with the start and end of each one in a sector. This is the same result we got from using the `mmls` tool in the command line where it asked us to select the mount point of each partition. In our case, we have only one NTFS partition, and we will mount this one as `C:` partition:

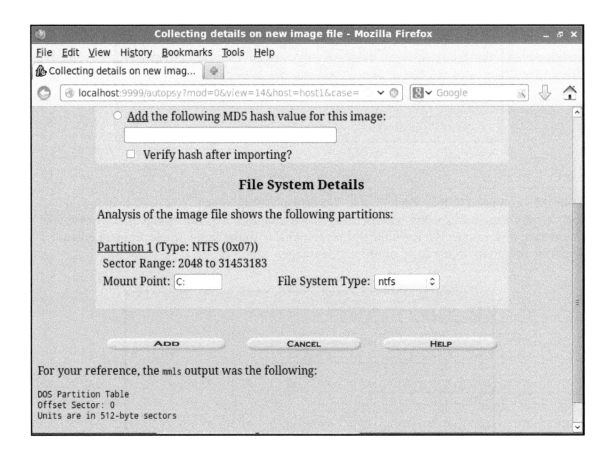

Mounting the allocated partition to the case

A confirmation message will summarize the configuration that you established:

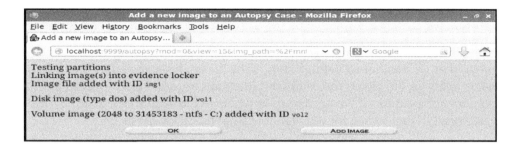

Confirmation message

Then, a home page for the case will be shown from where the investigator can select what he needs to do with the partition or the whole disk image:

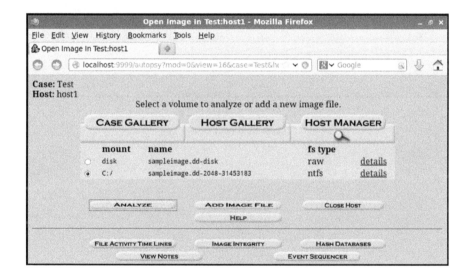

Start analysis on the case

Filesystem Analysis and Data Recovery

Now, we will go with the `C:` partition, it is the equivalent of specifying the offset with `-o` option in each command that we used in the command line tools, where we provided the offset of the working partition. Here, the upcoming analysis will target the contents of the `C:` partition.

After stating the analysis, the investigator will find some tabs targeting all the layers of investigation that we mentioned before, such as the file analysis, metadata analysis, and data clusters analysis. However, the command line tools are still better for results customization. For example, if we need to redo what we did with the `ntdll.dll` file using autopsy, we need to first search for the filename from the file analysis tab:

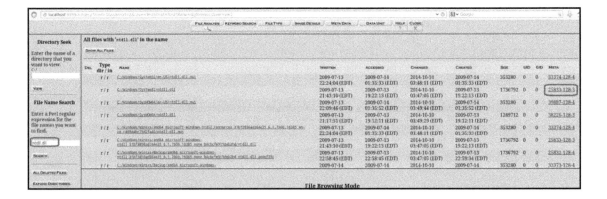

Search for the file by name

Chapter 6

We now have the metadata number `25833`. You can either click on this number or under the **Meta Data** tab to search for this number. This will list all the information of this file, including all the clusters that hold the contents of this file. We are interested in the first cluster number 1118226 as shown in the following image:

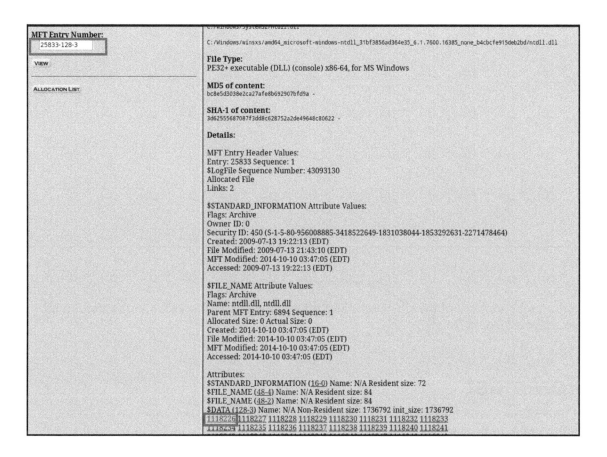

Listing the metadata information with the metadata ID

[127]

Filesystem Analysis and Data Recovery

Then, in the same way, either click on the cluster number or type its number under the DATA UNIT tab, it will display the contents the file in ASCII, Hex, or ASCII Strings views:

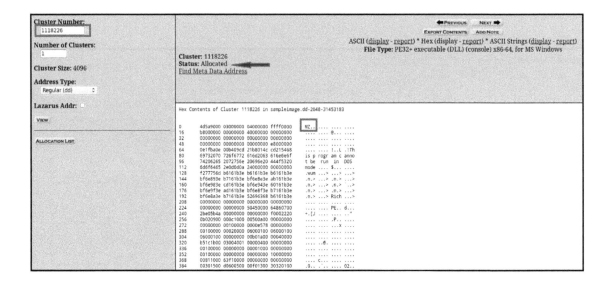

Listing the contents of cluster by cluster number

We can see the status of the cluster is allocated and the signature of the file as before in its hex view is 0x4D5A (MZ).

Foremost

With TSK, we could find and recover the deleted files. These deleted files still have their information in the metadata area, which is why we could identify their information and know their location in the data area. This leaves us with a simple step to recover these files by redirecting the contents of each file to a new file. What if there are no entries for the deleted file, and we only have the contents of the file in the data area and no metadata about this file (which under this assumption will be in the unallocated area of the hard drive)? In this case, the file carving technique will be useful to recover such files.

Each file has a different type, such as Microsoft Office, Adobe, exe, and AVI. The extension at the end of the filename is not what is needed to differentiate between one file type and another. There is a header in the beginning of each file which differs from one type to another. Some file types have a footer in the end of the file, but this is not mandatory. File carving techniques use these headers and footers to carve and identify the locations of the files in the unallocated area of the image or hard drive to recover these files.

Foremost is a Linux tool that is used to recover data based on file carving techniques. We can apply foremost to all the images, but we already know that the carving will work on the unallocated area. So, why don't we apply foremost against the unallocated area as a single file? This single file was produced from the image using the `blkls` tool from `tsk` named as `unallocated.blkls`. We can carve this produced file from the hard drive to find the deleted files, if there are any.

The output of foremost is different directories under the working directory, which are named after each file type when using the `--o` option. As we know that each file will start at the beginning of a cluster, we don't need to search the rest of the cluster contents. We can use the `--q` option to search the beginning of the clusters only for quick results:

```
digforensics@forensics:/mnt/hgfs/windows7$ mkdir foremost-results
digforensics@forensics:/mnt/hgfs/windows7$ foremost -q -o foremost-results/ unallocated.blkls
Processing: unallocated.blkls
|*****************************************|
digforensics@forensics:/mnt/hgfs/windows7$
```

Foremost to carve the unallocated area in the image

Filesystem Analysis and Data Recovery

Then, in the results of running this tool, we will find that one `audit.txt` file and one PDF directory were created under the foremost-results directory. Opening the `audit.txt` file will show us some information about the process of file carving, such as the time, size, and the extracted files. In our case, one single PDF file was extracted from the unallocated area in this image:

```
digforensics@forensics:/mnt/hgfs/windows7/foremost-results$ cat audit.txt
Foremost version 1.5.7 by Jesse Kornblum, Kris Kendall, and Nick Mikus
Audit File

Foremost started at Wed Oct 15 01:20:18 2014
Invocation: foremost -q -o foremost-results/ unallocated.blkls
Output directory: /mnt/hgfs/windows7/foremost-results
Configuration file: /etc/foremost.conf
------------------------------------------------------------------
File: unallocated.blkls
Start: Wed Oct 15 01:20:33 2014
Length: 4 GB (4339044352 bytes)

Num      Name (bs=512)         Size       File Offset     Comment

0:       00000145.pdf          82 KB      74240
Finish: Wed Oct 15 02:10:06 2014

1 FILES EXTRACTED

pdf:= 1
------------------------------------------------------------------
Foremost finished at Wed Oct 15 02:10:06 2014
digforensics@forensics:/mnt/hgfs/windows7/foremost-results$
```

Extracted files by foremost

Due to the absence of the metadata of this file as we discussed before, we won't be able to know any information about this file except for the size and the contents of this file. This PDF file was created for testing purposes and we assumed that it contains evidential data related to the case under investigation:

```
(EVIDENTIAL DATA RELATED TO THE
CASE UNDER INVESTIGATION)
```

Extracted PDF file

Summary

In this chapter, we saw how the files are organized in the filesystem, and how it differs from FAT to NTFS. Then, we learned about reading files from a forensic image using TSK and its GUI Autopsy. We also discussed file carving and how to recover a file, based on its signature using Foremost.

In the next chapter, we will learn about Windows registry—a complex yet very important artifact in the Windows operating system. We will learn about registry structure, and its important value to the investigation and different tools to parse and analyze the registry.

7
Registry Analysis

Understanding system configuration and settings and user activities is always an important step in the forensics analysis process. This configuration used to be stored in INI files, which were text files with a simple format. However, starting from Windows 3.1, the concept of registry was introduced to store the com-based components only. **COM** or **Component Object Model** was introduced by Microsoft in 1993 to enable inter-process communication and dynamic object creation in a wide range of programming languages. Since then, it has been used on a larger scale to include most of the Windows settings.

The registry can be considered as the Windows-structured database. It contains the operating system's configurations and settings, and also contains the settings of running services and installed applications along with users' preferences. It is not mandatory for the installed applications to use the registry to store its configurations and settings. Some programs use XML or text files to store their configurations.

Portable applications usually keep their configuration data within files in the directory or folder from where the application executable runs. The registry also keeps track of users' activities, stores their settings, and supports the multi-profile structure, where each user has their configuration for their account. The registry of each user stores under that user's directory in a separate file called `NTUSER.DAT`, which will be discussed in detail later in this chapter.

Registry analysis in the digital forensics process is a valuable source of evidential information for investigators. Malicious programs are like any other program. They use the system resources while running, so they may leave some traces in the registry. These traces will help in understanding the circumstances of the incident under investigation.

In this chapter, we will discuss the structure of the registry and some tools that are used to perform analysis.

The registry structure

The registry has a specific structure, which is divided into key and value. Like the directory structure, main root keys represent the root directory, sub-keys represent the sub folders, and values represent the files. Figure 1 depicts the registry structure opened from Windows native tool "registry editor". This tool can be opened in editable mode by typing regedit.exe in Run.

The items in the round-edged rectangle are the root keys, while the items in the rectangle below it are the sub-keys. The items inside the oval are the values of the registry. Each value has these three entries:

- Name
- Type
- Data

To access a specific value, the user needs to know the path to this value. The path can be found in the tail of the regedit window. In our example, the path is `Computer\HKEY_CURRENT_USER\Environment`:

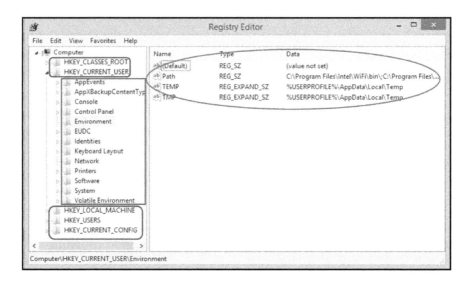

Figure1: The main components of the registry

Root keys

The Windows system, in this case Windows 8.1, has five root keys. Each root key stores different information and settings about the running system and the system's users. Each root key shown in the registry editor is actually a file in the filesystem called **registry hive**. The root keys are as follows:

- HKEY_CLASSES_ROOT
- HKEY_LOCAL_MACHINE
- HKEY_USERS
- HKEY_CURRENT_USER
- HKEY_CURRENT_CONFIG

In the following section, we will discuss each root key in brief and the registry hive structure, before discussing the analysis programs to explain how it could be useful in the analysis process.

HKEY_CLASSES_ROOT or HKCR

This key contains subkeys. Each subkey is named after one extension that can be found in the system, such as .exe and .jpeg. This root key describes the default program that has to be used to open this extension to the system. Also, this key stores the right-click menu's details and the icon of the program.

Consider that during an analysis, we (the investigator) need to know which program is used to open a specific file type, such as the executable files with the flv extension. We would then use the following process:

- First, we need to search for the subkey named .flv, without quotes, under the root key and locate the associated value of this subkey.

- Then, we need to search under the same root key for another subkey named after the associated value `VLC.flv`. This subkey contains some values about how the operating system deals with `.flv` media files:

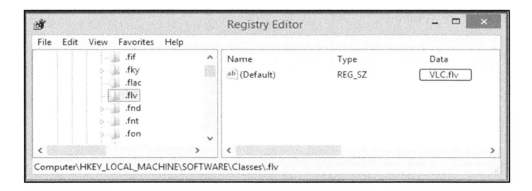

Figure 2: The flv extension associated value in the registry

- On searching for the `VLC.flv` value in the same registry key, we will locate the executable that was used to run the `.flv` file types. In this case, this is the VLC media player. It also mentions the location of the executable in the filesystem:

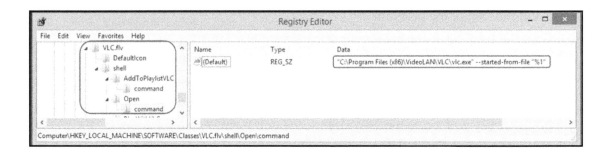

Figure 3: location of the VLC player used to run the .flv file type

For example, in a multiuser Windows environment, if two different users have installed two different programs to open PDF files, then when one user logs in to the system, the operating system will load the profile of this specific user, including their selected program to open the PDF file.

However, the information in the HKCR comes from two different locations:

- `HKEY_LOCAL_MACHINE\SOFTWARE\Classes`
- `HKEY_CURRENT_USER\SOFTWARE\Classes`

Usually, this is an alias to only `HKEY_LOCAL_MACHINE\SOFTWARE\Classes`. When a user registers a different association to specific file type, it uses the per-user class registration feature to register the new association to this user only.

In this case, if the user opens one file of a specific type, and this file type has two different associations in `HKEY_LOCAL_MACHINE\SOFTWARE\Classes` and `HKEY_CURRENT_USER\SOFTWARE\Classes`, then the one in `HKEY_CURRENT_USER\SOFTWARE\Classes`, which relates to this specific user, will be used.

HKEY_LOCAL_MACHINE

This key contains configuration and settings that are used by the system during start-up. It is independent from the user login. This root key contains the following five subkeys:

- **System**: This contains system configuration, such as the computer name, system time zone, and network interfaces.
- **Software**: This contains settings and configuration about the installed applications on the system and the operating system services.
- **SAM**: This is the Security Account Manager, and it stores the user and group security information. It summarizes the total rights of the user that are granted by the administrator on the local system and domain. It contains the username, the unique SID of the user, and a hash message of the user's password. This file will be empty if opened from a running system by the `regedit.exe` tool because of Windows security. It can be extracted and opened in a different analysis machine to display all its contents.
- **Security**: This contains the security policy in the system, if any. This is the same as SAM, its contents can't be viewed from a live system.
- **Hardware**: This holds information about the hardware devices connected to the system. This information is stored during the system boot.

Registry Analysis

HKEY_USERS or HKU

The HKU registry root key contains a number of subkeys. We will use Windows 8.1 for this example:

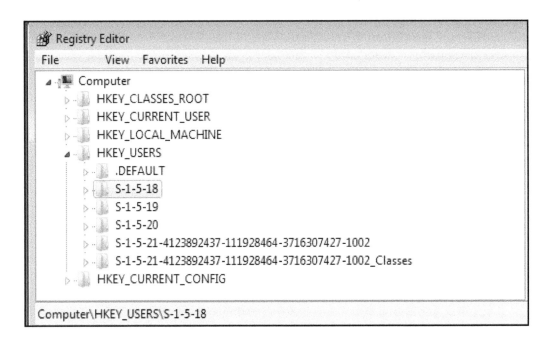

Figure 4: HKEY_USERS

Its subkeys are as follows:

- **S-1-5-18**: This is the system profile located at `%systemroot%\system32\config\systemprofile`.
- **S-1-5-19**: This is related to LocalService and located at `%systemroot%\C:\Windows\ServiceProfiles\LocalService`.
- **S-1-5-20**: This is related to the NetworkService and located under `%systemroot%\C:\Windows\ServiceProfiles\NetworkService`.
- **S-1-5-21-4123892437-111928464-3716307427-1002**: This is the currently signed in user with their full SID. Ours is located in the user directory `C:\Users\Forensics2`.

- **Default user**: This is the default profile for any new user. It is located at `%SystemDrive%\Users\Default`. When a new user was created, a copy of this profile is copied for this user, and all the changes in configuration made by this user are recorded under this profile. This process doesn't happen until the first login for this new user. The system starts building this user profile, as we can see in the following figure:

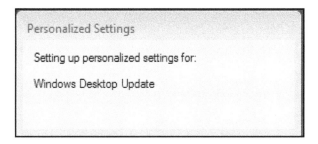

Figure 5: Creating a new user profile in Windows

Only the logged on user can be found under HKU, not all the users. However, on a live system, we can find the location and more details about the system's users in the `HKEY_LOCAL_MACHINE\SOFTWARE\Microsoft\Windows NT\CurrentVersion\ProfileList` key in the registry.

In this key, we can find basic information about all the system users' profiles, including the location of each profile, but not the configurations and settings of each user. In the following screenshot, we can find another user profile with SID ends with 1002, which we can't find under HKU:

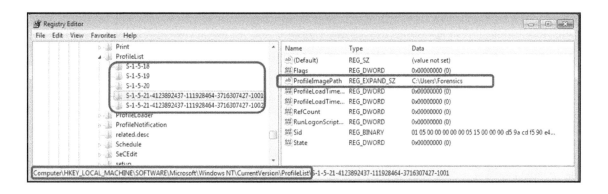

Figure 6: The list of system profiles

HKEY_CURRENT_USER or HKCU

HKCU is only a pointer to the current user under the HKU, with the same configuration and settings:

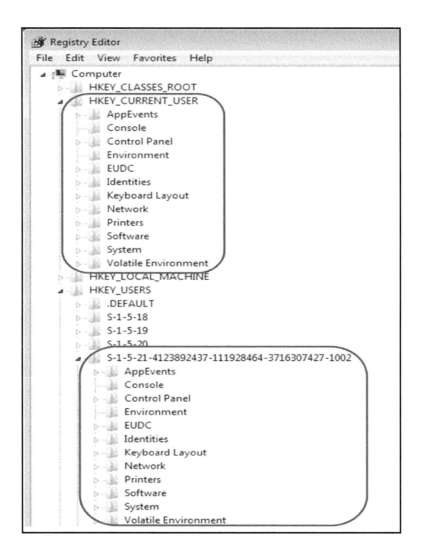

Figure 7: HKCU VS HKU

Mapping a hive to the filesystem

Each root key in the registry is actually mapped to a single file in the filesystem, which differs from one Windows version to another. In the following table, we target Windows NT to Windows 10. These files have specific formats, which the operating system parses for either read or write data in the registry.

We can view the location of each hive in the filesystem in the following table:

Hive name	Location in the filesystem
`HKEY_LOCAL_MACHINE\System`	`%WINDIR%\system32\config\System`
`HKEY_LOCAL_MACHINE\SAM`	`%WINDIR%\system32\config\Sam`
`HKEY_LOCAL_MACHINE\Security`	`%WINDIR%\system32\config\Security`
`HKEY_LOCAL_MACHINE\Software`	`%WINDIR%\system32\config\Software`
`HKEY_USERS\User SID`	This is the user profile (`NTUSER.DAT`); `Documents and Settings\User` (this was changed to `Users\User` in Vista). Each profile under HKU must be linked to one `NTUSER.DAT` file under the user profile directory. This directory can be determined, as in Figure 6, under: `HKEY_LOCAL_MACHINE\SOFTWARE\Microsoft\Windows NT\CurrentVersion\ProfileList`
`HKEY_CURRENT_USER`	This acts as a pointer to the HKU of the currently logged in user.
`HKEY_USERS\.Default`	`%WINDIR%\system32\config\default`

Table 1: Hive to filesystem mapping

Backing up the registry files

Windows OS backs up the hive files by default every 10 days. The backup files are located at `%WINDIR%\repair` in Windows XP and at `%WINDIR%\System32\config\RegBack` starting from Windows Vista. The backup hives are useful in determining the changed configuration from the last update. They are also useful in case the normal hives are corrupted.

Registry Analysis

The backup is done by the local system in Windows tasks under
`%WINDIR%\System32\Tasks\Microsoft\Windows\Registry`:

```xml
<Task xmlns="http://schemas.microsoft.com/windows/2004/02/mit/task">
  <RegistrationInfo>
    <Author>$(@%systemroot%\system32\regidle.dll,-600)</Author>
    <Version>1.0</Version>
    <Source>$(@%systemroot%\system32\regidle.dll,-601)</Source>
    <URI>Microsoft\Windows\Registry\RegIdleBackup</URI>
    <Description>$(@%systemroot%\system32\regidle.dll,-602)</Description>
    <SecurityDescriptor>O:BAG:BAD:P(A;;FA;;;BA)(A;;FA;;;SY)(A;;FR;;;IU)(A;
  </RegistrationInfo>
  <Triggers />
  <Settings>
    <Enabled>true</Enabled>
    <MultipleInstancesPolicy>IgnoreNew</MultipleInstancesPolicy>
    <AllowStartOnDemand>true</AllowStartOnDemand>
    <DisallowStartIfOnBatteries>true</DisallowStartIfOnBatteries>
    <StopIfGoingOnBatteries>false</StopIfGoingOnBatteries>
    <RunOnlyIfNetworkAvailable>false</RunOnlyIfNetworkAvailable>
    <ExecutionTimeLimit>PT0S</ExecutionTimeLimit>
    <Hidden>true</Hidden>
    <WakeToRun>false</WakeToRun>
    <StartWhenAvailable>true</StartWhenAvailable>
    <Priority>5</Priority>
    <RunOnlyIfIdle>false</RunOnlyIfIdle>
    <UseUnifiedSchedulingEngine>true</UseUnifiedSchedulingEngine>
    <MaintenanceSettings>
      <Period>P10D</Period>
      <Deadline>P14D</Deadline>
    </MaintenanceSettings>
  </Settings>
  <Principals>
    <Principal id="LocalSystem">
      <UserId>S-1-5-18</UserId>
    </Principal>
  </Principals>
  <Actions Context="LocalSystem ">
    <ComHandler>
      <ClassId>{ca767aa8-9157-4604-b64b-40747123d5f2}</ClassId>
    </ComHandler>
  </Actions>
</Task>
```

Figure 8: The registry backup task in Windows

Extracting registry hives

Performing a postmortem analysis on the system registry requires extracting the hives from the filesystem. In this section, we will look at extracting files from a live system and from a forensic image.

Extracting registry files from a live system

Copying the backup files on a live system is quite easy; simply copy and paste or type the following command in the administrator command prompt:

```
reg save HKLM\<hive name> <savename>
```

As discussed earlier, these files could be 10 days old. This may not contain any traces of the incident under investigation. So, we need to extract the working hive files, which won't be allowed by the system because these files are in use in the live system:

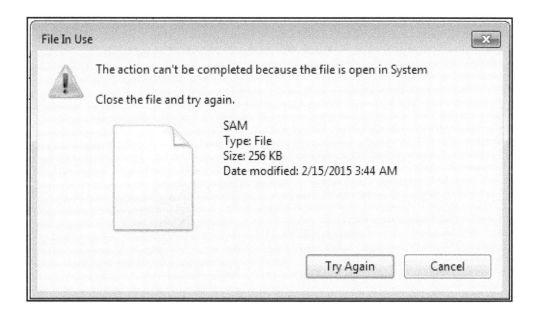

Figure 9: Error in copying registry files in live system

Registry Analysis

In order to copy registry files from the live system, we need to use a program, such as FTK imager. We will use the lite version in this exercise, which is better in case of live analysis because it does not leave large traces in the system as compared to the installation version:

1. In the Windows live system, open the FTK imager lite program.
2. Select **add evidence item** from **File**.
3. This will ask you to select a source. In this case, we can either select a physical or logical drive. It won't make a difference in our case here; we can anyway select a logical drive:

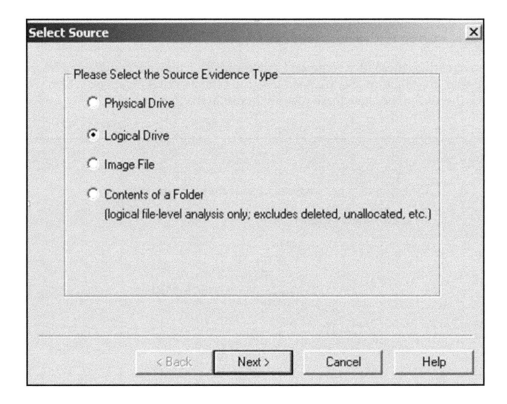

Figure 10: FTK source type

4. After this we need to select the source drive, and we need to select the Windows working partition, which in our case is partition C:

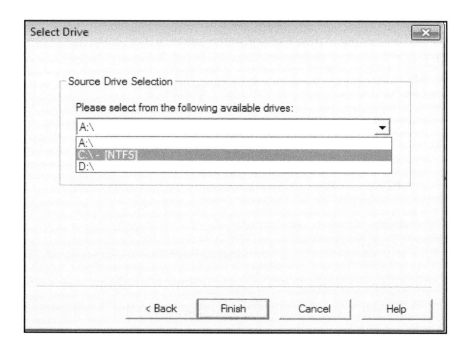

Figure 11: Source partition

The contents of partition C will be in the left pane of the program.

Registry Analysis

5. We need to browse to the registry files location. Select the hive file, and export these files to the external connected storage or shared folder over the network and not to the local machine. This avoids overwriting possible related evidential data, as shown in the following image:

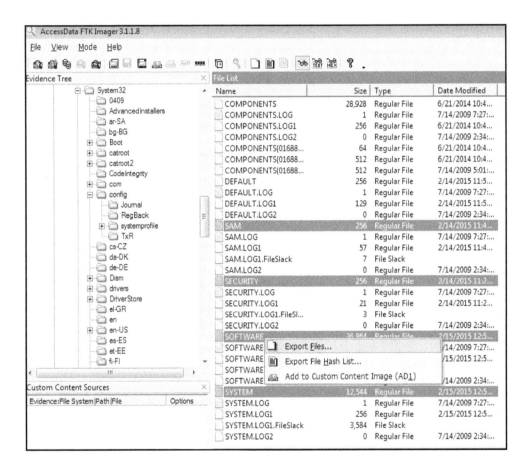

Figure 12: Exporting registry files by FTK imager

After this, we can take the extracted files to our Linux machine for analysis.

It is worth mentioning here that FTK Imager has a built-in feature to acquire all the registry files and protected system files. It can be accessed by navigating to File à Obtain protected system files from a live system without adding any devices or partitions.

Extracting registry files from a forensic image

To extract files from a forensic image in Linux, we need to mount the system partition to the system first as read only and then perform a simple copy and paste operation of the registry files.

To mount one partition from a forensic image in Linux, we need to know the offset of this partition in the forensic image in the first place. This task can be done using the mmls command from the TSK or The Sleuth Kit. TSK will be discussed later in detail:

```
digforensics@forensics:~$ mmls /mnt/hgfs/image/image.001
DOS Partition Table
Offset Sector: 0
Units are in 512-byte sectors

     Slot    Start        End          Length       Description
00:  Meta    0000000000   0000000000   0000000001   Primary Table (#0)
01:  -----   0000000000   0000002047   0000002048   Unallocated
02:  00:00   0000002048   0125827071   0125825024   NTFS (0x07)
03:  -----   0125827072   0125829119   0000002048   Unallocated
digforensics@forensics:~$
```

Figure 13: Windows partition

The results show that the system partition starts at sector 2048. Using this piece of information, we can mount this partition as read only:

1. First, we need to create a directory as the mount point at `</mnt/mountpoint>`, and then we run the mount command, as follows:

```
digforensics@forensics:~$ sudo mkdir /mnt/mountpoint
[sudo] password for digforensics:
digforensics@forensics:~$ sudo mount -t lowntfs-3g -o ro,loop,show_sys_files,ignore_case,offset=$((512*2048)) /mnt/hgfs/image/image.001 /mnt/mountpoint/
digforensics@forensics:~$
```

Figure 14: Creating a mount point and mounting the image

Registry Analysis

As we can see, the offset must be in bytes. So, we need to put it in this formula (512*2048), where 512 is the sector size and the 2048 is the sector number. In this command, we also selected to mount the image as read only, show system files, and ignore case, to make it easier to browse through the files without mistakes.

2. So, we can see that all the filesystem structure can be accessed easily from the mount point:

```
digforensics@forensics:~$ ls /mnt/mountpoint/
$attrdef    $boot              $extend       programdata          $recycle.bin             users
$badclus    bootmgr            $logfile      program files        $secure                  $volume
$bitmap     bootsect.bak       pagefile.sys  program files (x86)  system volume information windows
boot        documents and settings  perflogs recovery             $upcase
digforensics@forensics:~$
```

Figure 15: Mounted system partition

3. As we know the location of the registry files in the system, we can start copying them:

```
digforensics@forensics:/mnt/hgfs/image/registry$ cp /mnt/mountpoint/windows/system32/config/sam sam
digforensics@forensics:/mnt/hgfs/image/registry$ cp /mnt/mountpoint/windows/system32/config/system system
digforensics@forensics:/mnt/hgfs/image/registry$ cp /mnt/mountpoint/windows/system32/config/software software
digforensics@forensics:/mnt/hgfs/image/registry$ cp /mnt/mountpoint/windows/system32/config/security security
digforensics@forensics:/mnt/hgfs/image/registry$
```

Figure 16: Copying registry files

4. The same can be done with the users' profiles. Here, we have two users, forensics and forensics2:

```
digforensics@forensics:/mnt/hgfs/image/registry$ cp /mnt/mountpoint/users/forensics/ntuser.dat forensics.dat
digforensics@forensics:/mnt/hgfs/image/registry$ cp /mnt/mountpoint/users/forensics2/ntuser.dat forensics2.dat
digforensics@forensics:/mnt/hgfs/image/registry$
```

Figure 17: Copying users' profiles

[148]

Parsing registry files

Suppose that you have a corrupted registry file, or you need to recover some data, or you want to verify the results of a new analysis tool. All these reasons, besides your need to know how the analysis tools work to parse and recover registry files, make it important to understand the registry file structure.

The registry file consists of blocks with the same concept of clusters in the filesystem. The block size is 4Kb. The hive expands in the whole block, again like the clusters in the filesystem. The first cluster is called the **base block**.

The base block

The base block is the first 4KB of the hive file. It contains the following:

- The hive signature, which identifies this file as a hive file.
- A timestamp of the last write operation on this hive.
- Checksum.
- The hive format, which differs from one OS version to another. There are differences in how data treated in different versions.
- The real name of the hive file and its full path in the system.
- The offset to the root cell, which is relative to the beginning of the hbin. (Both will be explained shortly.)
- The two sequence numbers. We can consider the sequence number as a way to preserve the integrity of the hive file.

When one write operation needs to be performed in the registry hives, it is first done in memory. The operating system needs to write these changes to the nonvolatile on-disk file to keep it updated. The operating system keeps tracking all the sectors of the hive.

To write to the on-disk file, the operating system schedules what is called a lazy write operation or hive sync. The lazy write starts synchronizing the hive changes from memory to the on-disk file and updates the last write time. If something crashed during the synchronization process, the file will be corrupted.

Registry Analysis

In order to avoid this, the lazy write updates the first number of the sequence before it starts the synchronization process. After finishing the write process, it updates the second sequence number with the same value. If the operating system finds two different values in the sequence numbers, it knows that there was a crash during the last synchronization process. It then starts the recovery process following the log file of the hive to keep the file consistent.

In this section, we will consider an example of the `forensics2.dat` registry file. To view the registry file as raw data, we will use the hexdump utility or hd and start to interpret the registry file data.

From the forensic machine, run the following command to view only the first 200 bytes of the base block:

```
digforensics@forensics:/mnt/hgfs/image/registry$ hd -vn 200 forensics2.dat
00000000  72 65 67 66 55 00 00 00  55 00 00 00 e0 58 ba 17  |regfU...U....X..|
00000010  bc 48 d0 01 01 00 00 00  03 00 00 00 00 00 00 00  |.H..............|
00000020  01 00 00 00 20 00 00 00  00 50 07 00 01 00 00 00  |.... ....P......|
00000030  5c 00 43 00 3a 00 5c 00  55 00 73 00 65 00 72 00  |\.C.:.\.U.s.e.r.|
00000040  73 00 5c 00 46 00 6f 00  72 00 65 00 6e 00 73 00  |s.\.F.o.r.e.n.s.|
00000050  69 00 63 00 73 00 32 00  5c 00 6e 00 74 00 75 00  |i.c.s.2.\.n.t.u.|
00000060  73 00 65 00 72 00 2e 00  64 00 61 00 74 00 00 00  |s.e.r...d.a.t...|
00000070  bc 88 68 01 6f 6c de 11  8d 1d 00 1e 0b cd e3 ec  |..h.ol..........|
00000080  bc 88 68 01 6f 6c de 11  8d 1d 00 1e 0b cd e3 ec  |..h.ol..........|
00000090  00 00 00 00 bd 88 68 01  6f 6c de 11 8d 1d 00 1e  |......h.ol......|
000000a0  0b cd e3 ec 72 6d 74 6d  00 00 00 00 00 00 00 00  |....rmtm........|
000000b0  00 00 00 00 00 00 00 00  00 00 00 00 00 00 00 00  |................|
000000c0  00 00 00 00 00 00 00 00                           |........|
```

Figure 18: First 200 bytes of the base block

Now, let's interpret the values in the previous image. Note that now that these values are little endian, we need to read them byte by byte from right to left:

Offset	Length (Bytes)	Value	Description
0x0000	4	Regf	This is the registry file signature.
0x0004	4	0x00000055	This is the first sequence number that the OS writes before editing the registry.
0x0008	4	0x00000055	This is the second sequence number. The first and second sequence numbers are the same, which means that the last write operation was successful.

0x000C	8	0x01D048BC17BA58E0	This is the timestamp of the last write operation. This value can be decoded with the `dcode.exe` program, from http://digitaldetective.com/:
			Value to Decode: 01D048BC17BA58E0
			Date & Time: Sun, 15 February 2015 01:09:48 UTC
			www.digital-detective.co.uk Cancel Clear Decode
			From these results, we can see that the last write time was Sunday, February 15, 2015, at 01:09:48 UTC.
0x0014	4	0x00000001	This is the major version of the file. In this case, it is 1.
0x0018	4	0x00000003	This is the minor version of the file. In this case, it is 3. So, the file format version is 1.3.
0x0024	4	0x00000020	This is the offset of the first cell relative to the first hbin.
0x0030	64 maximum	`C:\Users\Forensics2\ntuser.dat`	This is the location and the name of the file. From this piece of information, we know that this file is the user's profile under `C:\Users\Forensics2`. Despite the name of the file under investigation, the file name is `ntuser.dat`.

Table 2 : Parsing base block

Hbin and CELL

The cell is the data container in the registry file; it contains a key, subkey, or value. Each type has a different signature and a different data structure within the cell. If the cell signature is kn or key node, then the following information will be interpreted as for a key. The operating system allocates these cells within another container called HBIN. The HBIN can contain more than one cell, and it has its own header in the signature file. For our example here, let's take the first cell within the first hbin.

The first hbin can be found directly after the base block, that is, 4,096 bytes from the beginning of the file. We will display the first 200 bytes after the first 4,096 bytes or 0x1000 in hex:

```
digforensics@forensics:/mnt/hgfs/image/registry$ hd -vn 200 -s 4096 forensics2.dat
00001000  68 62 69 6e 00 00 00 00  00 10 00 00 00 00 00 00  |hbin............|
00001010  00 00 00 00 e0 58 ba 17  bc 48 d0 01 00 00 00 00  |.....X...H......|
00001020  78 ff ff ff 6e 6b 2c 00  ef 12 c4 3f b0 48 d0 01  |x...nk,....?.H..|
00001030  00 00 00 00 00 06 00 00  0b 00 00 00 01 00 00 00  |................|
00001040  28 1e 01 00 68 02 00 80  00 00 00 00 ff ff ff ff  |(...h...........|
00001050  60 05 00 00 ff ff ff ff  28 00 00 00 00 00 00 00  |`.......(.......|
00001060  00 00 00 00 00 00 00 00  43 00 75 00 34 00 00 00  |........C.u.4...|
00001070  43 4d 49 2d 43 72 65 61  74 65 48 69 76 65 7b 44  |CMI-CreateHive{D|
00001080  34 33 42 31 32 42 38 2d  30 39 42 35 2d 34 30 44  |43B12B8-09B5-40D|
00001090  42 2d 42 34 46 36 2d 46  36 44 46 45 42 37 38 44  |B-B4F6-F6DFEB78D|
000010a0  41 45 43 7d fc 03 ca 01  a0 ff ff ff 6e 6b 20 00  |AEC}........nk .|
000010b0  65 20 a0 15 b9 48 d0 01  00 00 00 00 60 01 00 00  |e ...H......`...|
000010c0  20 00 00 00 01 00 00 00                           | .......|
```

Figure 19: The first 200 bytes of the first HBIN

Registry Analysis

We can interpret the information in the header as follows:

Offset	Length (Bytes)	Value	Description
0x1000	4	hbin	This is the beginning of the hbin signature.
0x1004	4	0x00000000	This is the offset, which is relative to the first hbin structure. The value here is 0, which means that this is the first hbin in the file.
0x1008	2	0x1000	This is the size of the current hbin. It is 4096 bytes. Usually, it is either equal to 4096 bytes or a multiple of this number.

Table 3: The header of hbin

From parsing the base block at 0x0024, the offset to the first cell is 0x20 relative to the first hbin.

So, to find the header of the first cell, we need to go to offset 0x1020 at the current hbin:

Offset	Length (Bytes)	Value	Description
0x1020	4	0xFFFFFF78	This is the size of the cell in negative implementation. The negative sign indicates that this cell is in use. The value here is (-136). This cell is used, and it has a size of 136.
0x1024	2	nk	This is the nk signature, which means that this cell contains a key node value.
0x1026	2	0x002C	This is the properties flag of the record; it has different values. The binary representation or the value here is 00101100, which indicates that the file is: CompressedName: $(00100000)_2$ NoDelete: $(00001000)_2$ HiveEntryRootKey: $(00000100)_2$ As we expected before, this entry holds root key information.
0x1028	8	0x01D048B03FC412EF	This is the timestamp of the last write time of this entry. The value is Sat, 14 February 2015 23:45:01 UTC, according to the decode value from Dcode.exe Value to Decode: 01D048B03FC412EF Date & Time: Sat, 14 February 2015 23:45:01 UTC
0x1034	2	0x0600	This value is the offset to the parent key record. As this is the parent kn record, this value can be ignored here as long as this is already the kn root key record.

[152]

0x1038	4	0x0000000B	This is the number or subkeys list under this root key. Here, the value is 11, so there are 11 subkey under this key.
0x1040	4	0x00011E28	This is a pointer to the list of the subkeys under this root key.
0x104C	4	0xFFFFFFFF	This is a pointer to the list of the values under this root key. The value here is 0xFFFFFFFF, which means that there are no values under this root key.
0x106C	2	0x0034	The size of the key name. In this case, it is 52 bytes.
0x1070	52	CMI-CreateHive{D43B12BB-09B5-40DB-B4F6-F6DFEB78DAEC}	This is the name of the root key. Its length is 52 bytes or character.

Table 4: Cell analysis

Now, we can conclude that this is a root key named `CMI-CreateHive{D43B12BB-09B5-40DB-B4F6-F6DFEB78DAEC}` with a size of 136 bytes, and this contains 11 subkeys and no values. Now, we need to find the names of the subkeys under this root key.

From the previous analysis, the offset to the subkeys list is 0x11E28 relative to the beginning of the hbin. So, we need to add 0x1000 to get it from the beginning of the hive file itself. The offset will be 0x12E28:

```
digforensics@forensics:/mnt/hgfs/image/registry$ hd -vn 200 -s 0x12E28 forensics2.dat
00012e28  a0 ff ff ff 6c 66 0b 00  c8 1d 01 00 41 70 70 45  |....lf......AppE|
00012e38  30 3c 00 00 43 6f 6e 73  b8 0e 00 00 43 6f 6e 74  |0<..Cons....Cont|
00012e48  18 03 00 00 45 6e 76 69  f0 8b 01 00 45 55 44 43  |....Envi....EUDC|
00012e58  f0 99 04 00 49 64 65 6e  f0 e2 01 00 4b 65 79 62  |....Iden....Keyb|
00012e68  20 68 00 00 4e 65 74 77  d8 6b 00 00 50 72 69 6e  | h..Netw.k..Prin|
00012e78  60 01 00 00 53 6f 66 74  60 0c 00 00 53 79 73 74  |`...Soft`...Syst|
00012e88  a0 ff ff ff 6e 6b 20 00  46 85 14 4a b0 48 d0 01  |....nk .F..J.H..|
00012e98  00 00 00 00 c8 1d 01 00  2f 00 00 00 00 00 00 00  |......../.......|
00012ea8  98 e8 01 00 ff ff ff ff  00 00 00 00 ff ff ff ff  |................|
00012eb8  48 8c 03 00 ff ff ff ff  30 00 00 00 00 00 00 00  |H.......0.......|
00012ec8  00 00 00 00 00 00 00 00  00 00 00 00 0b 00 00 00  |................|
00012ed8  45 76 65 6e 74 4c 61 62  65 6c 73 00 00 00 00 00  |EventLabels.....|
00012ee8  a8 ff ff ff 6e 6b 20 00                           |....nk .|
```

Figure 20: The subkeys list

Registry Analysis

We can see that this is a new cell that needs to be parsed, as follows:

Offset	Length (Bytes)	Value	Description
0x12E28	4	0xFFFFFFA0	This is the size of the cell in negative implementation. The negative sign indicates that this cell is in use. The value here is (-96). This cell is used, and it has a size of 96.
0x12E2C	2	lf	The lf signature indicates that this contains a list of subkeys.
0x12E2E	2	0x000B	This is the number of elements in the list. In this case, this is 11, which matches the value from the previous analysis.
0x12E30	—	---	Starting from this point, each 8 bytes represent one subkey. The first 4 bytes are the offset to the subkey location relative to the beginning of the hbin. The second 4 bytes are used as the checksum.

Table 5: The lf entry analysis

From the previous analysis, we can determine the location of each subkey to be to the following offsets:

- 0x00011DC8
- 0x00003C30
- 0x00000EB8
- 0x00000318
- 0x00018BF0
- 0x000499F0
- 0x0001E2F0
- 0x00006820
- 0x00006BD8
- 0x00000160
- 0x00000C60

To see the contents that are related to the beginning of the hive file, we need to add 0x1000 to each offset, which represents the size of the base block, and then view the first 100 bytes. We will see that each offset will point to another entry with a different name, as shown in the following screenshot:

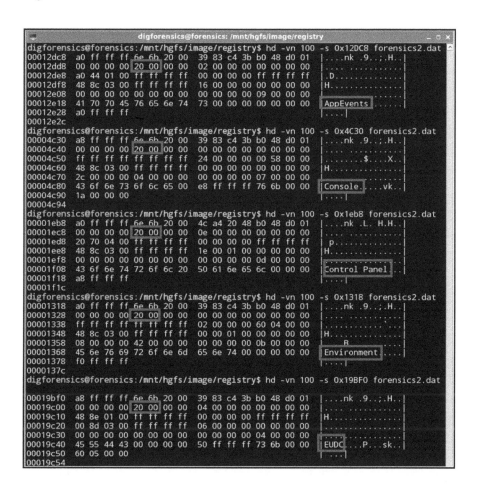

We can see that in the new entries, the parent cell offset in the new entries is 0x0020, which is the offset of the first entry named CMI-CreateHive{D43B12BB-09B5-40DB-B4F6-F6DFEB78DAEC}.

Registry Analysis

The complete list of subkeys is as follows:

- AppEvents
- Console
- Control Panel
- Environment
- EUDC
- Identities
- Keyboard Layout
- Network
- Printers
- Software
- System

To confirm these results with the actual case, we can display the registry in our test live machine using the native regedit tool. If the list matched the results, then the parsing went well, as we can see in the following screenshot:

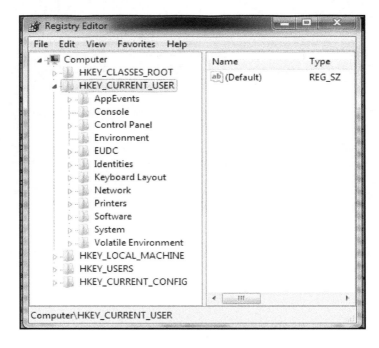

Figure 21: Actual subkeys from the live machine

Auto-run keys

Malware programs usually tend to preserve their existence in the system in case the system was rebooted or different users log on to the system. The following listing shows two important autorun keys that run when the system boots:

- `HKEY_LOCAL_MACHINE\System\CurrentControlSet\Services`
- `HKEY_LOCAL_MACHINE\SOFTWARE\Microsoft\Windows\CurrentVersion\ShellServiceObjectDelayLoad`

These locations can host malware that targets the machine itself, such as rootkit, botnet, or backdoor. Other malware executables target some users on the system and run when the specific user or any user logs on to the system.

They can be found in the following locations:

- `HKEY_LOCAL_MACHINE\Software\Microsoft\Windows\CurrentVersion\Runonce`
- `HKEY_LOCAL_MACHINE\Software\Microsoft\Windows\CurrentVersion\Run`
- `HKEY_CURRENT_USER\Software\Microsoft\Windows\CurrentVersion\Run`
- `HKEY_CURRENT_USER\Software\Microsoft\Windows\CurrentVersion\RunOnce`
- `HKEY_LOCAL_MACHINE\Software\Microsoft\WindowsNT\CurrentVersion\Winlogon\Userinit`

An example of these keys is the Zeus banking malware. It adds its executable in the Userinit key to run when anyone logs on to the system:

```
Userinit       : (S) C:\WINDOWS\system32\userinit.exe,C:\WINDOWS\system32\sdra64.exe,
```

Figure 22: The Zeus autorun technique

Registry analysis

After we have extracted the registry files from the live system or the forensic image, we need to analyze them.

We will use RegistryRipper, and sysinternals for registry parsing and analysis.

RegistryRipper

Regripper is a Perl open source and cross-platform tool by Harlan Carvey, which can be downloaded from `https://code.google.com/p/regripper/`. It parses the registry structure, searches for the forensically important areas, and lists the contents of these areas. The investigator needs to understand the results and extract the anomalies from the output.

The tool is a command line tool, and it also has a simple GUI to carve different types of hives. Through the GUI, the investigator will be able to select one hive file for analysis and the list of plugins to run against this hive file by selecting the type of the hive file from the Profile dropdown. The report will be created in the txt format, and a log file will be created through the analysis process in order to view the successful and failed plugins:

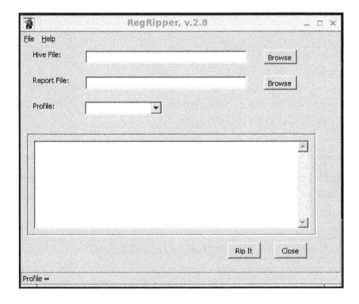

Figure 23: The RegRipper GUI

RegRipper also has a command line interface, which can be used with other Linux tools, such as grep, to directly filter the analysis results. The command line is simple, as follows:

- Run the complete profile against the hive file, where the profile will provide you with a list of the plugins that run against this specific hive:

```
forensics@forensics:~$ regripper -r /mnt/hgfs/image/registry/software -f software
Parsed Plugins file.
Launching appinitdlls v.20130425
appinitdlls v.20130425
(Software) Gets contents of AppInit_DLLs value

AppInit_DLLs
Microsoft\Windows NT\CurrentVersion\Windows
LastWrite Time Tue Jul 14 04:53:25 2009 (UTC)
  AppInit_DLLs : {blank}
  LoadAppInit_DLLs : 0
*LoadAppInit_DLLs value globally enables/disables AppInit_DLLS.
0 = disabled (default)

Wow6432Node\Microsoft\Windows NT\CurrentVersion\Windows
LastWrite Time Tue Jul 14 04:53:25 2009 (UTC)
  AppInit_DLLs : {blank}
  LoadAppInit_DLLs : 0
*LoadAppInit_DLLs value globally enables/disables AppInit_DLLS.
0 = disabled (default)

Analysis Tip: The AppInit_DLLs value should be blank; any DLL listed
is launched with each user-mode process.
appinitdlls complete.
----------------------------------------
Launching apppaths v.20120524
apppaths v.20120524
(Software) Gets content of App Paths subkeys

App Paths
Microsoft\Windows\CurrentVersion\App Paths
Sat Jun 21 22:40:14 2014 (UTC)
```

Figure 24: Run a complete profile against the hive file

Registry Analysis

- Alternatively, you can run only one plugin against a hive file to extract a single piece of information from this hive. In the following figure, only the appcompatcache plugin is running against the system hive:

```
forensics@forensics:~$ regripper -r /mnt/hgfs/image/registry/system -p appcompatcache | more
Launching appcompatcache v.20130425
appcompatcache v.20130425
(System) Parse files from System hive Shim Cache

Signature: 0xbadc0fee
Win2K8R2/Win7, 64-bit
C:\Program Files\VMware\VMware Tools\resume-vm-default.bat
ModTime: Fri Mar 21 13:31:33 2014 Z

C:\Windows\system32\StikyNot.exe
ModTime: Tue Jul 14 01:39:46 2009 Z

C:\Windows\System32\fsquirt.exe
ModTime: Tue Jul 14 01:39:10 2009 Z
Executed

C:\Windows\SysWOW64\DllHost.exe
ModTime: Tue Jul 14 01:14:18 2009 Z
Executed

C:\Windows\System32\net.exe
ModTime: Tue Jul 14 01:39:25 2009 Z
Executed

C:\Windows\WinSxS\amd64_netfx-clrgc_b03f5f7f11d50a3a_6.1.7600.16385_none_ada52b8ba0da82ba\clrgc.exe
ModTime: Wed Jun 10 20:39:44 2009 Z
Executed

C:\Windows\syswow64\WOWReg32.exe
ModTime: Mon Jul 13 23:16:09 2009 Z
Executed
```

Figure 25: Extracting single information from a hive file.

It is worth mentioning that appcompatcache parses the registry for the Application compatibility cache, which stores information about runnable programs in the system. It stores information about the path, size, the timestamp of the last modification, and the time of the most recent run of the executable file and also whether it was executed in the system.

One of the malicious results that can be an indication of malware installation on a system is theexecutable related to one of the banking malware in the following figure:

```
C:\Users\Alina\AppData\Local\Temp\malicious_name.exe
ModTime: Tue Feb 25 12:55:09 2015 Z
Executed
```

Figure 26: Malware in the Application compatibility cache

Here, we can find an executable in the temp folder, which can be an indication of downloading this executable from the Internet during browsing. It had a malicious name and was executed in the system under investigation.

Sysinternals

Sysinternals is a suite used to troubleshoot the Windows system. It was developed by Mark Russinovich and can be found at https://technet.microsoft.com/en-us/sysinternals/bb545021.aspx. It can be used in the forensic analysis to give an indication of infection. It usually runs and parses a live system, but it can also work on an offline system. We just need to point to the registry locations; these are Windows directory and username directory in the offline system.

In Linux, under the Wine environment, privilege escalation is not available, and this program needs to run as administrator. So, we need to run this tool on any Windows machine. It won't run if you provide the program with the read-only mounted image. From the forensics perspective, mounting an image as read/write is not acceptable.

In such cases, we only need to simulate the locations of the registry files:

- `Windows`: This should be a folder with the following subfolder:
    - `System32`: This should be a folder with the following subfolder and files:
        - `Config`: This should be a folder with the following files:
            - `SYSTEM`: This is an extracted registry hive
            - `SOFTWARE`: This is an extracted registry hive
            - `SAM`: This is an extracted registry hive
            - `SECURITY`: This is an extracted registry hive
            - `ntdll.dll`: Copy this file from the mounted image as well (or just empty file with that name)
- `<Username>`: This should be a folder with the following files:

Registry Analysis

- `NTUSER.DAT`: This is an extracted registry hive:

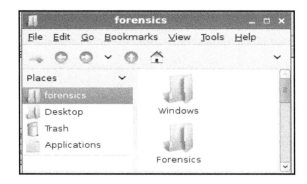

Figure 27: Simulate Windows registry folders

1. Then, we run the `autoruns.exe` within Wine. The `autoruns.exe` tool will display many autoruns registry keys and services along with much more useful information for analysis.
2. Select **Analyze Offline System…** from File and browse to the newly created folders:

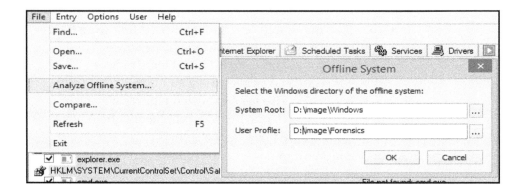

Figure 28: Open the simulated directories

The program has different tabs to filter the registry. For example, the Logon tab filters the entire registry, which runs while logging to the system. These keys are usually used by malware executables in order to preserve its existence in the system after a reboot, as discussed earlier:

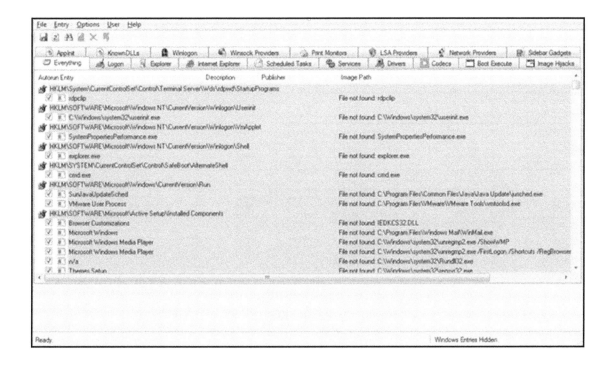

Figure 29: An example of offline system registry analysis

As we can see in Figure 29, for all the entries thst are in yellow and under Image Path we will find File not found. This is normal because the related system isn't actually running.

The Scheduled Tasks list is important; it needs to be checked. One technique for a malicious executable to preserve its existence is to add itself as a task to run every period of time.

MiTeC Windows registry recovery

MiTeC WRR is another registry analysis program worth mentioning. It opens one hive at a time, and you can open all the hives concurrently. Besides viewing the registry in its structured format, it filters the registry based on tasks, such as start-up programs and userdata. WRR can be run under Linux within the Wine environment:

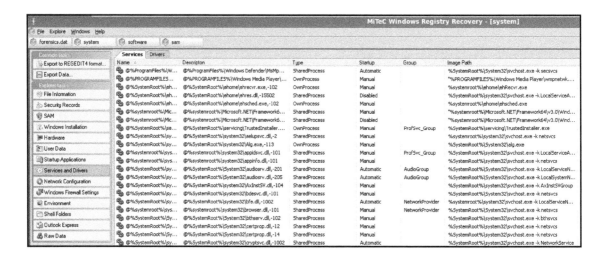

Figure 30: MiTeC WRR

Summary

In this chapter, we got introduced to the registry as one of the most important Windows artifacts, which holds most of the operating system and the installed programs' configurations and settings. We explained the function of each registry hive and its location in the filesystem. Besides this, we parsed the structure of one registry file as an important process in case a corrupted registry file or a recovered fragment of the registry file needs to be analyzed. Then, we explained how malware programs use the registry to preserve their existence in the system and how to discover their presence. We used different tools to view and analyze the registry files.

In the next chapter, we will cover another important artifact of the Windows operating system, the Event Log files. We will explore how to use event files to track the activities of the users in the system and how to discover malicious activities within the system.

8
Event Log Analysis

In this chapter, we will learn about Event Logs in the Microsoft operating system. We will discuss why it is important to cover issues related to event logs for successful investigation. We will consider differences between event logs depending on the MS Windows version.

Event Logs – an introduction

When an operating system works, a lot of events take place in the system. The range of these events is very large and a majority of them can be registered in the system. To register events on the system, there is a powerful mechanism called **Event Logging**. It presents a standard centralized way, which the operating system and applications use to record important information coming from software and hardware. An event can be something that occurred in the system or in some application, and it is necessary to notify the user. Information about every event should be recorded.

Events are collected and stored by the Event Logging Service. This keeps events from different sources in event logs. Event logs provide chronological information, which allows us to determie problems in the system environment and security and tracks users' activities and the usage of system resources. However, the kind of data that will be actually recorded in an event log is dependent on system configuration and application settings. For example, security event logs is turned off on old Windows operating systems by default.

Event logs provide a lot of data for investigators, and they can help with answers for the following issues:

- **What happened**: Some items of the event log record, such as Event ID and Event Category, help get information about a certain event.
- **When**: Timestamps are a key part of the event log and they provide the temporal context for an event. In a system where are a lot of events are generated, the timestamps could be very useful to narrow the timeframe of the search.
- **Who**: Which users are involved. All actions that are executed on the Windows operating system are committed in some account contexts. Some actions are committed not by the normal user but by the operating system, and this will be done in the system's account context, for example, System or Network Service. We can identify who is the user behind a certain event.
- **What systems are involved**: In the network environment, event logs usually have a lot of references to accounts from remote systems. Originally only the NetBIOS of workstations were recorded in event logs. However, it complicated the tracking of involved systems. In systems after Windows 2000, IP addresses are also kept in event logs.
- **What resources are accessed**: The Event Logging Service can be configured to store very granulated information about various objects on the system. Almost any resource of the system can be considered as an object and, thereby, we can detect any requests for unauthorized access to resources.

Event Logs system

Now that we've figured out that Windows event logs contain a lot of useful information and that they can be very valuable resources to detect security incidents, let's see where event logs can be found on different versions of MS Windows.

In the evolution of the MS Windows process, even the Event Logs system was changed. It originally appeared in MS Windows 3.1. Some minor changes occurred in every Windows version, but the names of event logs files and paths remained the same until Windows 2003. Initial versions used the .evt binary format. This format is not suitable to search for strings or to browse for information without special software. Also, these logs have size limitations in results; therefore, new upcoming events could rewrite old stored data.

Before Vista, the event logs were as follows:

```
%System root%\System32\config
```

However, starting from Vista and Server 2008, significant changes were implemented in the event logs structure, types, and locations on the filesystem. The original version of the Event Logs system was a heavy load for system performance. A new version was developed to fix some issues related to performance too. The new .evtx format of event logs was introduced. However, the most significant changes touched the structure of the event logs.

In Vista, many new types of event logs were added, their total number became more than 70. These event logs can be found at the following location:

```
%System root%\System32\winevt\logs
```

Moreover, the new Event Logs system allows sending events to a remote collector, so it's necessary to keep in mind that additional event logs can be found on another server. Note that the presented path for the storage of event logs is the default value and it may be changed through the registry key:

- HKLM\SYSTEM\CurrentControlSet\Services\Eventlog\Application
- HKLM\SYSTEM\CurrentControlSet\Services\Eventlog\System
- HKLM\SYSTEM\CurrentControlSet\Services\Eventlog\Security

Initially in MS Windows, three types of event logs existed:

- System
- Security
- Application

All other extra event logs can be united in the Custom group. Vista, Win7, Server 2008, Win 8, and Server 2008 now have many additional event logs, including specialized event logs for some processes, such as PowerShell, Task Scheduler, and Windows Firewall.

Let's take a look at what kind of information is recorded in various types of event logs:

- **Security Log**: This records events based on local and group policies.
- **System Log**: This records events from the operation system and its components, such as failure of a service on the boot system.
- **Application Log**: This records events from applications, such as failure of access to a file or an antivirus notification.
- **Directory Service**: This records events from Active Directory and some services based on it. It is a standard event logon Domain Controller.

- **File Replication Server**: This records events about updates between Domain Controllers. It is a standard event logon Domain Controller.
- **DNS Server**: This is a standard event logon server where DNS server software is running. It records events about the management of zones, and the start and stop of a DNS server.

The main reason to dedicate a separate directory for new event logs is their large number. As we already mentioned, it exceeds 70.

A new event log can be divided into the following categories:

- **Setup**: This is a new event log, in which information about Windows security updates, patches, hotfixes are stored
- **Forwarded Events**: This is also a new event log to record events coming from remote computers
- **Applications and Services**: This group includes all other new event logs, which were introduced in Windows 2008

Security Event Logs

The old Event Log system had some issues related to performance. In that version, the event log needed to be completely loaded into memory. Sometimes, just for one log, 300 MB of RAM had to be allocated. This behavior affected system performance very much, and it forced administrators to turn off event logging. In the new Event Log system, every event log file has a small header, which is followed by 64Kb chunks. Now, only the currently used chunk will be loaded into memory. This certainly improves performance and reduces resource usage. Also, an increased likelihood of logging will be enabled. Almost all event logs could prove to be useful during an investigation, nonetheless, most answers for the questions that we have in forensics can be found in Security Event Log. System and Application Event Logs are more useful for system administrators for troubleshooting.

Security Event Logs record audit events whenever they occur in the system or the user activity which is covered by local or group audit policies. They could present details about various user activities, including user authentication (logons, run as commands, and remote access) and user activities after logons. Using privileges and object auditing could be a trigger event that shows access to protected files, which user accessed it, and the date and time of when it happened. An audit allows applying security settings to itself so that all modifications of audit policy can be traced.

Keep in mind that security policies may register events with success and failure results. It allows adjusting policies and records only data of interest. From an investigator's point of view, we want to log as much data as possible. This could create additional load to system performance, and it requires significant disk space to store information. This is not possible in many environments. For some nonforensic professionals, it is not obvious why successful and failed attempts to log on should be recorded and how it can help detect a brute force attack. Also, it is possible to set additional audit policies for a specific user with a built-in `gpedit.msc` snap-in. So, we can set a more detailed audit for critically valuable users.

Due its nature, Security Log has more protections than System and Application event logs. Starting from Windows XP SP2, the API for applications that send events to the Security event log was deprecated, excluding the Windows Security Service. Now this possibility is available only for Local Security Authority System Service (LSASS) because it is responsible for applying security policies in the system. Moreover, only users with administrator permissions can review, export, or clear the Security event log.

Let's take a look at what kind of information is stored in the Security event log:

- **Account Logon**: These are events that are stored on the system and which authorize the user. So, it could be workstation or Domain Controller.
- **Account Mgmt**: This is account maintenance and modification.
- **Logon Events**: This is every logon or logoff event on the local system.
- **Directory Service**: These are attempts to access the objects of the Active Directory.
- **Object Access**: This is access to objects which have their own access control list.
- **Policy Change**: These are modifications of users' rights and audit policies.
- **Privilege Use**: This has each case of an account exercising a user right.
- **Process Tracking**: This stores the start, stop process, and objects access.
- **System Events**: This is the start and shutdown of the system.

The Security Event Categories give us understanding about what kind of events can be interesting for us. For every category, we can set an audit policy in the values No Auditing, Success, Failure, or Success and Failure both. Every time an event is recorded in the event log file, it is marked by the category to which it belongs. When the audit is turned off, we will not see any information about such types of events in the event log file.

One of the most disappointing things during an investigation is hitting a dead end. This often happens because we lack event logs. Some investigations, such as intrusion and event log analysis, are very important to track the activities of the intruder. In others, such as employee misuse, they present extra artifacts, which prove the case with significant information, such as time of log on, installation programs, and access to specific files. Unfortunately, audit policies don't have rules and event logs don't contain useful information. So, it is important to configure an audit policy, such that Windows records only what we need.

Also, the settings on systems executing various roles could be different. Audit policies and the number of event logs turned on by default on Workstations, Servers, and Domain Controllers will differ. The Event Logs system on Windows 7 or Windows 8 has minimal logs and it is turned off at all times on Windows XP and Vista by default. Due to the fact that Windows 7 and Windows 8 are becoming more and more common, we can expect more systems with Security, System, and Application event logs. It should be noted that in the corporate network, there are domain policies. Local policies will be rewritten by group policies and, thus, increase logging information.

Many investigators mistakenly believe that server versions of Windows have good settings for event logging out of the box. However, similar workstations standard configuration of server have a minimal set of logged data.

From Windows 2008 onward, every event category is divided into a subcategory called **extended audit policies**. These detailed options were introduced to allow better control over events that need to be monitored by administrators. This became available in Windows 7 and later.

Event types give us reasons as to why an event was recorded into an event log file. Also, they can provide important information about the severity of the event, allowing the administrator to focus on more critical events.

We have the following types of events:

- **Error**: These are significant problems, such as loss of data or functionality; for example, the server fails to load
- **Warning**: These are not significant problems but they can be a problem in the future; for example, low disk space
- **Information**: These are successful operations of applications or services; for example, a service was started

- **Success Audit**: These are notifications that audited events completed successfully, for example, successful user logon
- **Failure Audit**: These arenotifications that the audited event did not complete successfully, for example, failed access to device

Extracting Event Logs

When event logs are analyzed, the most common approach is to export logs and then review them on the forensics workstation. There are a few reasons for such an approach. Often, we need to analyze a few event logs (for example, System, Security, and Application) from several workstations and Domain Controller. So, it is very convenient to have all event log files in one place. Also, many forensics tools not enough good work with event logs.

There are two main approaches to export event logs:

- Live systems
- Offline systems

Both of them have their own set of features; let's see what they are.

Live systems

While working with live systems, remember that event log files are always used, which creates some additional challenges. One way of exporting data from a live system is using Event Viewer. If you right-click on the event log file, the **Save All Events As...** option will appear. Logs can be saved in various formats, including `.evtx`, `.csv`, `.xml`, or `.txt`. If you are concerned about possible log corruption, this is the safest way.

Another alternative for live systems is using FTK Imager so that you can mount the drive as a Physical Disk and export event log files. In practice, there may occur a situation when the event file is corrupted. However, it is still possible to analyze it. The MS Event Viewer may refuse to open such files. The situation with new `.evtx` format is a little bit better, as new file log corruption happens much more rarely, and MS Event Viewer is more tolerant of this format.

The MS Resource Kit includes the elogdump utility, which allows keeping containment of the event log from a local or remote computer. The PsLogList utility is the analog of elogdump with one difference: PsLogList allows logging in on a remote system and receives the message from the remote system in case the attempt failed. It is the best alternative to the live system, and it is a free tool from SysInternals. This command line tool has a lot of features. It can dump live event logs to `.csv` file, read, and output exported data in the native `.evt`/`.evtx` format, filter output and dump event logs from a remote system. By default, it outputs the system event log file.

Offline system

Event logs are binary databases, so to review `.evt`/`.evtx` files, we need tools that can parse these formats. There are a few good free tools which allow converting binary format of event logs to human readable text formats.

TZWorks released `evtwalk` and `evtx_viewer`. Harlan Carvey wrote a few Perl scripts to parse event log files, and Andreas Schuster released `evtx_parser`.

Extraction of event logs from an offline system is often the last hope for investigators who encounter corrupted event logs, but this approach has some benefits. For example, there is data stored in event logs, access to which is difficult using standard log viewers. The most important one of these is the *number of records* in an event log file. The number of records is assigned sequentially to an event within the log file. So, a missed number will be a marker for manipulation with events in the event log. The best way to get access to this data is to extract the specific events and sort it with a database or spreadsheet.

The TZWorks evtwalk tool can be used for both live and offline systems. For a live system, we can use the `-livesys` option; it will examine all the event logs on the host. The evtwalk tool will determine the version of operating system and scan the appropriate event log directory for that version of Windows.

For offline analysis, when event logs are gathered as part of an investigation, the evtwalk tool can be invoked with `-pipe`. The `-pipe` option allows `evtwalk` to receive a separate path or filename per line as input and process each of them separately.

For Windows, one can use the built-in `dir` command along with some of its companion switches to get the desired result. The following is an example of using this option:

```
dir c:\forensicscases\*.evtx /b /s | evtwalk –pipe
> events.txt
```

The `evtwalk` command can work with one or multiple event files specified with the -log option and is separated by the | character.

Another unique feature of the evtwalk tool is its ability to output data to the timeline format with the `cvsl2t` (log2timeline) and `bodyfile` (mactime) options. Due to this fact, we have the ability to combine event log activity with filesystem and registry activity that allows determining what happened on the computer.

Instead of displaying all the records that are presented in an event log, it is possible to filter a certain class of event data.

For evtwalk, the followingreport categories are available:

- Password changes
- Clock changes or updates
- User logon and logoff events
- System start and stop times
- User credential or permission changes
- USB events

An analyst may want their own report template. In this case, they can determine the report template and specify it using the cmdfile option. It should be noted that if you want to run evtwalk on a live system, you should run it with administrator permissions.

Evtx_view is the GUI version of the evtwalk tool. This is a good tool to exactly understand how events are recorded and what data is available. Both tools have unique features, allowing them to filter specific types of events according to the action which they represent. Investigators can make a request to report only particular events, for example logons, password changes, times of modifications, USB usage, and so on. TZWorks tools are nice, but they are not free.

Event Viewer

One tool that you can use for free is Event Viewer. One of the most interesting features of Event Viewer is that you can review events from remote PCs in a corporate network. This could be a good alternative to usage of Remote Desktop. This may be very useful in a live response when it is necessary to check something specific very fast. For example, if we need to know whether the compromised user account was used or whether some malware-specific service was started. The ability to have a quick answer for critically important questions has big value for effective incident response:

1. To review event logs from other computers, right-click on Event Viewer (Local) and choose Connect to Another Computer.
2. Select Another Computer, input IP Address or Hostname, and click on OK.

> Starting from Windows 7, Event Viewer allows specifying different accounts for remote authentication (similar to "run as").

Keep in mind that when your review event logs on a live system, all events with your activities will be recorded to event logs, including remote logons executed for review of logs. You may also see new 4624, 4776, 4769, and 4674 events in event logs, depending on network settings and audit policies.

The built-in Windows Event Viewer has significant disadvantages. It is very tedious to review a lot of events in the Event Viewer interface. There is no ability to load a few logs from different systems and to filter them and search in parallel. Besides this, Event Viewer has strict requirements for the format of event log files. In practice, you may have corrupted files, and some unexperienced analysts may give up an analysis of event logs when they cannot open them with Event Viewer.

Event Log Explorer

One more utility for Event Log analysis is Event Log Explorer. This is event log management software, which works over built-in Microsoft tools. It provides all the features that are needed by analysts to quickly analyze event logs. It supports all the current versions of MS Windows and the `.evt` and `.evtx` formats. However, what is more important is that it works with corrupted files. It has two options:

- To open event logs with API
- To open event files in direct parsing mode

Event Log Explorer allows opening a few event log files simultaneously and using an event to combine them. Moreover, it has rich filtering features, including access to the Event Description text field where significant forensics artifacts are. Also very useful is the feature of marking various Event IDs by different color. Event Log Explorer is free for personal use and costs around $100 for commercial use.

Useful resources

It is not possible to describe all events in one chapter, so you can find out more information about events that you are interested in some internet resources.

Here are useful resources with information related to the event logs topic:

- A good resource of information about a lot of forensics topics is the SANS Reading Room (https://www.sans.org/reading-room/). Here, are you can find many useful white papers and written analysts, students and forensics investigators. One of these is a white paper written by Russ Antony (http://www.sans.org/reading-room/whitepapers/logging/detecting-security-incidents-windows-workstation-event-logs-34262). It describes how useful Event Logs can be to detect anomalies in system and for investigations of security incidents.

> It is impossible and also not necessary to remember all Event ID and error codes that are related to them. Fortunately, we have a few online resources with such information.

- A good place to search for information about events is MS TechNet (https://www.microsoft.com/technet/support/ee/ee_advanced.aspx). This resource contains a lot of information on various Event IDs for numbers and different MS operation systems and applications.

    Event ID.net (http://www.eventid.net/) is another very good resource related to this topic. It contains useful information about different Event Logging issues.

- Ultimate Windows Security (www.ultimatewindowssecurity.com) contains databases which are supported and updated by the community.

Event Log Analysis

Analyzing the event log – an example

Let's take a look at a small example, how we can use the Event Log Explorer to analyze an event log. Assume that we have event log files from the analyzed system:

1. First, load the Security log. This displays all events relating to login, the creation of new accounts, and more. Let's try to display all the users who log in to the system. A login event has the 4,624 identifier. We can apply an Event ID = 4,624 filter. Note that we should adjust the time. Choose **Time Correction…** from View according to the offset from GMT on the forensics station. For instance, if you work on a system with GMT + 3, you need to input -3 to get time of events in the GMT time zone:

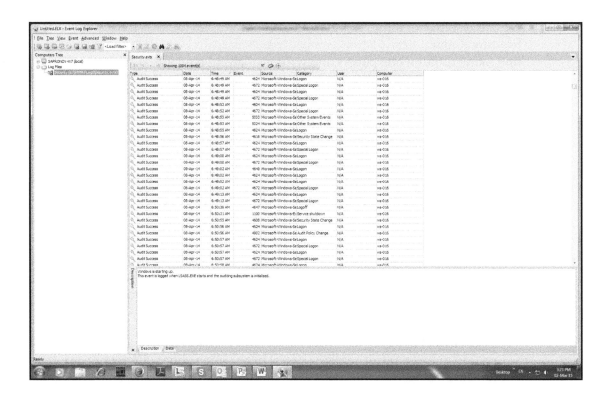

[176]

2. Now, we can sort out user accounts. We see that we have an unusual user, `SYSTEMSERVICE`. Let's filter all events with this account. We can filter by `SYSTEMSERVICE` in the **Description** field:

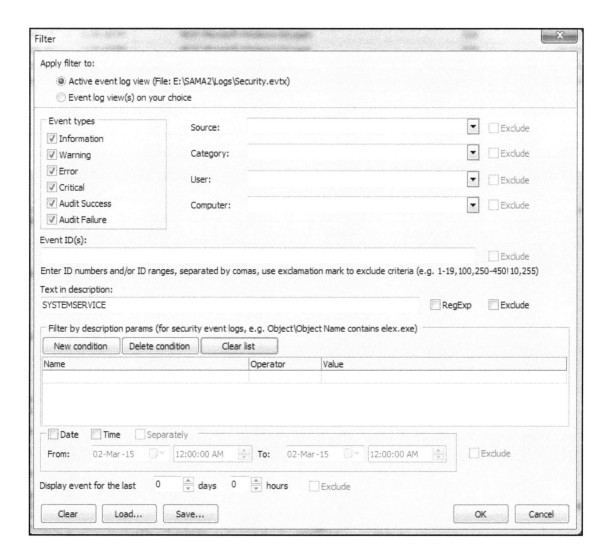

After applying this filter, we will have the following result:

We can see the following events with this account with a chronological timeline:

Event ID	Description
4624	This is a successful log in to the system
4634	This is a log off from the system
4647	This is a log off from the system
4648	This is an unsuccessful log in attempt
4672	This is an assignment of new privileges
4720	This is an account creation
4722	This is an account activation
4724	This is an attempt to change password
4726	This is an account deletion
4738	This is an account modification

We can see that the account was created on April 8, 2014 at 12:40:52 UTC.

Let's view the types of login (login using RDP has type 10); to do this, just filter Logon Type equal 10:

After applying the filter, we will have the following result:

This user remotely accessed the system on April 8, 2014 at 12:10:18 UTC.

So now, we can figure out this is a malicious account, when it was created, and when and how it logged in to the system.

Summary

In this chapter, we have seen that event logs can be a useful source of evidence for forensic investigations. We examined the structure of event logs and looked at the features of event log systems for various Windows operating systems. We looked at some tools, which you can use to analyze event logs.

In the next chapter, we will look at some files with which the Windows OS works. These files are artifacts of Windows live, and they reflect what occurred in the system. We will learn to analyze prefetch, links, and jobs files.

9
Windows Files

In the previous chapter, we discussed the Windows log files and discussed how important they are for analysis. However, Windows logs aren't the only important artifact in Windows. In this chapter, we will discuss more important Windows files that are usually created in the normal Windows operations but may have evidential importance from our prospective of the case under investigation.

Windows prefetch files

The Windows operating system uses what are called prefetch files to speed up the program starting process. It will store a list of all the files and DLLs used by the program when started in order to preload these files into the memory when the program starts to make it faster to start. Each executable has a prefetch file which contains the following:

- The executable's name
- The path to the executable
- The number of times that the program ran within the system
- The last run time
- A list of DLLs used by the program

Windows Files

The prefetch files are located at `%SystemRoot%\Prefetch`, and each file has a "pf" extension. The naming schema of these files consists of adding the executable name in capital letters, followed by -, and then an eight character hash of the application's start location, as shown in Figure1 for the `calc.exe` Windows native tool:

CALC.EXE-A7D3F5D3.pf	1/10/2016 2:37 PM	PF File	11 KB

Figure 1: A prefetch file example

If you find two different pf files on the same executable, this means that either there are two executables with the same name, or the same executable ran from two different locations. Also, the user who ran this program won't store this in the prefetch information. However, this can be compensated by correlating the last run time and the pf modification timestamp in the filesystem with the security logging information to see which user ran this executable the last time.

The maximum number of prefetch files is 1,024 starting from Windows 8. From Windows XP to Windows 7, it was 128 files only. When the maximum number of files is reached, Windows will delete the oldest file in order to create a new one. This means that in case you found the maximum number of prefetch files in the prefetch folder, you can assume that there might be another pf file for any existing executable and it was overwritten before and recreated again, so the first run and last run of the program might not be the right times.

Windows prefetch can be used in speeding up the booting process of the applications' start time or both. This information will be written in the following registry key: `HKEY_LOCAL_MACHINE\SYSTEM\CurrentControlSet\Control\Session Manager\Memory Management\PrefetchParameters`.

Under a `EnablerPrefetcher` registry value, you can find one of four data values:

- 0: This means that prefetching is disabled.
- 1: This means enable applications prefetching only.
- 2: This means enable boot prefetching only.

- 3: This means enable both boot and applications prefetching:

Name	Type	Data
(Default)	REG_SZ	(value not set)
BaseTime	REG_DWORD	0x1b982190 (462954896)
BootId	REG_DWORD	0x0000001f (31)
EnablePrefetcher	REG_DWORD	0x00000003 (3)

Figure 2: Prefetch in Registry

A piece of malware is a program as well. So, if the prefetch was configured to enable prefetching for applications, a prefetch file will be created for that malware in the `prefetch` folder. Finding a malware's prefetch file will add great evidential value as it will indicate all the files and DLLs that were used by the malware, which will give indications about its operations and a start point for the rest of the analysis.

Also, in some attacks, the kill chain requires running different tools on the local system to remotely control it by attackers. Ordering prefetch files by time and filtering the files by the incident time will give us the timely ordered tools which ran within the system and caused the infection. These facts will help us make better assumptions about an attack scenario and will help in the eradication and recovery phases of the incident response cycle.

Another file named `layout.ini` is located in the same `prefetch` folder as well. In this file, there are some paths to the files that are frequently used and loaded by the prefetching process. This file is used by the Windows Defragment process to move all the files that are opened frequently in a contiguous location physically in the system disk in order to load it quickly and reduce the time required to physically access these disk locations sequentially. This process's effect can be noticed in the HDD more than SSD, where the access to any physical location in the HDD requires mechanical motion.

Prefetch file analysis

It is worth mentioning that the structure of the prefetch file changes from one Windows version to another. To analyze the prefetch file, the investigator can open it manually with a hex-editor, for example, understand its structure, and start parsing the contents of the file and even create an automated tool to perform this function faster. Fortunately, there is a tool already created, and it supports the prefetch files up to Windows 10. The WinPrefetchView tool can be downloaded from `http://nirsoft.com/`.

WinPrefetchView automatically parses the location of the prefetch files in the live system and views it for further analysis. In order to parse prefetch files in a postmortem analysis on our Linux analysis machine, we can run the WinPrefetch program within the Wine environment and copy the `prefetch` folder from the mounted image.

The program interface consists of two small windows, one for the applications that are related to each prefetch file and another one to list all the files that are used by the selected program from the upper window. In Figure 3, we can see the ntosboot file, which refers to the boot process of the system and lists all the files that are opened during this operation. In Figure 3, the program is running from the Linux machine under the Wine environment:

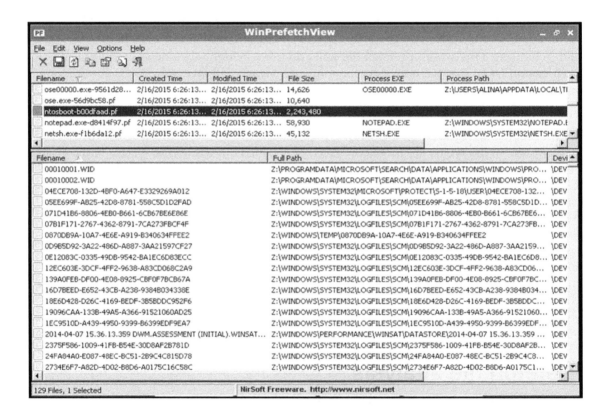

Figure 3: WinPrefetchView

Windows tasks

Some programs need to perform specific events at a specific time in the Windows environment. To do this, Windows allows programs to create what is called a **scheduled task**. Tasks are stored in `C:\Windows\System32\Tasks`. Each task is stored in the XML file format, which contains the user who created the task, the time or the trigger of the task to take place, and the path to the command or the program that will be executed, which is the task itself. Starting from Task Scheduler 2.0, which was first introduced with Windows Vista, the trigger can be calendar-based or an event, such as starting the task when a specific event is logged to the event log system. The actions can also be: running the program, sending an e-mail, or viewing a message to the user.

In the live system, the investigator can open the tasks using the usual `Task Scheduler`. From the forensic image, the investigator can extract the tasks from `C:\Windows\System32\Tasks`, where each file is a single task in the XML format. In Figure 4, we can see the task that is used by Google in the Windows operating system to update Google products in the system:

```
          <Enabled>true</Enabled>
        </LogonTrigger>
        <CalendarTrigger>
          <Enabled>true</Enabled>
          <StartBoundary>2014-05-08T13:04:00</StartBoundary>
          <ScheduleByDay>
            <DaysInterval>1</DaysInterval>
          </ScheduleByDay>
        </CalendarTrigger>
      </Triggers>
      <Settings>
        <Enabled>true</Enabled>
        <ExecutionTimeLimit>PT0S</ExecutionTimeLimit>
        <Hidden>false</Hidden>
        <WakeToRun>false</WakeToRun>
        <DisallowStartIfOnBatteries>false</DisallowStartIfOnBatteries>
        <StopIfGoingOnBatteries>false</StopIfGoingOnBatteries>
        <RunOnlyIfIdle>false</RunOnlyIfIdle>
        <Priority>5</Priority>
        <IdleSettings>
          <Duration>PT600S</Duration>
          <WaitTimeout>PT3600S</WaitTimeout>
          <StopOnIdleEnd>false</StopOnIdleEnd>
          <RestartOnIdle>false</RestartOnIdle>
        </IdleSettings>
      </Settings>
      <Principals>
        <Principal id="Author">
          <UserId>System</UserId>
          <RunLevel>HighestAvailable</RunLevel>
          <LogonType>InteractiveTokenOrPassword</LogonType>
        </Principal>
      </Principals>
      <Actions Context="Author">
        <Exec>
          <Command>C:\Program Files\Google\Update\GoogleUpdate.exe</Command>
```

Figure 4: Google Update Task

A piece of malware can create a task to start itself after a specific trigger, such as running the malware executable each morning, or after a specific period of time. This is another way used by malware authors to ensure the existence of the malware on the infected machine besides adding its executable to the startup registry keys or as a service in the system.

Windows Thumbs DB

When the user uses the **Thumbnails** or **Filmstrip** views from the Windows folder viewing options, a small thumbnail version of the pictures will be created and stored in a single file. This file is located in the same directory as the pictures in Windows XP and named Thumbs.db. The Thumbs.db file has a thumbnail version of the existing and also deleted pictures. Thumbs.db is a hidden file, and usually the user ignores it:

Figure 5: Files viewing options

If the user has deleted the pictures but hasn't delete the Thumbs.db file, it will be possible to recover the thumbnail version of the pictures deleted from that directory, which provide a good clue about the pictures' contents. Besides the thumbnail version of the picture, Thumbs.db contains the file name and the date and time of the last modification.

This Thumbs.db file is very important in cases related to pictures, such as child pornography cases.

Starting from Windows 7, the process of handling thumbnails files changed. All the Thumbs.db files are allocated in a single folder in C:\Users\<UserName>\AppData\Local\Microsoft\Windows\Explorer. This is better from the forensics prospective, as all the files are in the same place and there is no need to search for any Thumbs.db files in the whole partition or disk, and it won't be deleted if the user deleted the whole photos' folder. Also, the file name has changed to Thumbcache.db.

In the modern Windows version, the files' view has different sizes: small, medium, large, and extra-large. Different thumbcache files need to be allocated for each size of the viewing layout. Each size has a separate Thumbcache database, and the name of the Thumbcache file has a number, which indicates the size of the viewing layout, for example, thumbcache_32.db or thumbcache_256.db:

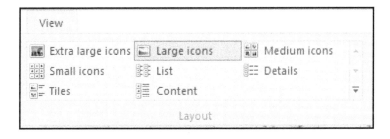

Figure 6: Files viewing options in modern Windows Oses

Thumbcache analysis

Thumbcache Viewer is a free tool, and it can be downloaded from `https://thumbcachev iewer.github.io/`. It extracts thumbnail images from Thumcache files, as shown in the following screenshot:

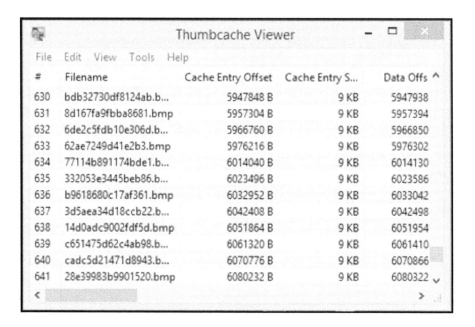

Figure 7: Thumbcache Viewer

Note that there is another version to parse `Thumbs.db` files.

The original file path is not stored in the `Thumbcache` file. To map the file to its original location, we can run the program in the target Windows system itself and start mapping from the live system. Or, we can extract and use the Windows search database `Windows.edb` file from the target system, the system under investigation. It is an ESE database located at `C:\ProgramData\Microsoft\Search\Data\Applications\Windows\`:

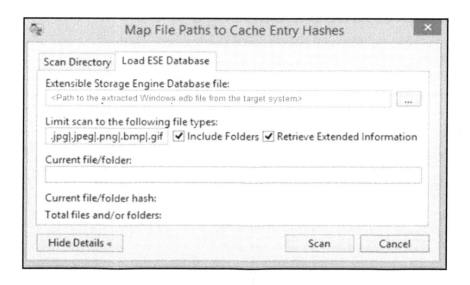

Figure 8: Mapping Thumbcache files to location

This is created by the Windows indexing service that is used to speed the search process in Windows OS. Thumbcache viewer uses this file to map the entries to their original locations in the target system. Thumbcache viewer can run on another Windows system and use only this database file from the target Windows system. However, in this case, the host Windows OS must be the same version or higher of the target Windows system. Not all the entries will be mapped based on the data in the `Windows.edb` file, but the successfully mapped entries will be viewed in green:

686	C:\Users\AymanT\Desktop\1.pn
687	52091c61604f8a38.bmp
688	C:\Users\AymanT\Desktop\Perf
689	C:\Users\AymanT\Desktop\Perf
690	C:\Users\AymanT\Desktop\Perf

Figure 9: Mapped entries using the Windows.edb file.

Windows Files

Corrupted Windows.edb files

Extracted `Windows.edb` files will be corrupted in some cases. If the `Windows.edb` file is corrupted, the tool will give you a warning about this and request a recovery first on this file to use it in mapping. Fortunately, the recovery of such a file can be done using the `esentutl.exe` Windows native tool with a /p switch:

Figure 10: Fixing corrupted Windows.edb file

Windows RecycleBin

When a user deletes file with the normal deletion process, the file actually doesn't leave the HDD. It will be only marked as deleted on the filesystem, and all the file's metadata and contents will continue existing on the hard disk until it is overwritten by another file's metadata and content. This will allow the user to recover such a file if it was deleted by mistake, for example. The deleted files will be located in what is called a **Recycle Bin** in the Windows OS.

Usually, the advanced forensics tools will be able to find and view the deleted files if the system still has their metadata and can read them without carving. However, if the investigator only has the recycle bin file and needs to understand which files were deleted, this can be done by analyzing the `Recycle Bin` folder.

The name of the Recycle Bin differs from one version of Windows to another. In Windows versions 95 and 98, the location is under the system partition in a folder named `RECYCLED`. From Windows XP until before Vista, the location was the same, but the folder name changed to `RECYCLER`. Starting from Windows Vista, the name was changed to `$Recycle.Bin`.

The ordinary user on a live system can browse to the Recycle Bin, but they need to display hidden files and protected system files from the Explorer's view menu. From the Recycle Bin, the user can recover the file to its previous location by simply right-clicking on the file. As long the file exists in the Recycle Bin, it is still recoverable.

In postmortem analysis, the files won't be shown as in the live system, and it will need more understanding of its structure, which differs from one Windows version to another.

Windows Files

RECYCLER

In the `RECYCLER` folder, there are other subfolders named after the users' IDs. In these folders, the deleted files don't have their normal names, but rather they have sequential names: DC1, DC2, and so on. There is another binary file named INFO2, which maps the Recycle Bin files to the real filename, date and time, and the recycler name of the file. In the following screenshot, we can see the structure of `RECYCLER` using FTK imager while opening a live Windows XP system:

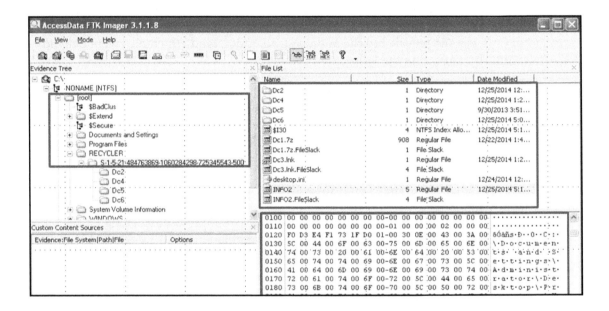

Figure 11: Recycler in Windows XP with FTK Imager

Chapter 9

As we can see, the files have no names, only sequential DC# names. The INFO2 file has all the names and paths of the actual file mapped to their DC names. We can see that by opening the INFO2 file with any hex editor or by the FTK Imager itself:

```
0100  00 00 00 00 00 00 00 00-00 00 00 00 00 00 00 00  ................
0110  00 00 00 00 00 00 00 00-01 00 00 00 02 00 00 00  ................
0120  F0 D3 E4 F1 73 1F D0 01 00 30 0E 00 43 00 3A 00  ðÓäñs·Ð··0··C·:·
0130  5C 00 44 00 6F 00 63 00-75 00 6D 00 65 00 6E 00  \·D·o·c·u·m·e·n·
0140  74 00 73 00 20 00 61 00-6E 00 64 00 20 00 53 00  t·s· ·a·n·d· ·S·
0150  65 00 74 00 74 00 69 00-6E 00 67 00 73 00 5C 00  e·t·t·i·n·g·s·\·
0160  41 00 64 00 6D 00 69 00-6E 00 69 00 73 00 74 00  A·d·m·i·n·i·s·t·
0170  72 00 61 00 74 00 6F 00-72 00 5C 00 44 00 65 00  r·a·t·o·r·\·D·e·
0180  73 00 6B 00 74 00 6F 00-70 00 5C 00 50 00 72 00  s·k·t·o·p·\·P·r·
```

Figure 12: INFO2 file in Hex

The values can be parsed, as follows:

- The file sequence number in the Recycler: Dc1
- Deletion date: Wed, 24 December 2014 12:20:03 UTC. The deletion time can be decoded using the Dcode program, as follows:

- Actual file size in bytes: 929792 =908 KB
- File location and name:C:\Documents and Settings\Administrator\Desktop\<FileName>

[193]

Windows Files

$Recycle.bin

This was used starting from Windows Vista. Instead of the DC naming schema and the INFO2 file from RECYCLER, for each deleted file, there will be an INFO2-like file and another file that holds the content of the file instead of DC files. The content of each deleted file will be found under a file with a name that starts with $R, and its INFO2-like file will start with $I with the same name, as shown in the following screenshot:

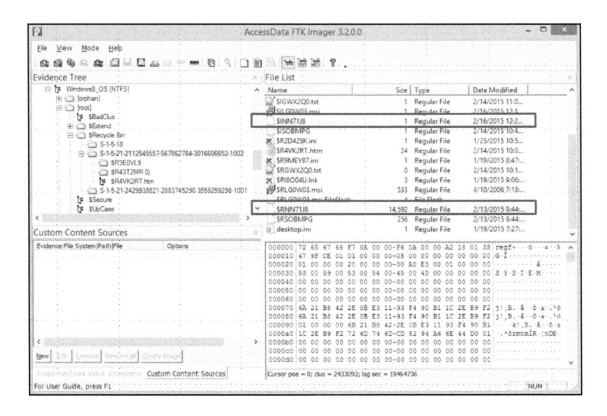

Figure 13: Recycle.bin in Windows 8.1

If we tried to parse the INFO2-like file and the $I file, we can extract the following information as before but from different offsets:

```
000 01 00 00 00 00 00 00 00 00 00 E4 00 00 00 00 00  ........ä.....
010 40 F1 62 63 7E 49 D0 01 43 00 3A 00 5C 00 55 00  @ñbc~IÐ.C.:.\.U.
020 73 00 65 00 72 00 73 00 5C 00 41 00 79 00 6D 00  s.e.r.s.\.A.y.m.
030 61 00 6E 00 54 00 5C 00 44 00 65 00 73 00 6B 00  a.n.T.\.D.e.s.k.
040 74 00 6F 00 70 00 5C 00 53 00 59 00 53 00 54 00  t.o.p.\.S.Y.S.T.
050 45 00 4D 00 00 00 00 00 00 00 00 00 00 00 00 00  E.M.............
060 00 00 00 00 00 00 00 00 00 00 00 00 00 00 00 00  ................
070 00 00 00 00 00 00 00 00 00 00 00 00 00 00 00 00  ................
```

Figure 14: $I file opened in Hex

- $I file header: 0x0000000000000001
- Actual file size in bytes: 14942208 = 14592 KB
- Deletion date: Mon, 16 February 2015 00:20:37 UTC
- File location and name:`C:\Users\AymanT\Desktop\SYSTEM`

Windows shortcut files

The ordinary user of the Windows system can create a shortcut to any file in the system. The shortcut is like a pointer to a specific file from another location in the filesystem. The user creates this file to achieve easy access to some locations or files in the filesystem.

The Windows operating system creates shortcut files for the recently opened files by default in the following locations:

- `C:\users\<username>\AppData\Roaming\Microsoft\Windows\Recent`
- `C:\users\<username>\AppData\Roaming\Microsoft\Office\Recent`

Windows XP saves the shortcut files at the following location:

- `C:\Documents and Settings\<username>\Recent\`

Windows Files

Windows stores these shortcut files if the user has opened data or media files in the system. It stores the timestamps, the name and location of the original file, and the volume name.

The importance of these link files is that they won't be deleted even if the original file was deleted from the system specially in the automatically created shortcut files in the 'Recent' folder in the Windows OS. In this case, you can prove that a specific file, maybe an infected pdf file, has been opened in the system under investigation even if the file has been opened from an external storage that is now removed from the system. Also, in this case, you will find the path to this file in the external storage saved in the link file.

Shortcut analysis

The filesystem timestamps of the shortcut file can reveal some information about the file itself. We can consider the creation time of the shortcut file as the first time the file was opened and the modification time is the last time the file was opened. If both timestamps are the same, this indicates that the file was opened only once from the location mentioned in the shortcut file:

Date created	Date modified	Type	Size
12/27/2015 4:44 PM	12/27/2015 4:44 PM	Shortcut	1 KB
12/21/2015 12:09 PM	1/7/2016 5:41 PM	Shortcut	1 KB
12/22/2015 3:19 PM	12/25/2015 2:50 PM	Shortcut	1 KB
12/30/2015 11:49 AM	12/30/2015 11:52 ...	Shortcut	1 KB

Figure 15: Filesystem timestamps for shortcut files

To show the contents of the shortcut file in postmortem analysis, we can show it in a live system. However, the content may change to match some paths in the running Windows machine, or we can use a tool, such as Exiftool tool from http://www.sno.phy.queensu.ca/~phil/exiftool/. Exiftool is a platform-independent Perl library that was designed to read and edit Meta information for a wide variety of files, including photos with different formats and the .lnk files. All the supported files can be found at http://www.sno.phy.queensu.ca/~phil/exiftool/#supported.

We can use the command line version of this tool in opening any shortcut file, and it will display different information, including the original file location and the timestamps of the shortcut file:

```
C:\Users\AymanT\Downloads\exiftool-9.86>"exiftool(-k).exe" C:\Users\AymanT\AppData\Roaming\Microsoft\Office\Recent\app.xml.LNK
ExifTool Version Number         : 9.86
File Name                       : app.xml.LNK
Directory                       : C:/Users/AymanT/AppData/Roaming/Microsoft/Office/Recent
File Size                       : 1223 bytes
File Modification Date/Time     : 2015:02:23 16:16:43+02:00
File Access Date/Time           : 2015:02:23 16:16:43+02:00
File Creation Date/Time         : 2015:02:23 16:16:43+02:00
File Permissions                : rw-rw-rw-
File Type                       : LNK
MIME Type                       : application/octet-stream
Flags                           : IDList, LinkInfo, RelativePath, Unicode
File Attributes                 : Normal
Create Date                     : 2015:02:23 16:15:55+02:00
Access Date                     : 2015:02:23 16:15:55+02:00
Modify Date                     : 1980:01:01 00:00:00+02:00
Target File Size                : 987
Icon Index                      : (none)
Run Window                      : Normal
Hot Key                         : (none)
Target File DOS Name            : app.xml
Drive Type                      : Fixed Disk
Volume Label                    : Windows8_OS
Local Base Path                 : C:\Users\AymanT\Desktop\Compound file - Copy\docProps\app.xml
Relative Path                   : ..\..\..\..\Desktop\Compound file - Copy\docProps\app.xml
Machine ID                      : ayman
```

Figure 16: Exiftool opening a lnk file

Summary

So, in this chapter, we discussed different extra Windows artifacts that are important to digital forensics analysis. We discussed the prefetch files, and how they can be used to track a malicious executable that ran within the system. We also showed the Windows tasks that can be used to preserve a malware existence in the infected Windows system. Then, we showed you how to investigate the photos existing in the system even after deletion using the Thumbcache files. By mentioning deletion, we discussed the Recycle Bin and its structure in different Windows OS versions. In the end, we discussed the shortcut or `.lnk` files and illustrated how to read their data and their forensic importance.

As opening a malicious URL or opening malicious attachments are the most common ways to infect a machine, in the following chapter, we will discuss browser forensics and show you how to track user activities and investigate the visited websites using different tools with different browsers. Also, we will explain how to conduct e-mail forensics and investigate received e-mails and their attachments or embedded links.

10
Browser and E-mail Investigation

The Internet and World Wide Web is the main way to search and view data and information nowadays. Browsers are the most common tools to do this. So, investigating browsers is important when an analyst tries to investigate a user's activity to profile this user. This isn't an easy task because of the huge number of browsers in the market nowadays and the different artifacts structure in each browser. In this chapter, we will highlight three of the most used browsers: Internet Explorer, Firefox, and Chrome.

E-mail is still the main way to communicate among many people in the digital world, especially in the corporate environment. This chapter will cover the different formats of e-mail clients' archives, and explain how to read e-mails from these archives for analysis or tracing senders.

Browser investigation

Tricking a user into visiting a malicious link and downloading a malicious executable is one of most used techniques by offenders to infect users' machines. Analyzing the browsing activities of the victim can identify the first infection vector and how it worked. Also, in case of analyzing a criminal machine, browsing through the history would help profile the user and clarify their intentions by identifying the types of websites that they usually visit and the contents of their downloaded files.

Analyzing browser activities requires that the investigator understand the different artifacts of the browser with their locations and the data structure of each one. From this, we can see why it is tricky to conduct in-depth browser forensics. There are many browsers that are currently on the market, and a single user can be using more than one browser.

In this section, we will explain different browser's artifacts and look at how to extract all these artifacts from the local browser files.

Microsoft Internet Explorer

Microsoft Internet Explorer aka IE or MSIE is one of the first internet browsers on the market. It comes by default with the Windows operating system. Version 1 was released in 1995, and the latest version at the time of writing this book is version 11. Between version 1 and version 11 and between the different versions of Windows, the artifacts of the MSIE have been reformed.

Also, starting from Windows Vista the directory structure and artifacts' locations have been changed in the filesystem. So, there are two factors that control the Internet Explorer analysis process:

- The version of the installed Internet Explorer
- The version of the running Windows operating system

History files

Using browsing history, the investigator can profile system users and track their activities to narrow the investigation process. Windows keeps the browsing history for 20 days by default, which can be edited from the program itself or from the registry.

The investigator can use this piece of information to see whether the user recently cleared their browsing history or the history that the investigator found is the maximum history record that can be found in the system. The number of days to keep the history records of MSIE can be found under a value named `DaysToKeep` in the software hive under `\Microsoft\Windows\CurrentVersion\Internet Settings\Url`.

The location of History files differ from one Windows version to another, as follows:

- Before Windows Vista, the History file called `History.IE5` in `C:\Documents and Settings\<Username>\Local Settings\History.IE5`

- In Windows Vista and Windows 7, the locations changed but it uses the same file structure `History.IE5`:
    - `<SystemPartition>\Users\<Username>\AppData\Local\Microsoft\Windows\History\History.IE5`
    - `<SystemPartition>\Users\<Username>\AppData\Local\Microsoft\Windows\History\Low\History.IE5`

- In Windows 8, Windows 8.1, and Windows 10, the location and the structure changed:
`<SystemPartition>\Users\<Username>\AppData\Local\Microsoft\Windows\WebCache\WebCacheV#.dat`

> Starting from MSIE Version 7 under Windows Vista and then Windows 7, MSIE runs in protected mode to improve security. This protected mode is turned on by default, and it can be turned off by the user. It runs the MSIE with low privilege, which makes any malicious software that is installed by MSIE during browsing run with the same low privilege, which doesn't allow the malware to access and manipulate sensitive areas in the operating system, such as system files or registry keys. All the activities of the MSIE in protected mode in Windows Vista or Windows 7 are located under the `Low` folder:
> `<SystemPartition>\Users\<Username>\AppData\Local\Microsoft\Windows\History\Low\History.IE5`.

History.IE5

This was used by MSIE from Version 5 to Version 9 to store browsing history. On a live system, browsing to this location will display different folders indicating different periods of browsing. Each folder contains links to the visited websites. The user can reopen these websites from this location:

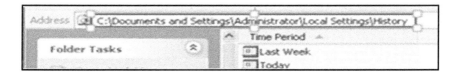

History on a live system

Now, let's try to open the same location with the command line. We will list the files under the `content.IE5` directory using the `dir` command line:

```
C:\Documents and Settings\Administrator\Local Settings\History\History.IE5>dir
 Volume in drive C has no label.
 Volume Serial Number is 105A-2378

 Directory of C:\Documents and Settings\Administrator\Local Settings\History\History.IE5

02/28/2015  11:22 PM            32,768 index.dat
               1 File(s)         32,768 bytes
               0 Dir(s)  40,548,528,128 bytes free
```

Listing the contents of History using the dir command

We can see that there is a different structure with only one file named `index.dat`. However, if we tried to list the directory structure by the `dir` command with an `/a` switch to list all directories, we will get different results, as shown in the following screenshot:

```
C:\Documents and Settings\Administrator\Local Settings\History\History.IE5>dir /a
 Volume in drive C has no label.
 Volume Serial Number is 105A-2378

 Directory of C:\Documents and Settings\Administrator\Local Settings\History\History.IE5

02/28/2015  11:54 PM    <DIR>          .
02/28/2015  11:54 PM    <DIR>          ..
09/29/2010  07:26 AM               113 desktop.ini
02/28/2015  11:22 PM            32,768 index.dat
02/28/2015  10:39 PM    <DIR>          MSHist012015021620150223
02/28/2015  11:54 PM    <DIR>          MSHist012015022820150301
               2 File(s)         32,881 bytes
               4 Dir(s)  40,548,528,128 bytes free
```

The dir command with an /a switch

We can see two new directories with names that start with `MSHist01`. These two folders represent the two folders in the preceding screenshot. The rest of the name represents the period of time that each folder contains of browsing history with the following structure:

The constant `MSHist01`, *four digits for the start year, two digits for the start month, two digits for the start day, four digits for the end year, two digits for the end month, and two digits for the end day*

So, these two files represent the following browsing history:

- The first file shows the dates from 16-2-2015 to 23-2-2015, which indicates that this is a weekly history
- The second file indicates a daily history for February 28, 2015.

In Linux, if we tried to open the same `History` directory, we would see all the details using the `ls` command:

```
digforensics@forensics:~$ cd history/
digforensics@forensics:~/history$ ls
desktop.ini  History.IE5
digforensics@forensics:~/history$ cd History.IE5
digforensics@forensics:~/history/History.IE5$ ls
desktop.ini  $I30  index.dat  MSHist012015021620150223  MSHist012015022820150301
digforensics@forensics:~/history/History.IE5$ ls MSHist012015022820150301/
index.dat
digforensics@forensics:~/history/History.IE5$
```

Listing the History contents with the ls command in Linux

So, from this short listing, we can see that there are three different types of `index.dat` files, which can be summarized, as follows:

- Main `index.dat`, which is located directly under `History.IE5`
- Weekly `index.dat`, which is located under the `weekly` folder
- Daily `index.dat` file, which is located under the `daily` folder

Each index file contains entries about the visited websites. Each entry starts with a URL as a signature. Each entry contains the website title, URL, username, number of hits, and two timestamps—one at offset 8, and the second one at offset 16 from the start of each entry. Each timestamp is 32 bits or 8 bytes long:

```
digforensics@forensics:~/history/History.IE5$ hd MSHist012015021620150223/index.dat
00000000  43 6c 69 65 6e 74 20 55  72 6c 43 61 63 68 65 20  |Client UrlCache |
00000010  4d 4d 46 20 56 65 72 20  35 2e 32 00 00 80 00 00  |MMF Ver 5.2.....|
00000020  00 40 00 00 80 00 00 00  24 00 00 00 00 00 00 00  |.@......$.......|
00000030  00 00 80 00 00 00 00 00  00 00 00 00 00 00 00 00  |................|
00000040  00 00 00 00 00 00 00 00  00 00 00 00 00 00 00 00  |................|
*
00000250  ff ff ff ff 0f 00 00 00  00 00 00 00 00 00 00 00  |................|
00000260  00 00 00 00 00 00 00 00  00 00 00 00 00 00 00 00  |................|
*
00004000  48 41 53 48 20 00 00 00  00 00 00 00 00 00 00 00  |HASH ...........|
00004010  03 00 00 00 03 00 00 00  03 00 00 00 03 00 00 00  |................|
*
00004470  00 95 e7 16 00 50 00 00  03 00 00 00 03 00 00 00  |.....P..........|
00004480  03 00 00 00 03 00 00 00  03 00 00 00 03 00 00 00  |................|
*
00004c50  01 00 00 00 00 51 00 00  03 00 00 00 03 00 00 00  |.....Q..........|
00004c60  03 00 00 00 03 00 00 00  03 00 00 00 03 00 00 00  |................|
*
00004e10  00 00 00 00 00 00 00 00  00 00 00 00 00 00 00 00  |................|
*
00005000  55 52 4c 20 02 00 00 00  50 7c ab 59 5b 4c d0 01  |URL ....P|.Y[L..|
00005010  c0 b3 2c a3 96 53 d0 01  00 00 00 00 00 00 00 00  |..,..S..........|
00005020  00 00 00 00 00 00 00 00  00 00 00 00 80 51 01 00  |.............Q..|
00005030  60 00 00 00 68 00 00 00  fe 00 10 10 00 00 00 00  |`...h...........|
00005040  04 00 20 00 00 00 00 00  00 00 00 00 00 00 00 00  |................|
00005050  5c 46 ed a4 01 00 00 00  00 00 00 00 00 00 00 00  |\F..............|
```

Hex dump of the weekly index.dat file

Knowing the timezone of the machine is a very critical piece of information for the analysis process, but you must also know how each artifact in Windows is storing its timestamps—either in UTC or local time. In `History.IE5`, there are three different `index.dat` files, each file stores timestamps in a different way:

Type of index.dat file	First timestamp at offset 8	Second timestamp at offset 16
Main	Last access (UTC)	Last access (UTC)
Daily	Last access (local time)	Last access (UTC)
Weekly	Last access (local time)	Creation time of the `index.dat` file (UTC)

Different timestamps for different index.dat files

The timestamp can be converted to a human readable format using the `DCode.exe` tool (http://www.digital-detective.net/digital-forensic-software/free-tools/):

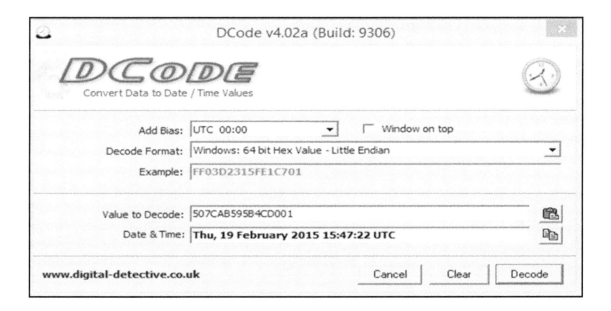

The first timestamp in weekly index.dat decoded using the DCode.exe tool

The first timestamp of the weekly `index.dat` entry shows the date on which it was last accessed in local time. So, this page was last accessed on **Thu, 19 February 2015 13:47:22 UTC**, considering that the machine's timezone was UTC+2.

In the same way, the second timestamp is **Sat, 28 February 2015 20:39:24**, which is the creation date of the weekly `index.dat` file itself in UTC.

In case we don't know the timezone of the machine, the difference in time between the first and the second timestamp in the same entry in the daily `index.dat` file is the difference between the UTC and the local time of the machine.

IEHistoryView

IEHistoryView (http://www.nirsoft.net/utils/iehv.html) can open the history file and parse it from live system or within the Wine environment in Linux with the History folder. It can parse history up to MSIE Version 9:

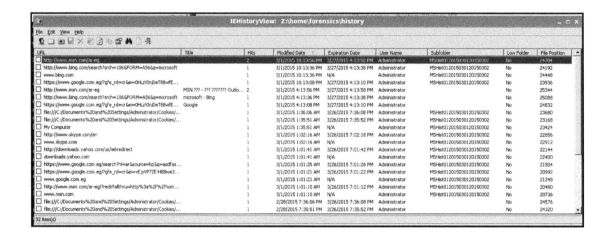

The IEHistoryView tool (index.dat parser)

BrowsingHistoryView

BrowsingHistoryView (http://nirsoft.net/utils/browsing_history_view.html) is another program that can parse all versions of the MSIE, and it has two versions for 32-bit and 64-bit systems. Also, it can work on a live system and in a postmortem analysis by providing the program with the webcache directory location. It also can parse the history of different other browsers:

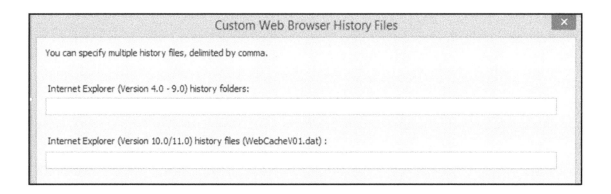

BrowsingHistoryView custom analysis

MiTeC Internet History browser

MiTeC InternetHistory browser is free software from MiTeC (`http://www.mitec.cz/ihb.html`). This works on all MSIE versions and on other browsers as well. It parses the machine and displays the results of different browsers in the same output:

MiTeC IHB output (three different browsers) on Windows 8.1

Cache

When the user visits Internet pages, these pages will be cached to the system in order to speed up browsing. For example, if the user pressed the back button in the browser, then the browser will fetch the page from the local system instead of requesting it again from the remote server. From the forensics perspective, this is useful to find a way to rebuild the contents of the pages that a user has been visiting. Cached data allow us to do this.

The cached data location differs from one version of Windows to another, as follows:

- Before Windows Vista, the cache file was called `Content.IE5` and was located at `<SystemPartition>\Documents and Settings\<Username>\Local Settings\Temporary Internet Files\Content.IE5`
- In Windows Vista, Windows 7, and Windows 8:
    - `<SystemPartition>\Users\<Username>\AppData\Local\Microsoft\Windows\Temporary Internet Files\Content.IE5`
    - `<SystemPartition>\Users\<Username>\AppData\Local\Microsoft\Windows\Temporary Internet Files\Low\Content.IE5`
- In Windows 8 or with the beginning of MSIE V10.0, the cache is combined with the `WebCacheV#.dat` file, but the old locations still exist with only a file with size of 0 bytes named `container.dat`:

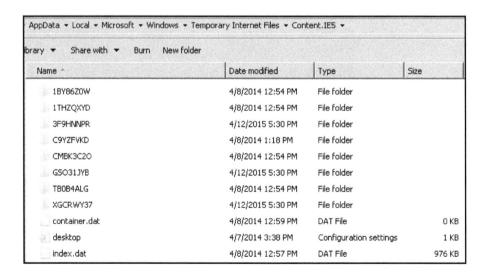

Content.IE5 for MSIE Version 11 running on Windows 7

- In Windows 8.1, the `WebCacheV#.dat` file is still also used by the operating system to save a cache, but the old location has been changed to the `INetCache` directory starting from MSIE V11.0:
    - `<SystemPartition>\Users\<Username>\AppData\Local\Microsoft\Windows\INetCache\IE`
    - `<SystemPartition>\Users\<Username>\AppData\Local\Microsoft\Windows\INetCache\Low\IE`

The following screenshot shows the new cache location in Windows 8.1:

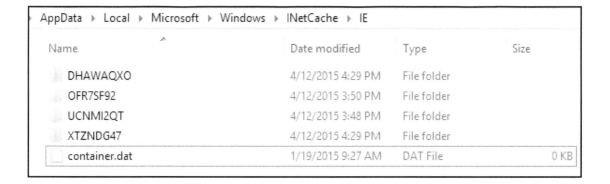

Windows 8.1 cache location

Content.IE5

The `Content.IE5` folder was used starting from MSIE5 and it contains randomly named folders that contain the actual data of the visited pages. The `index.dat` file, located in the Content.IE5 folder, contains the metadata of each cached file. This file tracks the cached contents and identifies which files are located under the sub-directories.

It contains the following:

- The original address with the HTTP header returned from the request
- The location of the file cached for this URL

- The type of cache record, that is, URL and LEAK for normal record, REDR for redirected pages, and HASH to index the contents of the file:

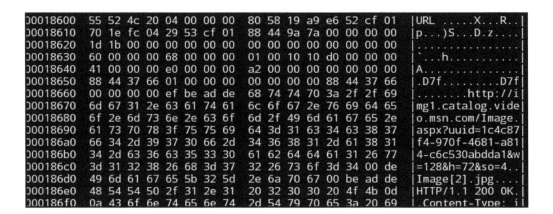

A sample URL entry in index.dat file

Along with this information, there are some timestamps stored in the `index.dat` file as well.

IECacheView

The IECacheView program from `http://www.nirsoft.com` can parse the cache information on a live Windows system. In case of live analysis, it will detect the right location of the cached information. However, in a postmortem analysis, it should be provided with the location of the cached data:

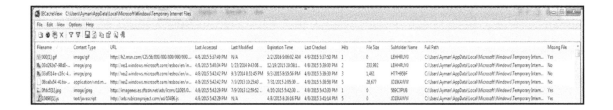

IECacheView parsing cached data of MSIE V8 on Windows 7

This program can do many things to each entry in the context menu, such as viewing the actual code of the page, which will be useful in identifying malicious redirection in the page with iframe.

Msiecf parser (Plaso framework)

We will highlight the Msiecf parser or the MSIE Cache File parser from Plaso framework, which we used in Chapter 5, *Timeline*, which parses the cache file from the system partition from the forensics image or backup and includes all the results in the storage file created by the log2timeline tool.

We can create the storage file for this parser, which will take little time as compared to the creation of a complete storage file by, for example, Win7 parser. In this case, we need to mount the image and point to the user profile location in the mounted image:

```
digforensics@forensics:~$ log2timeline.py --parsers MsiecfParser -z UTC history.plaso /mnt/mountpoint/users/forensics
[WARNING] (MainProcess) Appending to an already existing file.
[INFO] (MainProcess) Starting storage thread.
[INFO] (MainProcess) Starting to collect files for processing.
[INFO] (MainProcess) Starting to extract events.
[INFO] (Worker_0  ) Worker 0 (PID: 3673) started monitoring process queue.
[INFO] (MainProcess) Collection is hereby DONE
[INFO] (MainProcess) Waiting until all processing is done.
[INFO] (Worker_0  ) Worker 0 (PID: 3673) stopped monitoring process queue.
[INFO] (MainProcess) Processing done, waiting for storage.
[INFO] (StorageThread) [Storage] Closing the storage, nr. of events processed: 1612
[INFO] (MainProcess) Storage process is done.
[INFO] (MainProcess) Run completed.
```

Msiecf Parser from Plaso framework

Then, we can use the `psort.py` tool to filter the created storage file as before.

Cookies

Cookies are used by the remote site to track the user activities on the site. The remote site adds some information to a single file called a cookie. This information differs from one site to another.

For example, a user uses an online shopping site, starts adding items to their cart, and browses between different sections on the site without losing previously added items and without signing in to the site. One way to do this is by adding cookies to the user's machine.

There are two different types of cookies:

- **Session cookies**: These are stored only in the memory of the running machine. This type can be investigated during memory forensics.
- **Persistent cookies**: These will be stored to the local filesystem, and this type of cookie is what we are interested in this section.

Like history and cache, the location of the cookies in the machine differs between different versions, as follows:

- Before Windows Vista: `<SystemPartition>\Documents and Settings\<Username>\Cookies`
- In Windows Vista, Windows 7, and Windows 8:
    - `<SystemPartition>\Users\<Username>\AppData\Roaming\Microsoft\Windows\Cookies`
    - `<SystemPartition>\Users\<Username>\AppData\Roaming\Microsoft\Windows\Cookies\Low`

Starting with Windows Vista, Microsoft made some changes to the user profile folder structure and operations in the operating system to increase security. One improvement was to make more use of the roaming profile, which allows users to access machines in the same domain with their profile data. During this remote access some data, including the cookies of the user browsing, is stored locally in the roaming directory and not in the remote machine.

- In Windows 8.1:
    - `<SystemPartition>\Users\<Username>\AppData\Local\Microsoft\Windows\INetCookies`
    - `<SystemPartition>\Users\<Username>\AppData\Local\Microsoft\Windows\INetCookies\Low`

IECookiesView

IECookiesView is a program (http://www.nirsoft.net/utils/internet_explorer_cookies_view.html) that directly detects the location of the cookies in a live system, and it can be provided with the location of the cookies extracted from a forensic image in a postmortem analysis:

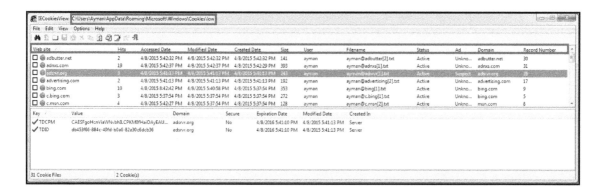

IECookiesView on live Windows 7 running MSIE V8

The output of the IECookiesView contains the following:

- The website this cookie was created for
- The number of visits to this website (number of hits)
- Timestamps for the cookies stored in UTC
- The user who accessed the URL, which can be seen mentioned as part of the filename in the following pattern: `<UserName>@<SiteURL>`

Favorites

Favorites are some websites that are stored by the user for future use. These favorites can help in identifying and profiling user activities. The location of the favorites changed after Windows Vista as follows:

- **Before Windows Vista:** `<SystemPartition>\Documents and Settings\<Username>\Favorites`
- **After Windows Vista:** `<SystemPartition>\Users\<Username>\Favorites`

FavoritesView

FavoritesView is another program from Nirsoft (`http://www.nirsoft.net/utils/faview.html`) that parses the bookmarks of Mozilla Firefox and Netscape in the same window. In some cases and if the program is running under live system, it won't open the correct location of the favorites or bookmarks, so the investigator needs to open the correct locations:

FavoritesView on Windows 8.1

Session restore

Starting from MSIE V8.0 Microsoft implemented a recovery mode to recover the opened tabs if MSIE crashed:

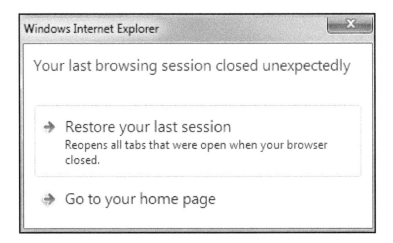

Crash recovery message of MSIE

Each opened tab has a file describing the pages opened with this tab. The location that contains data differs from one Windows version to another, as follows:

- Before Windows Vista and with MSIE V8: `<SystemPartition>\Documents and Settings\<Username>\ Local Settings\Internet Explorer\Recovery`
- Windows Vista, Windows 7, Windows 8, and Windows 8.1: `<SystemPartition>\Users\<Username>\AppData\Local\Microsoft\Internet Explorer\Recovery`

This will provide great help to the investigator, especially if the history was turned off. Each file is an OLE-structured storage file with the signature of `0xD0CF11E0A1B11AE1`. This type of file needs a special parser.

MiTeC SSV

MiTeC Structured Storage Viewer, from `http://www.mitec.cz/ssv.html`, can read the structured storage format and parse it.

By opening one of the last active files in the recovery directory by the SSV, we can find some timestamps of the file itself:

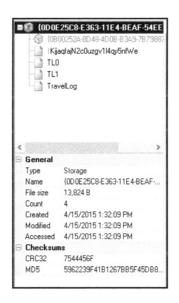

Timestamps in SSV

The creation time indicates the time when the session was ended as long as the file was found under the last active folder. If we investigate the active folder, the time will indicate when the tab was opened:

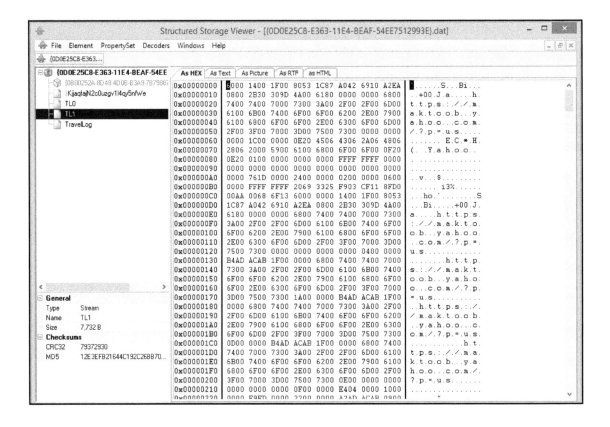

An example of the last active sessions of MSIE

In the previous figure, two pages were opened in this tab. We are now interested in two files:

- `|KjjaqfajN2c0uzgv1l4qy5nfWe`: This contains the last opened URL in the tab
- `TL#`: This is the page that opened in the tab. Instead of the # sign, there will be a number, which indicates the order of the tab in the session

Each TL# page has the page title, page URL, and the referring site if there is one.

Inprivate mode

Inprivate or **Incognito** modes are in almost all browsers nowadays. In the Inprivate mode, no artifacts are saved to the hard drive. All the artifacts are in memory, including the session cookies. Memory forensics can provide good results in such cases. This is another reason why we need to capture the memory of a running system and not shut it down.

The session recovery files during the Inprivate mode are created in the same location but deleted after closing the session. With MSIE Inprivate mode, recovering these files can provide some information about the visited sites during the Inprivate sessions. Carving the unallocated space for the OLE file header can be enough to recover these files.

WebCacheV#.dat

MSIE Version 10 was released with Windows 8. Starting from this version, a relatively new artifact was introduced, the `WebcacheV#.dat` file. `WebcacheV#.dat` is a single file that contains many browser data, that is, history, cache, and cookies together. Instead of the # in the file name, there is a two digit number, this number may differ from one system to another, but there will be only one file with this name at `<SystemPartition>\Users\<Username>\AppData\Local\Microsoft\Windows\WebCache\`:

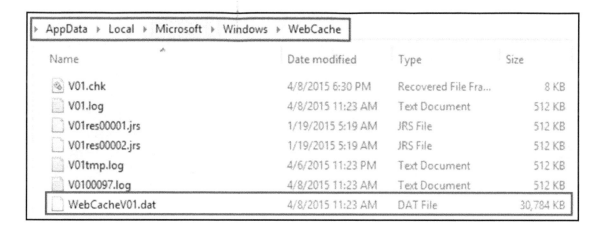

WebCacheV#.dat in Windows 8.1

Browser and E-mail Investigation

This file is an **Extensible Storage Engine** (**ESE**) database file or EDB. This type of database is used in many Microsoft applications, such as Windows search, Active directory, and Windows Mail.

Although this file contains many browser artifacts combined, the old locations of the browser artifacts still have the old files, but they are unused (we will explain this later).

Most of the artifacts won't be extracted from a live system because they are already in use by the operating system. They can be extracted from the forensic image. Otherwise, we can use programs, such as **FTK imager**, if we have the suitable privilege to dump these files from the live system as discussed earlier.

As it is an ESE database, the `WebcacheV#.dat` file can be tested to see whether it is corrupted with the Windows utility, `Esentutl`:

```
C:\Users\AymanT\Desktop>esentutl /m WebCacheV01.dat

Extensible Storage Engine Utilities for Microsoft(R) Windows(R)
Version 6.3
Copyright (C) Microsoft Corporation. All Rights Reserved.

Initiating FILE DUMP mode...
        Database: WebCacheV01.dat

DATABASE HEADER:
Checksum Information:
Expected Checksum: 0x0904c1e7
  Actual Checksum: 0x0904c1e7

Fields:
        File Type: Database
         Checksum: 0x904c1e7
   Format ulMagic: 0x89abcdef
   Engine ulMagic: 0x89abcdef
 Format ulVersion: 0x620,17
 Engine ulVersion: 0x620,20
Created ulVersion: 0x620,17
     DB Signature: Create time:04/08/2014 14:59:41.000 Rand:111234 Computer:
         cbDbPage: 32768
           dbtime: 2896 (0x1ed8)
            State: Clean Shutdown
     Log Required: 0-0 (0x0-0x0)
    Log Committed: 0-0 (0x0-0x0)
```

The Esentutl utility to test the WebCacheV01.dat file

ESEDatabaseView

ESEDatabaseView from Nirsoft can be used to open the .dat file. Once opened, we can find many containers (tables) in the database. We can list all the containers in the containers table:

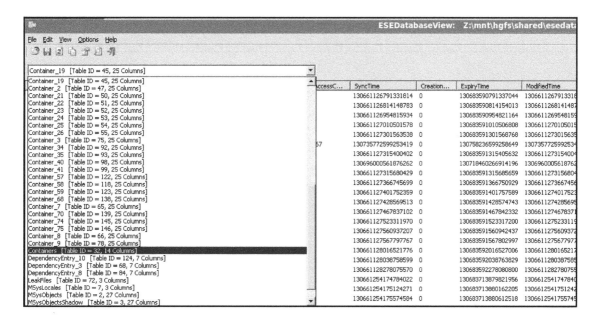

The list of containers in the WebCacheV01.dat file

Browser and E-mail Investigation

We can see all the artifacts that are located in the `WebCacheV#.dat` file, such as the highlighted history data in the following screenshot:

The history containers within the WebCacheV01.dat file (cropped image)

Then, using the container ID we can list the table or the container which contains the actual data. For example, container 1 contains the `History.IE5` data:

The History.IE5 container in the WebCacheV01.dat file (cropped image)

Firefox

Firefox is a widely-used browser that started in 2004 and has kept developing since. Starting from version 3, it started to use the SQLite format to store the usage artifacts except for the cache, and since this version the location of these artifacts is the same.

The location of the cache is at the following places:

- **Before Windows Vista:** `<SystemPartition>\Documents and Settings\<Username>\Local Settings\Application Data\Mozilla\Firefox\Profiles\<profile folder>`
- **Since Windows Vista:** `<SystemPartition>\Users\<Username>\AppData\Local\Mozilla\Firefox\Profiles\<profile folder>`

The rest of the artifacts are at the following locations:

- **Before Windows Vista:** `<SystemPartition>\Documents and Settings\<Username>\Application Data\Mozilla\Firefox\Profiles\<profile folder>`
- **Since Windows Vista:** `<SystemPartition>\Users\<Username>\AppData\Roaming\Mozilla\Firefox\Profiles\<profile folder>`

> The `<profile folder>` folder consists of `<RandomText>.default`, such as `918159wp.default`.

Places.sqlite

`Places.sqlite` contains the browsing history of the Firefox browser. It contains a lot of information including the following:

- URL
- First visit date/time
- Last visit date/time
- Visit count
- Referrer
- Title of the visited page
- Visit type, which includes the following:
    - Clicked link
    - Typed URL
    - Redirected
    - Opened from bookmarks

MozillaHistoryView

To parse Firefox history, we can use MozillaHistoryView (`http://www.nirsoft.net/utils/mozilla_history_view.html`). This usually runs on a live system and automatically detects the location of the profiles in the running system, or it provides the SQLite database location:

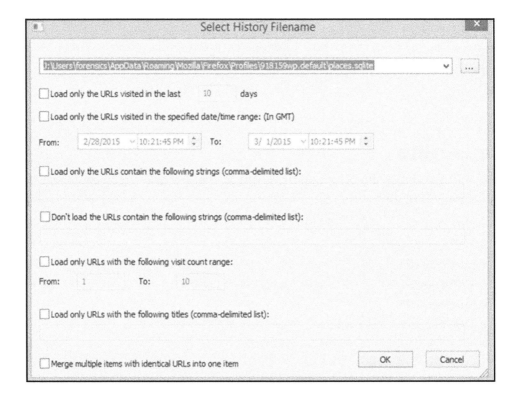

The MozillaHistoryView options

Cookies.sqlite

`Cookies.sqlite` contains the browsing cookies of Firefox. It stores the following information:

- Remote website
- Cookie name
- Creation time

- Last accessed time
- Connection type—either secure or not secure
- Stored data from the website

MozillaCookiesView

To parse the Firefox Cookies, we can use MozillaCookiesView from `http://www.nirsoft.net/utils/mzcv.html`. It parses and lists the cookies in the running system or in the profile directories that are pointed to:

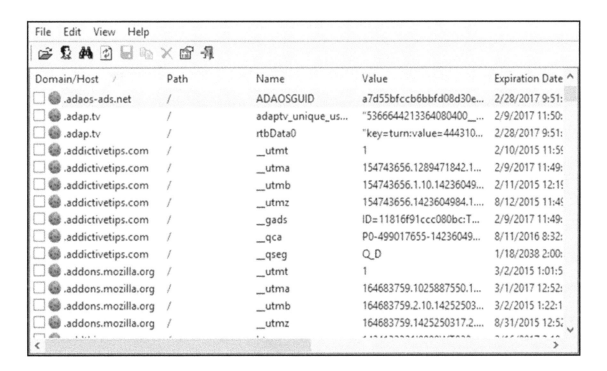

MozillaCookiesView

Cache

The Firefox cache format is the same for all versions. Its location hasn't changed from one version to another. It contains the following information about the cached files in the system:

- Name
- Type
- Source URL of the download
- Size
- Timestamps (last modification, last request, and expiration time)
- Count (how many times this file was used from the cached data)

MozillaCacheView

MozillaCacheView (`http://www.nirsoft.net/utils/mozilla_cache_viewer.html`) can parse and view the cached data of Firefox. It can also export any file from the cached data for examination:

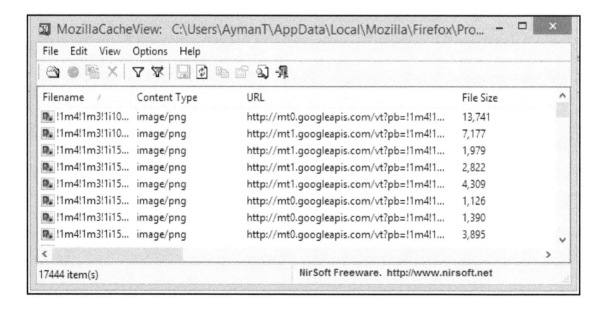

MozillaCacheView

Other browsers

From the previous analysis of MSIE and Firefox, we can understand how it is a challenge for digital forensics investigators to conduct browser forensics because of the huge number of browsers on the market and the difference in storing their browsing artifacts in the system. Nirsoft.net contains many other tools to parse different browsers at http://www.nirsoft.net/web_browser_tools.html for Google Chrome, Opera, and Safari.

E-mail investigation

E-mail is one of the most-used methods of communication nowadays, especially in corporate environments. Sending, receiving, or reading e-mails leaves traces in the electronic devices. These traces could help in analyzing cases of targeted attacks, blackmail, espionage, information leakage, and harassment. Traces of e-mail differ according to the way of using the e-mail account, either by webmail or an installed e-mail client.

In webmail, browser investigation and memory forensics could help in retrieving some e-mail data and even in some cases recover access credentials for the e-mail account. In this section, we will discuss the Outlook e-mail client artifacts on the machine.

Outlook PST file

There are many e-mail clients on the market. Outlook from Microsoft is one of the most-used clients. Outlook stores all the messages, contacts, and calendar in a **Personal File Folder** (**PFF**) file. One of the PFFs is the **Personal Storage Table** (**PST**) file and is saved by default in the following location:

- My Documents\Outlook Files in Windows XP
- Documents\Outlook Files starting from Windows Vista

Users can archive e-mails to their machine and free their space on the mail server. The archived e-mails will be stored in the PST file as well. The archived PST file won't be connected to the server and won't be associated to the user account. It will only be available on the user's local computer and won't be available on any other devices associated with the user and synced with their account, unless the user copies the archived PST file to another device.

The archived file locations are, as follows:

- `<SystemPartition>\Documents and Settings\<username>\Local Settings\Application Data\Microsoft\Outlook` in Windows XP
- `<SystemPartition>\Users\<username>\AppData\Local\Microsoft\Outlook` starting from Windows Vista

A PST file can be imported to Outlook, but it won't be uploaded to the server. It will be only available on the local running client.

Outlook OST files

Another PFF file is the **Offline Storage Table** (**OST**) file. It is mostly used with the Microsoft exchange server account. It allows the user to create, edit, or delete messages on the local computer without connecting to the server; and once the connection is established, the client syncs with the server and updates all the new changes made by the user to make both copies on the server and the client the same.

The OST file can be located at the following locations:

- `<SystemPartition>\Documents and Settings\<username>\Local Settings\Application Data\Microsoft\Outlook` in Windows XP
- `<SystemPartition>\Users\<username>\AppData\Local\Microsoft\Outlook` starting from Windows Vista.

Unlike the PST files, OST can't be imported to Outlook; it needs to be converted to the PST file format first. Different commercial tools can make this conversion.

EML and MSG files

An EML file contains single messages saved by the user. The EML file is a plain text file that contains the message details, including the header, body, and attachments. An EML file can be opened with Outlook or any compatible e-mail clients. Also, there are some EML viewers.

Another format for saved e-mails is the MSG format. MSG is a binary format and can be treated as a compound file for analysis with a compound file parser, such as the **Libolecf** by Joachim Metz:

```
digforensics@forensics:~$ olecfinfo test.msg
olecfinfo 20131108

OLE Compound File information:
        Version              : 3.62
        Sector size          : 512
        Short sector size    : 64

Storage and stream items:
Root Entry (6592 bytes)
  __properties_version1.0 (1072 bytes)
  __nameid_version1.0 (0 bytes)
    __substg1.0_00020102 (32 bytes)
    __substg1.0_00030102 (32 bytes)
    __substg1.0_00040102 (28 bytes)
    __substg1.0_10140102 (8 bytes)
    __substg1.0_10150102 (8 bytes)
    __substg1.0_10020102 (8 bytes)
    __substg1.0_10090102 (8 bytes)
  __substg1.0_0E04001F (26 bytes)
  __substg1.0_0E03001F (0 bytes)
  __substg1.0_0E02001F (0 bytes)
  __recip_version1.0_#00000000 (0 bytes)
    __properties_version1.0 (136 bytes)
    __substg1.0_0FFF0102 (120 bytes)
    __substg1.0_3001001F (24 bytes)
    __substg1.0_3002001F (8 bytes)
    __substg1.0_3003001F (58 bytes)
    __substg1.0_300B0102 (35 bytes)
    __substg1.0_0FF60102 (4 bytes)
  __attach_version1.0_#00000000 (0 bytes)
    __properties_version1.0 (232 bytes)
    __substg1.0_0FF90102 (4 bytes)
    __substg1.0_37010102 (10 bytes)
    __substg1.0_3704001F (24 bytes)
    __substg1.0_3707001F (58 bytes)
    __substg1.0_370A0102 (9 bytes)
    __substg1.0_370E001F (20 bytes)
  __substg1.0_001A001F (16 bytes)
  __substg1.0_0037001F (8 bytes)
  __substg1.0_003B0102 (36 bytes)
  __substg1.0_003F0102 (124 bytes)
  __substg1.0_0040001F (26 bytes)
  __substg1.0_00410102 (124 bytes)
  __substg1.0_0042001F (26 bytes)
  __substg1.0_00430102 (124 bytes)
  __substg1.0_0044001F (26 bytes)
  __substg1.0_00510102 (36 bytes)
  __substg1.0_00520102 (36 bytes)
  __substg1.0_0064001F (8 bytes)
  __substg1.0_0065001F (60 bytes)
  __substg1.0_0070001F (8 bytes)
  __substg1.0_00710102 (22 bytes)
```

Libolecf against an MSG file

DBX (Outlook Express)

Outlook Express was used before Windows Vista, and then was replaced with Microsoft Outlook. Outlook Express uses DBX files as the message storage. A DBX file is stored at `<SystemPartition>\Documents and Settings\<username>\Local Settings\Application Data\Identities\<Identity number>\Microsoft\Outlook Express`. The Outlook Express folder has the following files:

- `Folder.DBX`: This is the master file in Outlook Express. It contains the tree structure of the folders in the mail. There is a different DBX file for each folder in the mail structure, including `Inbox.DBX`, `SentItems.DBX`, and `Drafts.DBX`.
- `Cleanup.log`: This is used to log the cleanup operations in the deleted files. Outlook Express creates a log for the last archive. During archiving, Outlook Express actually cleans up deleted items. In normal behavior, it just marks an item as deleted and keeps it in the DBX file.

PFF Analysis (libpff)

Library libpff (`https://github.com/libyal/libpff/`) is a cross-platform library to open and parse the PFF files. This library has two tools: `pffinfo` and `pffexport`.

Let's try to investigate an OST file retrieved from the forensic image of Windows 7. First, let's find information about the OST file using `pffinfo`:

```
digforensics@forensics:~$ pffinfo test.ost
pffinfo 20120802

Personal Folder File information:
        File size:              1541120 bytes
        File content type:      Offline Storage Tables (OST)
        File type:              64-bit
        Encryption type:        compressible

Message store:
        Password checksum:      0xffffffff
```

Getting information from the OST file

Chapter 10

Now, we know that there is no encryption on the OST file, so let's export the data from the file:

```
digforensics@forensics:~$ pffexport -f html -l log.txt test.ost
pffexport 20120802

Opening file.
Exporting items.
Exporting folder item 1 out of 2.
Exporting folder item 2 out of 2.
Exporting email item 1 out of 1.
Exporting recipient.
Exporting email item 1 out of 2.
Exporting recipient.
Exporting email item 2 out of 2.
Exporting recipient.
Exporting email item 1 out of 1.
Exporting recipient.
Exporting appointment item 1 out of 324.
Exporting appointment item 2 out of 324.
Exporting appointment item 3 out of 324.
Exporting appointment item 4 out of 324.
Exporting appointment item 5 out of 324.
Exporting appointment item 6 out of 324.
Exporting appointment item 7 out of 324.
Exporting appointment item 8 out of 324.
Exporting appointment item 9 out of 324.
Exporting appointment item 10 out of 324.
Exporting appointment item 11 out of 324.
Exporting appointment item 12 out of 324.
```

Exporting the data from the OST file

A new folder, `<OSTfilename>.export`, will be created under the working directory. In our case, it will be `test.ost.export`. As there are many items in the OST file, we created the `log.txt` file to log all these exported items, and then we can filter the log file and locate the items of interest. In our case, if we are interested in e-mails only, we can `grep` the `log.txt` file for e-mail:

```
digforensics@forensics:~$ grep email log.txt
Processing email: 00000 in path: test.ost.export/Root - Mailbox/IPM_SUBTREE/Deleted Items/
Processing email: 00000 in path: test.ost.export/Root - Mailbox/IPM_SUBTREE/Inbox/
Processing email: 00001 in path: test.ost.export/Root - Mailbox/IPM_SUBTREE/Inbox/
Processing email: 00000 in path: test.ost.export/Root - Mailbox/IPM_SUBTREE/Sync Issues/
Processing email: 00000 in path: test.ost.export/Root - Mailbox/MSNConStream/
Processing email: 00001 in path: test.ost.export/Root - Mailbox/MSNConStream/
Processing email: 00000 in path: test.ost.export/Root - Mailbox/MSNConCategoriesStream/
```

E-mails in the OST file

[229]

Browser and E-mail Investigation

So, there are some e-mails in different folders, such as Deleted Items and Inbox. In case we are interested in the received e-mails, which could contain malicious links or attachments that deceived the user to infect the machine, we can check the e-mails in the Inbox folder.

In the created export folder, we will find the same folder structure in the OST. We can navigate to one message location and view the contents of this message's folder, as shown in the following screenshot:

```
digforensics@forensics:~$ cd test.ost.export/Root\ -\ Mailbox/IPM_SUBTREE/Inbox/Message00002/
digforensics@forensics:~/test.ost.export/Root - Mailbox/IPM_SUBTREE/Inbox/Message00002$ ls
ConversationIndex.txt  InternetHeaders.txt  Message.html  OutlookHeaders.txt  Recipients.txt
digforensics@forensics:~/test.ost.export/Root - Mailbox/IPM_SUBTREE/Inbox/Message00002$
```

The contents of each message

We will find different files for each message, including the message header and the message body itself. Using the header, we can track the sender. The message body will help us check for malicious or phishing links. If the message has an attachment, another directory with the attached files will be found under the message directory. The attachment could be malicious.

Other tools

There are many tools used to read and parse different e-mail files. Some of these of tools can run on a live system for live analysis.

Some of these tools are, as follows:

- MiTeC mail viewer for Microsoft Outlook Express 4, 5, and 6 message database [`*.idx`/`*.mbx`/`*.dbx`], Windows Vista Mail/Windows Live Mail, and Mozilla Thunderbird message databases as well as standalone EML files. You can download this from `http://www.mitec.cz/mailview.html`.
- Different tools from `http://www.freeviewer.org` to view PST, OST, EML, and DBX files:
    - PST File Viewer
    - OST File Viewer
    - EML File Viewer
    - Outlook DBX Viewer

- Different tools from `http://www.nucleustechnologies.com` to view PST, OST, and EML files:
    - Kernel PST viewer
    - Kernel OST viewer
    - Kernel EML Viewer

Summary

In this chapter, we discussed the importance of browser analysis, browser artifacts, and how to find and parse these artifacts in different browsers. Then, we learned about parsing PFF files for Microsoft Outlook and different e-mail files, such as MSG and EML.

In the next chapter, we will go through Windows memory analysis and show you how it is not optional anymore to perform memory forensics.

11
Memory Forensics

System memory is the working space of the operating system. The operating system uses memory to place the data that is needed to execute programs and the programs themselves. This is why acquiring the system memory is one of the steps that must be performed when applicable in digital forensics. Analyzing the memory may reveal the existence of a malicious process or program that has no traces in the machine hard disk. Memory also contains the opened network connections, which could include the connection of an attacker controlling the machine or stealing user data and information.

In this chapter, we will briefly discuss the Windows memory structure, some techniques that are used by attackers to hide their malicious activities and existence, and the tools that are used to investigate memory dump.

Memory structure

Each process that runs in memory allocates space in memory to store its code and data. This space consists of memory pages. Each memory page is 4 KB in size in x86 systems. All the processes address their memory spaces with virtual addresses, which are translated into physical addresses by the system itself with no interaction by any process.

In modern operating systems, there are two categories of the running processes: processes run in user mode and others run in kernel mode. The difference between both modes is the level of access that is granted to the operating system. In the user mode, the processes can't modify paging or access other processes' memory locations except some inter-process communications using Windows APIs. All the processes start in user mode, except the SYSTEM process.

Kernel mode is used by the Windows kernel at system booting to set up memory space and paging. In some situations, such as executing the Windows API, the processor receives interrupt, which requires it to switch to kernel mode to execute the interrupt and then return back to the user mode.

Memory acquisition

We discussed memory acquisition previously in volatile evidence acquisition in *Chapter 3, Volatile Data Collection*. However, we now need to highlight this in a modern Windows operating system, the different security controls which forbid processes to access the whole memory, and the step which is required by any acquisition tool to acquire the system memory. This may cause a system crash and the loss of system memory, or the whole hard disk in the case of active hard disk encryption.

So, modern digital forensics acquisition tools tend to install a driver first to the operating system and then use this driver to access the system memory, which will need higher privileges on the system.

The sources of memory dump

We can consider a memory dump during the incident response process as the main source for memory forensics. However, what if we have a powered off machine or, for any reason, we couldn't acquire the memory of the machine? The question here is do we have any other way to conduct memory forensics? Fortunately, we have a positive answer for this question in many situations. Let's see what they are.

Hibernation file

Hibernation is a power option in most operating systems, including Windows OS. In this mode, the system copies the memory, which is volatile, to a single file named `hiberfil.sys`, which is located under the system root in the hard disk, which is non-volatile, and completely shuts down the machine. When the user turns the machine on again from hibernation, the system copies the contents of this file again to memory and resumes the execution of the previous processes.

If the investigator has a forensic image of the victim's or suspect's hard disk, they can extract the hibernation file and conduct memory forensics on this file using the memory analysis tools that we will be discussing later in this chapter. The hibernation file will provide the investigator or the analyst with a memory image from specific time in the past that may contain traces to the malicious activities or important evidence related to the case under investigation.

The filesystem's last modification time of the hibernation file will indicate the time when the hibernation was used in the system. Fortunately, the structure of the hibernation file is different but known, which makes it possible to convert it to a raw memory image in order to conduct analysis on it using the memory forensics tools. Although it contains most of the memory data, the hibernation file won't contain some data, such as the dynamically obtained network information using DHCP. We need to consider this during analysis.

Crash dump

If the Windows system crashed, it is designed to store information about the system state at the time of the crash for future troubleshooting of the crash after recovering the system. Crashing the system was an old way to dump the memory to the crash dump file, which can be done using the NotMyFault tool from Sysinternals (http://download.sysintern als.com/files/NotMyFault.zip). However, better methods and tools are available nowadays. The crash dump file is named MEMPRY.DMP by default and is located under system root directly. The crash dump file can hold different data depending on the settings of the crash dumps, as follows:

- **Complete memory dump**: This contains the physical memory at the time of the crash with a 1 MB header. This type is not common because it has a large size especially for systems with a large memory.
- **Kernel memory dump**: This is when the system dumps the memory pages in the kernel mode only and ignores the pages in the user mode.
- **Small dump files**: These are small files that have a size of 64 KB in 32bit systems and 128 KB in 64bit systems. This contains information about running processes and loaded drivers in the system.

For the investigator to know which type of dump file is present in the case, they can determine this from the size of the file. They can also open the registry location of `HKEY_LOCAL_MACHINE\SYSTEM\CurrentControlSet\Control\CrashControl`, under a value called **CrashDumpEnable**, which will be one of the following four values:

- 0: This is when debugging information is not written to a file
- 1: This is when the complete crash dump is written to a file
- 2: This is when the kernel memory dump is written to a file
- 3: This is when a small memory dump is written to a file

After extracting the crash dump file, the investigator can use the `dmp2bin.exe` tool from Moonsols to convert the dump.

Page files

Paging is a memory management technique that works as a secondary storage for Windows memory. It speeds up the system by moving the least-used pages in memory to the hard drive in a file named `pagefile`. By applying such techniques, the user will have more memory space to use. When the user starts using the saved pages again, the system restores these pages to memory again. This can be noticed in small lagging while accessing some opened applications that haven't been used for some time.

The page files on the hard drive can be up to 16 files, and not only under the root directory. To find out the locations of the page files from the registry, check `HKEY_LOCAL_MACHINE\SYSTEM\CurrentControlSet\Control\Memory Management\ExistingPageFiles` and `PagingFiles`. Some memory acquisition tools, such as FTK imager can add the page file to memory image during live acquisition:

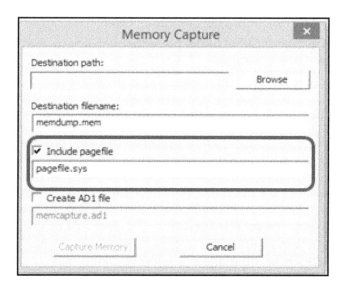

Figure 1: FTK imager; adding page files during memory acquisition

Page files store unordered data, which make it more difficult for in-depth analysis. This means that string search in the page files may give some clues about the contents of the page files and the case under investigation, such as the IP, path, or the registry key. File carving also can be conducted in the page files in order to recover some related files. Scanning the page files for a malware signature may uncover malware running in memory.

Processes in memory

A process is an instance of a program that has been executed in the system. Each process in memory has a private isolated memory space. A process contains the execution code and the data that is required to complete the execution of the code, such as files, DLLs, and user input. All this data and code are located in a memory space allocated for this process.

Many processes can be in the memory at the same time. All the processes are listed in one structure called _EPROCESS in the memory of the running Windows operating system.

Each entry of the _PROCESS structure holds one process with its metadata; the process name, its executable path, parent process, start time, and in some cases, the exit time. The metadata can be used as an indication of the presence of malicious activity if the parent process of a well-known process is different. For example, the `lsass.exe` process has parent process of `Explorer.exe`, while its parent process should be `Wininit.exe`. We can assume here that this `lsass.exe` process is not the genuine `lsass.exe` process and it is trying to deceive the user by taking the name of a legitimate process.

The _EPROCESS structure is similar to a double-linked list, each process points to the previous and the next process in a chain-like structure. This is used to circulate the processing time between different processes. The normal Windows command that is used to list the system processes uses the EPROCESS structure to read all the processes in a sequential way. So, if a malicious process was able to change the addresses in two processes before and after its location to point to each other, it won't be shown in the processes list. This is one way used by some malware samples to hide their existence. This technique is called **Direct Kernel Object Manipulation** or **DKOM**.

To overcome this technique and because the _EPROCESS entry has a specific structure, instead of depending on the manipulated EPROCESS structure, we can carve the memory file for all the _EPROCESS entries by their signature. In this case, the carving tool won't go through EPROCESS sequentially and won't miss any hidden processes. This can also display some closed processes which were removed from _EPROCESS but their entries still exist in memory.

Network connections in memory

Usually, networks are used by attackers to control the machine remotely, to send captured user information, or to receive new commands. Checking the network connections, which were opened in the system at the time of acquisition, would provide clues about the attack.

Network activities in general leave traces in memory. Investigating network connections could lead to discovery of a hidden connection created by rootkits. These connections can be hidden from normal listing tools in the same way that can be done with the processes. Carving for the network connection structure in memory can reveal such connections.

Another technique to hide a connection is to inject code into a legitimate process to open a malicious connection, so we need to check all the connections in the memory file.

The DLL injection

DLL or **Dynamic Link Libraries** are resources and functions that are shared among different processes running within the system. Some processes and programs require special external DLLs, which can be included with the program to run properly. As DLLs usually run within the processes in memory, they are usually targeted by the malware as a way to access and control other processes in memory. DLLs are loaded into the process with different ways:

- **Dynamic linking**: This is when an executable has an **Import Address Table** (**IAT**), which describes the resources needed for this executable to load along with their addresses, which are loaded in the process memory space.
- **Runtime Dynamic Linking**: Some DLLs may not be mentioned in the IAT, but are called out by the program itself during execution, by calling out one of the Windows functions such as `LoadLibrary`.
- **Injection**: DLLs can be injected into a process by different techniques. Let's see what they are.

Remote DLL injection

A malicious process allocates memory space in a legitimate process with read/write protection and writes the path to the malicious DLL in the legitimate process memory space. Then, the malicious process opens a remote thread to force open the DLL in the legitimate process and then removes the DLL path. In this way, the malicious process controls the legitimate one by the code in the DLL.

It won't be easy to detect this type of injection. We need to list all the DLLs loaded by the legitimate process and check the names, paths, and time of loading of all the DLLs.

Remote code injection

We follow the same steps of the Remote DLL injections, but instead of writing the path to the DLL in the hard drive, the malicious process injects the code directly to the allocated memory space. Here, the protection of the allocated memory space will be read/write and execute. This protection scheme, which isn't popular, is found a lot in memory that is used to detect this kind of injection.

Reflective DLL injection

The hybrid technique combines the previous two methods. The malicious process loads the DLL directly into the legitimate process's allocated memory space. In this way, DLL won't ever be written to the hard drive and won't go through the normal loading process, so it won't be found while listing the process's loaded DLLs.

API hooking

Hooking is usually used by rootkits, forcing the kernel to hide all activities that are related to the malware and to intercept the user input in order to steal sensitive information from the user. This used to be achieved by manipulating the output of the API calls by the system kernel. This can be deceptive in live analysis during the incident-handling process. In depth analysis of the memory image acquired during the evidence acquisition of the infected system would making it much easier to detect such behavior. Hooking is done simply by redirecting the normal flow of one process execution to execute malicious code in another location in the memory, and then return back to complete the normal process code.

Memory analysis

After a successful memory acquisition process, the investigator will have a single dump file that contains the full memory. Fortunately, the structure of the memory can be parsed by many analysis programs, including volatility, which is the most famous memory analysis framework nowadays.

The volatility framework

A free memory forensics framework can be downloaded from `http://www.volatilityfoundation.org`. This framework supports many versions of Windows, Mac, and Linux operating systems. An independent book called *Art of Memory Forensics* was released with volatility 2.4. It explains in detail different operating systems' artifacts in memory and how to extract and analyze them using the volatility framework. In this section, we will discuss the usage of volatility framework and how it detects the malicious activities in memory dump.

Each operating system has a different memory structure. Volatility has the ability to understand different structures. Using this profile, volatility can understand the correct data structures of the image under investigation and apply the right analysis and parsing tools.

Volatility works with plugins, each plugin performs specific tasks with the memory dump file. You can add or write your own plugin and add it to your version. In the following sections, we will discuss some volatility plugins.

Volatility plugins

A complete list of volatility plugins can be found in the tool's documentation. Here, we will discuss some plugins which are usually used to discover the discussed malware techniques.

imagecopy

In case the available memory file is a hibernation file or a crash dump file, volatility can convert this file to the raw format using the imagecopy plugin.

Usage: `vol.py -f <Hiber|DumpFile> --profile=<ImageProfile> imagecopy -O <OutputFile>`

raw2dmp

In some situations, you need to convert the dumped raw memory file to the crash dump format in order to use it with other tools, such as WinDBG, the Windows debugger. In such cases, the raw2dmp plugin can do this job.

Usage: `vol.py -f <ImageFile> --profile=<ImageProfile> raw2dmp -O <OutputFile>`

imageprofile

Before starting the analysis and in case you don't know the right image profile or don't know how to write it in a volatility command, you can run the imageinfo plugin against the image file and volatility will suggest the right profile to you. Imageinfo actually uses another plugin called **kdbgscan**, which scans a part of the NT kernel module for specific unique strings which identifies the image profile. The profile provided by one string, such as Win7SP0X86, and the profile which Volatility uses by default is WinXPSP2x86.

Usage: `vol.py -f <ImageFile> imageinfo`

pslist

This plugin lists the processes from the memory image file. It walks through the double-linked list in the _EPROCESS structure and prints all the processes in the list. It displays the process name, ID, offset, parent process ID, number of threads and handles, and timestamp of the start and end of the process. This plugin's output has the logical offset of each process in the _EPROCESS structure. If we need to view the physical offset, we can use the -P option. If there are hidden processes that were unlinked from the list, this plugin won't detect them.

Usage: `vol.py -f <ImageFile> --profile=<ImageProfile> pslist -P <OptionalPhysicalOffset>`

The following is the output of the preceding command:

```
Volatility Foundation Volatility Framework 2.3.1
Offset(P)   Name            PID   PPID   Thds   Hnds   Sess   Wow64 Start                         Exit
---------- --------------- ----- ------ ------ ------ ------ ----- ----------------------------- -----
0x3ff6a020 System             4      0     85    498   ------    0 2014-04-09 07:04:40 UTC+0000
0x3ed30b98 smss.exe         260      4      2     29   ------    0 2014-04-09 07:04:40 UTC+0000
0x3e491728 csrss.exe        352    344      9    487        0    0 2014-04-09 07:04:43 UTC+0000
0x3eca40c8 wininit.exe      392    344      7     96        0    0 2014-04-09 07:04:44 UTC+0000
0x3e490030 csrss.exe        404    384      9    235        1    0 2014-04-09 07:04:44 UTC+0000
0x3e363d40 winlogon.exe     452    384      6    131        1    0 2014-04-09 07:04:44 UTC+0000
0x3e38c030 services.exe     496    392      8    190        0    0 2014-04-09 07:04:44 UTC+0000
0x3e3a06c0 lsass.exe        512    392     10    481        0    0 2014-04-09 07:04:44 UTC+0000
0x3e3a5030 lsm.exe          520    392     14    214        0    0 2014-04-09 07:04:44 UTC+0000
0x3e3eca30 svchost.exe      624    496     15    367        0    0 2014-04-09 07:04:45 UTC+0000
```

Figure 2: An example of running the pslist plugin

psscan

This plugin lists the processes in the memory dump file by carving the dump for any process structure, and it doesn't consider the EPROCESS structure. It can get all the processes in the memory, including active, terminated, and hidden processes.

Usage: `vol.py -f <ImageFile> --profile=<ImageProfile> psscan`

pstree

The pstree plugin lists the processes in a tree view, identifying the parent and child processes. It lists the process using the same method that is used by the pslist plugin, so it won't detect hidden or unlinked processes. The output is structured in levels to show the different levels of parenthood between processes.

Usage: `vol.py -f <ImageFile> --profile=<ImageProfile> pstree`

psxview

The plugin psxview compares the results of different process-viewing techniques, for example, using pslist and psscan. This helps in detecting hidden and unlinked processes from one output window.

Usage: `vol.py -f <ImageFile> --profile=<ImageProfile> psxview`

The following is the output of the preceding command:

```
Volatility Foundation Volatility Framework 2.3.1
Offset(P)  Name                    PID  pslist psscan thrdproc pspcid csrss session deskthrd
---------- ---------------------- ----- ------ ------ -------- ------ ----- ------- --------
0x3de63340 SearchIndexer.         2940  True   True   True     True   True  True    True
0x3df72a40 taskhost.exe           1184  True   True   True     True   True  True    True
0x3df12a08 VSSVC.exe              516   True   True   True     True   True  True    True
0x3dcd28e0 SearchProtocol         3088  True   True   True     True   True  True    True
```

Figure 3: An example of running psscan

getsids

Each process has the privilege of the user who started it. The security identifier of the user, the SID, describes the user's privilege in the system. The process has a copy of the access token that is created for the user when they logged on to the system.

Use the getsids plugin and the process ID to provide the SID of the user who started the process.

The SID can be mapped easily from the system registry along the following path: `HKEY_LOCAL_MACHINE\SOFTWARE\Microsoft\Windows NT\CurrentVersion\ProfileList`.

It can also be extracted from the opened registry in memory, which will be discussed later.

Usage: `vol.py -f <ImageFile> --profile=<ImageProfile> getsids -p <optionalPID>`

dlllist

This plugin lists all the DLLs that are called and added to the process using the normal way in the operating system. It shows all the DLLs for all the processes in memory. If the investigator used the -p option with specific PID, then in this case, this will list only the DLLs of that specific process.

While addressing hidden of unlinked processes, we need to use the physical address of its structure in memory. So, if we need to list the DLLs of an unlinked or hidden process, we need to provide the plugin with the physical offset of the process in the psscan plugin output, with the `--offset= option`.

Usage: `vol.py -f <ImageFile> --profile=<ImageProfile> dlllist -p <OptionalPID> --offset= <PhysicalOffsetOfTheProcessFromPsscan>`

handles

A process can have many handles to many objects in the operating system. Analysis of these handles can be difficult because of the huge number of handles for each process. However, this could play an important role in proving a theory about the incident. It could provide the investigator with proof that one process has requested a handle to access a specific file in the filesystem or to create a specific mutant used as a signature for specific malware.

Using the handles plugin in volatility, we can display all the plugins of one process by the process ID and choose which type of handles will be displayed in the results.

Usage: `vol.py -f <ImageFile> --profile=<ImageProfile> handles -p <optionalPID> -t <OptionalHandleType>`

filescan

For any process to create or read a file, it needs to open this file first in memory. The volatility plugin, filescan, parses for the file object tag in memory and lists all the opened files or the files hidden from ordinary file-scanning tools by the rootkit.

This plugin will display the physical offset of the detected file object and the filename with the permissions on the file. Like the handles plugin, filescan will be useful in confirming the existence of specific malware by scanning for its specific files that are opened in memory. We can pipeline the output of this plugin with the `grep` command in Linux to filter on a specific filename.

Usage: `vol.py -f <ImageFile> --profile=<ImageProfile> filescan | grep "<FileName>"`

procexedump

When an executable runs in system, a version of this executable is copied to memory. During analysis, we can dump the executable from memory in order to investigate the executable code, or fix the code and run it within a controlled environment, such as a sandbox. Volatility has the procexedump plugin to dump any process executable from memory. It must be provided with the process ID.

Another plugin that does the same thing, but dumps the slack space along with the executable, is procmemdump and this is used in the same way. This will be helpful if the malware is manipulating the PE header in order to deceive the dumping tools.

Usage: `vol.py -f <ImageFile> --profile=<ImageProfile> procexedump -p <PID> -D <OptionalOutputDir>`

memdump

When the process starts executing, it uses some space in memory to store its code and data that is required during execution. This area could contain important information about the malware, such as strings, code, file paths, contents of files, and so on.

Volatility can dump this whole area into a single file for further analysis. We can run this file against the Linux native command-Strings in order to extract all the strings in the file.

Usage: `vol.py -f <ImageFile> --profile=<ImageProfile> procexedump -p <PID> -D <OutputDir>`

The following is the output of the preceding command:

```
Volatility Foundation Volatility Framework 2.3.1
****************************************************************
Writing ZkPECED.exe [   2224] to 2224.dmp
```

Figure 4: Dumping malicious process for further analysis

Memory Forensics

svcscan

Windows services are usually run in the background with higher privileges than other programs, which are run by system users. Some malware samples run as services to work in the background and to ensure the malware's existence in the system after reboot. Rootkits can manipulate the Windows native service-monitoring tools in order to hide some services. Volatility has a plugin called **svcscan**, which, besides listing the services by normal means, also parses the memory space that is owned by the `services.exe` process, searching for unique tags for services. This method will reveal any hidden process in memory.

The output displays the process ID of each service, the service name, service display name, service type, and current status. It also shows the binary path for the registered service, which will be an `EXE` for user mode services and a driver name for services that run from kernel mode.

Usage: `vol.py -f <ImageFile> --profile=<ImageProfile> svcscan`

connections

As discussed earlier, network traces are very important while analyzing memory samples. Volatility has plugins to scan opened TCP connections in memory with different methods. The first plugin is connections, which displays the TCP connections as Windows tools would do. This lists the all the connections in a linked list structure.

This plugin only works with Windows XP and the Windows 2003 server, only x68 or x64.

Usage: `vol.py -f <ImageFile> --profile=<ImageProfile> connections -P <OptionalPhysicalOffset>`

connscan

Just like the psscan plugin, connscan searches for connection object structure instead of listing all the connections in the linked list only. It will also list the terminated connections.

Some connections may have been fully or partially overwritten. So, we need to pay attention during analysis and compare the results with the normal connections plugin.

Usage: `vol.py -f <ImageFile> --profile=<ImageProfile> connscan`

sockets

Another plugin from volatility to network is sockets, which lists all the opened sockets on the system with any protocol. This lists the connection in the way that any Windows API would use for this purpose by walking though the sockets-linked list. This won't be able to find closed sockets or residuals from old sockets.

This plugin only works with Windows XP and the Windows 2003 server, either x68 or x64.

Usage: `vol.py -f <ImageFile> --profile=<ImageProfile> sockets`

sockscan

Like the connscan plugin, sockscan searches for the socket structure in memory, which makes it possible to recover residual sockets that were previously opened.

Usage: `vol.py -f <ImageFile> --profile=<ImageProfile> sockscan`

Netscan

For memory dumped from Windows Vista and higher, both x68 and x64 systems, the netscan plugin checks network traces. This plugin finds TCP endpoints, TCP listeners, UDP endpoints, and UDP listeners. It distinguishes between IPv4 and IPv6, prints the local and remote IP, the local and remote port, and the time when the socket was bound or when the connection was established.

Some fields could be missed, as netscan parses through the memory for tags of network data structure and views all the results in the same output.

Usage: `vol.py -f <ImageFile> --profile=<ImageProfile> netscan`

hivelist and printkey

The registry hives are opened in memory. To locate the hive files in memory, we can use the hivelist volatility plugin, which will list the addresses of the hive files in memory with virtual and physical addresses with the full path of the hive files on the hard drive.

We can use the printkey plugin to display the subkeys, values, and data in one specific registry key. This will parse all the hives to locate the key that you want, and it may be located in more than one hive.

Memory Forensics

If you want to limit the search to one hive, you can provide the virtual address to the plugin with the -o option.

Usage: `vol.py -f <ImageFile> --profile=<ImageProfile> hivelist`

Usage: `vol.py -f <ImageFile> --profile=<ImageProfile> printkey -o <OptionalVirtualOffsetOfTheHiveFile> -K "PathWithinTheregisty"`

malfind

The malfind volatility plugin finds hidden injected code or DLLs that are based on the permissions granted for specific pages in memory. It detects DLLs or code injected in a suspicious way, for example, using the `CreateRemoteThread` or `LoadLibrary` functions.

The output of the malfind plugin disassembles the code in the detected area. This output could contain malicious code or an executable file that starts with an executable signature that starts with MZ.

A copy of the identified memory segments can be extracted for further analysis using -D or -dump-dir=<Dir> and the extracted segment will be located under <Dir>.

Usage: `vol.py -f <ImageFile> --profile=<ImageProfile> malfind -p <PID> -D <OptionalOutputDir>`

The following is the output of the preceding command:

```
Volatility Foundation Volatility Framework 2.3.1
Process: wininit.exe Pid: 392 Address: 0x210000
Vad Tag: VadS Protection: PAGE_EXECUTE_READWRITE
Flags: CommitCharge: 1, MemCommit: 1, PrivateMemory: 1, Protection: 6

0x00210000   64 a1 18 00 00 00 c3 55 8b ec 83 ec 54 83 65 fc   d......U....T.e.
0x00210010   00 64 a1 30 00 00 00 8b 40 0c 8b 40 1c 8b 40 08   .d.0....@..@..@.
0x00210020   68 34 05 74 78 50 e8 83 00 00 00 59 59 89 45 f0   h4.txP.....YY.E.
0x00210030   85 c0 74 75 8d 45 ac 89 45 f4 8b 55 f4 c7 02 6b   ..tu.E..E..U...k

0x210000 64a118000000          MOV EAX, [FS:0x18]
0x210006 c3                    RET
0x210007 55                    PUSH EBP
0x210008 8bec                  MOV EBP, ESP
0x21000a 83ec54                SUB ESP, 0x54
0x21000d 8365fc00              AND DWORD [EBP-0x4], 0x0
0x210011 64a130000000          MOV EAX, [FS:0x30]
0x210017 8b400c                MOV EAX, [EAX+0xc]
```

Figure 5: An example of malfind

In the preceding screenshot, an area of memory with the `0x00210000` base address and the `PAGE_EXECUTE_READWRITE` permissions in the `wininit.exe` process (ID `392`).

vaddump

The **VAD** (**Virtual Address Descriptor**) is used in Windows memory to describe memory locations that are allocated by a process running in memory. Every time the process allocates new memory, a new VAD entry is created in what is called a VAD tree. Each VAD entry has a start and end, and it covers a specific area in the process memory space.

The volatility framework has a plugin, vaddump, which can dump each VAD area separately if we are interested in only one VAD entry. This is usually helpful if code or DLL injection has occurred, where we can extract the VAD that contains the malicious code.

Each VAD has metadata, including a start and end. The vadinfo volatility plugin can provide more information about VADs in one process.

Usage: `vol.py -f <ImageFile> --profile=<ImageProfile> vaddump -p <PID> -b <VADStartAddressInHex> -D <OutputDir>`

apihooks

The apihooks volatility plugin detects hooks. It detects CALLs and JMPs to other locations in memory. The function being imported or exported begins with the following instructions:

- CALL addr
- JMP addr
- PUSH addr; RET
- MOV reg, addr; CALL reg
- MOV reg, addr; JMP reg,

If the plugin detects an addr outside of the process memory space, it reports a hook.

Usage: `vol.py -f <ImageFile> --profile=<ImageProfile> apihooks`

mftparser

The maftparser volatility plugin scans memory file for master file table MFT entries using the FILE or BAAD entry signature. This can list information from the `$FILE_NAME`, `$STANDARD_INFORMATION`, and `$DATA NTFS` attributes.

The output of this plugin can be in text format by the `--output=text` option. It can also format the body, which is compatible with The Sleuth Kit 3 using the `--output=body` option.

In the case of a body file we can use the mactime tool to create one timeline of all the MFT activities in memory which will be useful in tracking activities by time.

Usage: `vol.py -f <ImageFile> --profile=<ImageProfile> mftparser --output=<body|text> --output-file=<OutputFile>`

Summary

In this chapter, we discussed the importance of memory forensics in discovering malicious activities, briefly explained the memory structure, and went through volatility as one of the most-famous and effective memory forensics tools.

In the next chapter, we will be discussing the network forensics tools and techniques in order to extract evidential data from any network dump.

12
Network Forensics

Network forensics is a separate large area of Computer Forensics. It also includes various fields. Under network forensics, we should understand forensics where the main evidence is researched digital network traffic logs of network equipment, network applications, such as proxies, firewalls, servers, and so on.

Together with a conventional host-based network, forensics allows us to resolve the incident more efficiently. Information from the network layer provides a complete picture of what happened. Moreover, in some cases the analyst does not have access to these compromised machines because attackers use encryption, delete files, or use other techniques to hide information.

In cases of complex targeted attacks, initial network intrusion is only the first stage of an attack. The next steps for the promotion of the network, the development of the attack, the collection of information, and data exfiltration occur with the use of the network.

Network traffic data relates to the volatility, therefore, to collect network traffic that is necessary to perform a series of preparatory measures for the collection of data.

Network data collection

All data that can be retrieved from the network traffic can be divided into several levels:

- Full Packet Capture 100%
- Packet String Data 4%
- Sessions 0.1%
- Statistics
- Logs

It is obvious that, from the point of view of a forensics analyst, the most preferred method is to collect full traffic, as in this case, we obtain the most complete dataset.

However, along with the obvious advantages, this approach has a number of drawbacks. A large amount of data for storage and subsequent analysis requires a lot of time and resources.

At the same time, other forms of data, such as NetFlow, in many cases is a reasonable alternative, and it requires fewer resources for the collection and storage and to process.

Compared to other forms of full traffic, data altogether constitutes only a few percent. It require less space for storage and, therefore, can be stored for a longer time period.

For clarity, consider the following example. Let's suppose an organization has a daily volume of network traffic in a 1 TB per day on weekdays and 100 GB over the weekend, while the weekly storage data volume requires 5.2 TB.

The data in other formats require *5200 * 0.041 = 213.2 MB* per week. Thus, the total amount required for data storage is the weekly amount 5.4 TB or an average of approximately 770 MB per day.

If we talk about the need to ensure a minimum of three months storage, it will require 69 TB space on the disc. In addition to the processing of such large amounts of data, it requires a lot of time and power equipment.

However, this problem can be solved by a combined approach to the collection and analysis of network data. Namely, it is possible to store a complete traffic only for a week and the rest of the data for the year.

Thus, the storage network data for the year 5200 will need *0.041 + 5200 * / 7 * 365 = 16.32 TB*.

As mentioned earlier, the Full Packet Capture data collection and NetFlow prerequire arrangements to collect the data before the incident. Unfortunately, often at the time of the incident, it appears that the organization has no Full Packet Capture, no NetFlow data. In this case, our only hope is that the processes of logging has been enabled on the server and networking equipment.

Next, consider the work with different data types, as often forensics analysts work with data that is available at the moment of working on the incident.

Exploring logs

The most ubiquitous connectivity options of the corporate network to the Internet is to use a proxy server. Moreover, all protocols except HTTP and HTTPS are blocked by a firewall. Therefore, we consider this particular scheme. A proxy server is a server that is an intermediary between the client and server. Proxies can be used for almost any network protocol, but they are most often used for the web traffic for HTTP and HTTPS.

In this case, a forensics analyst usually has a data proxy server. Proxy logs are invaluable in analyzing what URL is accessing the corporate network machines. Analysis of the logs of the proxy server allows you to quickly identify which workstations are exposed to a malicious resource. This is done much faster than in the analysis of each client machine.

Typically, proxy logs include not only the time and IP address of the client and the URL, but they also include the status of the HTTP response and the username:

- Unix timestamp (`sec.ms`)
- Response time (`ms`)
- Requestor IP/name
- Cache status and HTTP status code
- Reply size (bytes)
- Request method (GET, POST, and so on)
- URL requested
- Username (if available)
- Squid hierarchy status and Server IP / peer name
- MIME type

Also, caching the proxy server allows you to store additional copies of all the requested objects. In some cases, this is the only way to obtain the necessary files and perform the analysis.

Today there are many different proxies, both commercial and free. However, probably the most popular at the moment is Squid. Among the free servers, NGINX can also be noted.

There are also a number of commercial solutions both hardware and in software form. Among commercial proxies, one of the most popular is the BlueCoat proxy. Among its advantages is its ability to proxy SSL traffic.

Other popular solutions in the corporate environment are ForeFront Threat Managment Gateway (formerly, Microsoft ISA Server) and the decision of the Barracuda Network.

All of them have their own formats of log files, and we will not consider all of these decisions. We will focus on a detailed examination of Squid.

As noted earlier, Squid is one of the most popular and free solutions formed around a large community of users. This decision can be found in both small networks and large enterprises. Squid has great potential, and it is relatively easy to install.

An experienced administrator can configure Squid as a caching server with different filtering rules for different file types and a large number of additional options. All these settings are in the Squid configuration file, and they must be copied for analysis along with the log files. The default configuration file is located in /etc/squid/squid.conf. This file is well documented and explains many settings in the configuration file, specified as the location of the log files and cache.

Log files contain information about all client requests made via the HTTP protocol. The cache directory contains responses from web servers to clients. During the investigation, the analyst can get all the files and analyze them.

By default, Squid provides a lot of information about every request it receives from customers. Thus, during the investigation, the analyst can get all objects from HTTP traffic passing through the proxy. Attackers often use the HTTP protocol to deliver malicious software as well as as a means of communication to communicate with the C & C servers, so proxy is a good place to collect information about such activity.

Usually entry in the log file of the proxy server Squid (access.log) is as follows:

```
|12345678910.134|534|129.134.21.51|TCP
MISS/200|1345|GET|http://www.123.cc|-|DIRECT/134.41.65.13|text/htm|
```

It is worth noting that the query string is logged and does not default. To remedy this situation, it is necessary to make a corresponding change in the configuration file, namely this line:

```
strip_query_terms off
```

Besides this, it is also useful to include logging the following information:

```
User_Agent
Referer
```

These options can be particularly useful in investigations. Also, since the Squid 2.6 version, you now have the opportunity to ask your own log format via the `logformat` option in the configuration file.

Thus, the administrator can specify an alternate log file and format string.

Let's take the following example:

```
logformat customlogformat %tl %a> "%rm %ru HTTP/%rv"
%>Hs %<st "%{Referer}>h""%{User-Agent}>h" %Ss:%Sh
access_log /var/log/squid/access.log customlogformat
```

As the Squid log file is simply a text file, it is easy to automate using scripting languages and command-line utilities. There is also a large number of different log file analyzers in Squid. Here are some of them:

- Squidview: http://www.rillion.net/squidview/
- Calamaris: http://cord.de/calamaris-english
- SARG: http://sourceforge.net/projects/sarg/

Each has its advantages and disadvantages, so you need to choose the most appropriate:

Full Packet Capture

Consider the case when the disposal of such, analysts have a full dump of the network traffic. In some cases, recording network traffic is included in the investigation of the incident after the incident and detection. Even in this situation, network traffic analysis can greatly enhance the effectiveness of the investigation.

To capture network traffic, the most often used format is the PCAP format. This format is supported by most of the tools for data collection, analysis, and detection.

Most of the popular utilities are built on the `libpcap` library, including `tcpdump` and `wireshark`, and they have similar functionality.

Using tcpdump

The `tcpdump` tool is used to collect and analyze network packets. It is ideal for the analysis of individual packages and for their consistency. In the case of automatic processing, `tcpdump` has several advantages.

To read a previously recorded `pcap` file, you can use the following command:

```
tcpdump -nnr dump.pcap
```

The default `tcpdump` displays information about each packet, while the output format is protocol-dependent:

TCP:

```
[Timestamp] [Layer 3 Protocol] [Source IP].
[Source Port]> [Destination IP]. [Destination Port]:
[TCP Flags], [TCP Sequence Number],
[TCP Acknowledgement Number], [TCP Windows Size] ,
[Data Length]
```

UDP:

```
[Timestamp] [Layer 3 Protocol] [Source IP].
[Source Port]> [Destination IP]. [Destination Port]:
[Layer 4 Protocol], [Data Length]
```

In addition to make the output more informative, `-v` `-vvv` can be used, as in the following example:

```
tcpdump -nnvvvr dump.pcap
```

With the `-x` option, you can make `tcpdump` output packets in the `heh` format or into ASCII using `-A` or `-X`, and `tcpdump` allows you to output in two formats simultaneously.

In many cases, especially when handling large `pcap` files, the ability to use filters to discard unnecessary data is particularly useful. The `tcpdump` tools allows BPF filters. For example, to filter only TCP packets to port `80`, you can use the following command:

```
tcpdump -nnr dump.pcap tcp dst port 80
```

To write the filtered data to a file you must use the `-w` option, as follows:

```
tcpdump - nnr dump.pcap 'tcp dst port 80' -w 80_tcp_dump.pcap
```

Sometimes, it is necessary to use a set of filters, and in this case, it is more convenient to write the filter set in the file and, thus, to use a file with the `-F` optional filters:

```
tcpdump -nnr dump.pcap -F filter.bpf
```

For more information on the various keys to use `tcpdump`, use the `man tcpdump` command.

Using tshark

Another useful tool for the analysis of pcap files is tshark.

The tshark tool is a console version WireShark. tshark has virtually the same functionality as tcpdump, but it adds the possibility of a WireShark protocol analyzer and uses syntax to filter.

To read a previously recorded pcap file the -r option is also used. The output format depends on the protocol. Thus, tshark shows application-level information.

To obtain additional information, use the -V option. To display packets in hex and ASCII formats, use the -x option.

Tshark allows the use of filters capture when using syntax that is similar to tcpdump's BPF, and display filters can be used when the built-in protocol analyzers.

For the use of, filters should be used with the -f option and the -R recording and read option. So to read pcap file of DNS traffic, you can use the following command:

```
tshark -r dump.pcap -R 'udp && dst.port == 53'
```

Another useful feature is the ability to generate tshark statistics from the analyzed traffic. To do this, use the -z option. A full list of the available statistics are available through the man pages on tshark.

For example, to view statistics on http traffic, you can use the following command:

```
tshark -r dump.pcap -z http, tree
```

- **IO,phs**: This displays the results in a pcap file protocols
- **HTTP,tree**: This displays statistics from HTTP requests and responses
- **SMB,srt**: This displays statistics relating to the SMB commands

However, even so, despite the fact that in some cases command-line utilities are well suited for the analysis of packets at a fundamental level, it is better to use GUI tools such as WireShark for some tasks.

Using WireShark

WireShark is used to address various issues that are related to the functioning of the network by network administrators, but it also plays an invaluable role in cases of network traffic analysis in investigations of incidents.

The WireShark interface can be divided into three main parts.

The upper part displays the list of packages. Each package information is available. By default, the packet number, timestamp, source, and destination address, protocol, packet length, and special protocols for different information.

The middle section displays detailed information about the package, which is selected in the upper part.

The bottom window displays the individual bytes package to hex and ASCII formats such as conclusions team tcpdump, -x.

The data in all windows are connected to each other; thus, when we choose data in one window, associated data is highlighted in the other windows.

Wireshark has a lot of possibilities to analyze network packets. Therefore, to describe them in a single chapter is almost impossible. There are several good books that reveal these features in detail, namely *Practical Packet Analysis* and *Wireshark Network Analysis*.

In some cases, the timestamps are the only binding element in the investigation. For example, sometimes the analyst knows only the approximate time of the incident and that they have to filter traffic for a certain period of time. The default WireShark displays the timestamps of packets in seconds from the start of the recording of traffic in the `pcap` file. Changing the display format of this can be done through the menu, as follows: **View** | **Time Display Format** | **Date and Time of Day**.

In order not have to perform this action every time, you can change these settings in Wireshark, as follows: **Edit** | **Preferences**

In some cases, it is important to get a general idea of the analyzed traffic.

You can use the **Statistics** menu item. This displays a wealth of information and statistics on the traffic collected.

For example, Protocol Hierarchy provides a list of all identified in the traffic reports and statistics on them. Very often, this helps identify anomalies in the traffic, for example, in the case of tunneling via DNS or ICMP.

In addition to this, WireShark allows you to group the traffic on the traffic between the different hosts. Thus, it is possible to determine the amount of transferred data between different machines. Statistics on the machines can be viewed via **Statistic | Endpoints**, and various conversations can be viewed through **Statistics | Conversations**.

In some cases, there are situations when it is necessary to analyze the data exchanged between two specific hosts. You can use the `Following TCPStream` option. WireShark allows you to perform such actions for UDP, HTTP, and SSL.

Another useful WireShark option that should be mentioned is the extraction of the responses from the network traffic. WireShark allows you to extract objects from the HTTP, SMB, and DICOM streams. To do this, use navigate to **File | Export | Objects | HTTP**.

Then, select a file from the displayed list of files, and use the **Save As** to save the file. It should be noted that the need to extract the file, all packets of network traffic in the case of at least one `otsutviya` package relating to the transfer of the file to get it will not succeed.

Note that you can extract files from traffic using a number of other utilities, such as NetworkMiner or Bro. We discuss On Bro in more details later in this chapter.

The default setting displays a specific list of columns in WireShark with the data about the packets, as follows:

- The batch number
- The timestamp
- The source address
- The location receiver
- Protocol
- The length of the packet

Fields with more information

In some cases, this may require additional information, such as port numbers of the receiver and the source or method of the HTTP request.

Consider the following steps that must be completed in order to add a new column with the data on the method that is used by HTTP:

1. Start with the WireShark `pcap` traffic test.
2. Find the HTTP packet containing the HTTP request method, such as GET or POST. This can be done manually or by entering the `http.request` filter.
3. Select the HTTP packet in the window with packets, then expand the HTTP header, and find a site with the **Method Request** field.
4. Select the field, and right-click on it to select Â«**Apply as Column**Â».

After these actions a new column should appear. You can later change the name and other attributes of the column.

Often, WireShark plays an invaluable role in the analysis of network traffic that is required to handle large quantities of data and rich filtering. To filter data using Wireshark BPF filters. BPF filters are the most common method of filtering network utilities, including Wireshark, tcpdump, tshark, and so on.

BPF filters can be used both during the traffic data collection and the analysis data. Consider the structure BPF filter, and a folder created by the BPF, which is called expression syntax. The expression includes one or more primitives that can be combined by operators. The primitives, in turn, are made up of qualifiers and the following values.

There are three types of qualifier, as follows:

- **Type:** `host`, `net`, and `port`
- **Dir:** `src` and `dst`
- **Proto:** `ether`, `fddi`, `ip`, `arp`, `rarp`, `decnet`, `lat`, `sca`, `moprc`, `mopdl`, `tcp`, and `udp`.

Here is an example with several primitives:

- dst host host
- src host host
- host host
- ether src ehost
- gateway host

A full list of primitives can be found in the main pages for the `tcpdump` utility.

Primitives are grouped and can be combined using the following operators:

- Negation (`!` Or `not`)
- Concatenation (`&&` or `and`)
- Alternation (`||` or `or`)

More information about the BPF syntax can be found on the main page.

Knowing Bro

Another tool to analyze network traffic is Bro. Bro is a very powerful tool, which is often positioned as an IDS, but the possibilities are much wider with Bro. Discussing all of them in a single chapter is almost impossible, so we will consider only some of them. One of the many advantages of Bro is the ability to use ready-made parsers different protocols.

For example, the following are some of them:

- DHCP
- DNS
- FTP
- HTTP
- POP3
- SMTP
- SSH

The list of these protocols is constantly expanding.

By default, Bro applies the protocol analyzers to traffic, and it records the results in the log files that correspond to different protocols.

Network Forensics

Bro also allows you to write your own handlers in a language called Bro. For each event that occurs during the processing of the event may be caused by its handler.

For example, consider the following simple event handler discovery file:

```
event file_new (f: fa_file) {
local fname = fmt ("% s", f $ id)
Files :: add_analyzer (f, Files :: ANALYZER_EXTRACT, [$ extract_filename = fname])
}
```

Next, remove all files from the traffic to keep this code in a file, run the `getfiles.bro` command:

```
bro -C -r traffic.pcap getfiles.bro
```

The following is the output of the preceding command:

```
forensics@forensics:~/netlab$ bro -C -r /mnt/hgfs/evidence/netlab_20140408.pcap
/home/forensics/forensictools/bro_extplugins/getfiles.bro
forensics@forensics:~/netlab$ ls -al
total 3132
drwxrwxr-x  4 forensics forensics    4096 Apr  9 10:01 .
drwxr-xr-x 23 forensics forensics    4096 Apr  9 09:56 ..
-rw-rw-r--  1 forensics forensics  323044 Apr  9 10:01 conn.log
-rw-rw-r--  1 forensics forensics  203120 Apr  9 10:01 dns.log
drwxrwxr-x  2 forensics forensics  135168 Apr  9 10:01 extract_files
-rw-rw-r--  1 forensics forensics  507119 Apr  9 10:01 files.log
-rw-rw-r--  1 forensics forensics 1898512 Apr  9 10:01 http.log
-rw-rw-r--  1 forensics forensics     253 Apr  9 10:01 packet_filter.log
-rw-rw-r--  1 forensics forensics  103913 Apr  9 10:01 ssl.log
drwx------  3 forensics forensics    4096 Apr  9 10:01 .state
-rw-rw-r--  1 forensics forensics    4915 Apr  9 10:01 weird.log
forensics@forensics:~/netlab$
```

After running this command, the catalog files are created, as follows:

- `conn.log`
- `files.log`
- `http.log`
- `ssl.log`
- `ftp.log`
- `dns.log`
- `weird.log`

These files contain information about the network traffic for certain protocols. For example, `http.log` contains the following fields.

In addition to the log files in the startup directory that is created by Bro, `extract_files` lists which files are extracted from the traffic. For each file in this directory, you can find the corresponding entry in the `files.log` file. This entry contains a number of attributes, which are useful.

To analyze the contents of these log files in the distribution utility has Bro `bro-cut`. The input to this utility is passed through the pipe contents of the log file, and it specifies the list of fields to be filtered.

For example, to list the types of files extracted from the traffic, you can use the following command:

```
cat files.log | bro-cut mime_type | sort | uniq
```

The following is the output of the preceding command:

```
forensics@forensics:~/netlab$ cat files.log | bro-cut mime_type | sort | uniq
-
application/jar
application/octet-stream
application/vnd.ms-cab-compressed
application/vnd.ms-fontobject
application/x-dosexec
application/x-elc
application/xml
image/gif
image/jpeg
image/png
image/x-icon
text/html
text/plain
text/troff
text/x-c
text/x-c++
video/mp4
forensics@forensics:~/netlab$
```

Let's assume that we are investigating an incident of a viral infection, in which case the most interesting types of files are as follows:

```
application / jar
application / x-dosexec
```

These are executable files on MS Windows files and the Java virtual machine.

Then, we learn more about the following files of interest:

```
cat files.log | bro-cut -u ts, rx_hosts, tx_hosts,
source, mime_type, total_bytes, fuid | grep -iE "{jar |
x-dosexec}"
```

The following is the output of the preceding command:

```
forensics@forensics:~/netlab$ cat files.log | bro-cut -u ts,rx_hosts,tx_hosts,source,mime_type,total_bytes,fuid | grep -iE "/(jar|x-dosexec)"
2014-04-08T12:31:23+0000        172.16.11.101   85.17.137.151   HTTP    application/jar  14052   FUJlhk2BEJTsb8tozk
2014-04-08T12:31:31+0000        172.16.11.101   85.17.137.151   HTTP    application/x-dosexec    411648  FSZKuj2Za5hFRvZWSl
2014-04-08T12:53:26+0000        172.16.11.101   92.123.155.154  HTTP    application/x-dosexec    31892616        Fy9phB2NNXKNHKuyHb
forensics@forensics:~/netlab$ cp ./extract_files/FUJlhk2BEJTsb8tozk ./susp/FUJlhk2BEJTsb8tozk.jar
forensics@forensics:~/netlab$ cp ./extract_files/FSZKuj2Za5hFRvZWSl ./susp/FSZKuj2Za5hFRvZWSl.exe
forensics@forensics:~/netlab$ cp ./extract_files/Fy9phB2NNXKNHKuyHb ./susp/Fy9phB2NNXKNHKuyHb.exe
forensics@forensics:~/netlab$
```

These results allow the team to set time, download the resource files, and download the protocol by which to transfer these files. You can then find these files in the `extract_files` directory and analyze them.

For more information about the resource files, go to the IP address `85.17.137.151` `92,123,155,154`, and you can use the data from the `dns.log` file.

The `dns.log` file is the result of Bro, and it describes the events, permits, and changes domain names into IP addresses and vice versa. The request to the DNS server is represented by a query attribute. The server's response attribute is `answer`, and `ts` is the timestamp request:

```
cat dns.log | bro-cut -u ts, query, answer | grep -iE
"85.17.137.151 | 92.123.155.154 "
```

The following is the output of the preceding command:

```
forensics@forensics:~/netlab$ cat dns.log | bro-cut -u ts, query, answers | grep -iE "85.17.137.151|92.123.155.154"
2014-04-08T12:31:13+0000         finansial.gov    85.17.137.151
2014-04-08T12:31:13+0000         finansial.gov    85.17.137.151
2014-04-08T12:31:31+0000         w282d1wb.athleticsdrycleaner.pw 85.17.137.151
2014-04-08T12:53:23+0000         download.microsoft.com  download.microsoft.com.nsatc.net,main.dl.ms.akadns.net,download.
microsoft.com.edgesuite.net,a767.dscms.akamai.net,92.123.155.154,92.123.155.25
2014-04-08T12:54:18+0000         download.microsoft.com  download.microsoft.com.nsatc.net,main.dl.ms.akadns.net,download.
microsoft.com.edgesuite.net,a767.dscms.akamai.net,92.123.155.154,92.123.155.25
forensics@forensics:~/netlab$
```

The result is that the IP address `85.17.137.151` resolves to domains `finansial.gov` and `w282d1wb.athleticsdrycleaner.pw`.

The IP address `92.123.155.154` belongs to `microsoft.com`, which greatly reduces the likelihood that the downloaded file is malicious.

On the basis of the allocated domain names of the `http.log` file can obtain the following information:

```
cat http.log | bro-cut -u ts, id.orig_h, method, uri,
response_body_len, resp_fuid, host | grep -iE
"finansial.gov $"
```

The following is the output of the preceding command:

```
forensics@forensics:~/netlab$ cat http.log | bro-cut -u ts,id.orig_h,method,uri,response_body_len,resp_fuids,host | grep -iE "finansial.gov$"
2014-04-08T12:31:13+0000         172.16.11.101    GET    /              564    FIQI8C4ZLoTH5SDUg       finansial.gov
2014-04-08T12:31:22+0000         172.16.11.101    GET    /favicon.ico   288    FA1pOug3ReasDDiAj       finansial.gov
2014-04-08T12:31:22+0000         172.16.11.101    GET    /utisl.jar     14052  FUJlhk2BEJTsb8tozk      finansial.gov
forensics@forensics:~/netlab$ cat http.log | bro-cut -u ts,id.orig_h,method,uri,response_body_len,resp_fuids,host | grep -iE "w282d1wb.athleticsdrycleaner.pw$"
2014-04-08T12:31:31+0000         172.16.11.101    GET    /f/1389931620/4067114524/2    411648  FSZKuj2Za5hFRvZWSl  w282d1wb.athleticsdrycleaner.pw
2014-04-08T12:31:31+0000         172.16.11.101    GET    /f/1389931620/4067114524/2/2  322     FKd0142qSK4dz0i12f  w282d1wb.athleticsdrycleaner.pw
forensics@forensics:~/netlab$
```

Network Forensics

This suggests that the user downloaded a file from the resource `finansial.gov utisl.jar` protocol HTTP (the previously mentioned `FUJlhk2BEJTsb8tozk.jar.jar` file). Then, from the same resource, the `'2'` (`Fy9phB2NNXKNHKuyHb.exe`) file was downloaded:

```
forensics@forensics:~/netlab$ cat http.log | bro-cut id.orig_h,method,uri,response_body_len,resp_fuids,id.resp_h | grep -iE "85.17.137.151$" | sort | uniq
172.16.11.101    GET     /                             564       FIQI8C4ZLoTHS5DUg        85.17.137.151
172.16.11.101    GET     /f/1389931620/4067114524/2/2  322       FKd0142qSK4dz0i12f       85.17.137.151
172.16.11.101    GET     /f/1389931620/4067114524/2    411648    FSZKuj2Za5hFRvZWSl       85.17.137.151
172.16.11.101    GET     /favicon.ico                  288       FA1pOug3ReasDDiAj        85.17.137.151
172.16.11.101    GET     /utisl.jar                    14052     FUJlhk2BEJTsb8tozk       85.17.137.151
172.16.11.101    POST    /gate.php                     0         -                        85.17.137.151
172.16.11.101    POST    /gate.php                     234188    Fagqif3bfcVyWom8Xc       85.17.137.151
172.16.11.101    POST    /gate.php                     92        FjYtFU1JDHE93S12hf       85.17.137.151
172.16.11.101    POST    /gate.php                     92        FQKk2maipJsnPko8f        85.17.137.151
172.16.11.101    POST    /gate.php                     92        FSmaQF2advqwYP0kI1       85.17.137.151
forensics@forensics:~/netlab$
```

Additionally, you must pay attention to suspicious HTTP-POST `gate.php` requests.

The `resp_fuids` attribute identifies a response from the Web server, and this indicates any appropriate entry in the `files.log` file. Thus, the `FI ... Ug` identifier can get the `finansial.gov` server's response in the GET request:

```
forensics@forensics:~/netlab$ cp ./extract_files/FIQI8C4ZLoTHS5DUg ./susp/FIQI8C4ZLoTHS5DUg.html
forensics@forensics:~/netlab$ cat ./susp/FIQI8C4ZLoTHS5DUg.html
<!DOCTYPE HTML>
<html>
 <head>
  <meta charset="utf-8">
  <title>Financial news</title>
 </head>
 <body>
  <iframe src="http://www.efinancialnews.com/events" width="100%" height="1200" align="left" frameborder="no" scrolling="no">
    No frames!
  </iframe>
  <applet archive="utisl.jar" code="A_dsgweed" width="1" height="1">
<param name="ldcrlio" value="AhhjyHHQwqwYxQv8EhAbphcutYisubpE7pi8jQH5HxLqDDLx4wlHGl43xxGrwGHw"></param>
    <param name="t" value="0"></param>
      <param name="tt" value="0"></param>
  </applet>
 </body>
</html>
forensics@forensics:~/netlab$
```

From the replies provided, it is clear that `utisl.jar` is a java-applet. The client opens a page in a frame of the legal site, `www.efinancialnews.com`.

This small example is a clear demonstration of how it is possible to investigate with only file traffic using Bro.

However, the example shows only a small part of all possibilities of Bro. To learn about Bro's other capabilities, you can visit `https://www.bro.org/`, where you can find a lot of additional material.

Summary

In this chapter, we discussed some topics on network forensics. We learned what kind of data we could collect from a network and how to analyze logs from a proxy server. Also from this chapter, we learned how to collect `pcap` files and how to analyze them with WireShark and Bro.

In the following chapter, you will learn how to build a forensic environment. We will describe two approaches; one of them is virtualization, and another one uses distributed systems. We will describe GRR as an example of a distributed system.

A
Building a Forensic Analysis Environment

After the previous chapters, we should now have realized how important incident response is for digital forensics processes and how necessary it is to deal with both of them accurately. In this appendix of the book, we will discuss the creation of a convenient work environment to conduct the digital forensics analysis, the digital forensics lab, at enterprise scale.

Before we start building our lab, let's answer the following questions:

- What are the lab's purposes, and what kind of devices will we analyze (computers, mobiles, and so on)? This will help us determine the suitable tools for our lab.
- How many cases can we expect to receive, and what is the expected expansion in our scope and lab?
- Do we have trained individuals yet? If not, how will we select them, and what training will they need? What operating systems will they need to be familiar with, either to work with or to analyze?

Answering these questions will make it easier to take decisions. Also, there are some guidelines and standards, such as ISO/IEC 17025:2005, which can be followed in order to create accredited digital forensics lab.

Factors that need to be considered

Besides the essential tools, including hardware and software, which will be discussed later, there are some other factors to consider while building the lab. The investigator usually will spend a long time in the lab workspace. So, it should be comfortable enough and they must have full control over its environment. In the next section, we will highlight some factors that need to be considered in the planning phase.

Size

It is always a good idea to prepare for future expansion while planning for the lab from the beginning. If you are expecting an expansion, for example, the number of current team members will be raised by 50% in two years, you will need to consider a larger lab size in the planning phase so that you can have all your members working in the same place, instead of two separate locations.

Suitable lab size can be affected by the following factors:

- The number of the investigators working concurrently, and the overlapping between different work shifts if any
- Besides the size of the hardware tools that could occupy large space in the lab, the size of the evidence could be large enough to occupy additional space in the lab in case you don't plan to have a separate locked evidence storage room
- During the acquisition and analysis phases, some disassembly work can take place in the lab; thus, having a separate workbench for such tasks will be better for the sake of lab organization

All these points must be considered while asking for lab size.

Environment control

Many devices that will be running in the lab will generate a lot of heat. Controlling the room temperature and keeping it at an acceptable level will prevent the devices from failure due to overheating, and it will make the lab comfortable for team members.

Appendix A

Besides the digital evidence acquisition process, which is a time-consuming process because it may take hours to image some evidence, the analysis process itself may take longer time in some processes, such as Indexing. During the lab planning, considering an alternative power source and a backup power plan along with a reliable main power source to keep all these processes to continue without interruption is critical to save time and keep operations smooth.

In some environments with a big number of cases received in parallel, it will be hard to follow up with these cases and their progresses without automated management software. To control the workflow and prevent unauthorized access, a case management system that provides administrative control over the cases and the ability to assign access to investigators to work on specific cases must be installed in the lab. The management system can measure the work progress, and they can create statistics about workflow to notice weaknesses for future improvements.

Security

Usually, cases in the lab are related to criminal actions. This makes it important to secure the working location from any physical or virtual unauthorized access to prevent any possible manipulation to the evidence or the analysis results. The physical location of the lab needs to be chosen with care. These are some of the parameters that are needed to maintain physical security:

- The ground floor in your building is easier to access for outsiders. Locating the lab at a higher floor in a no-windows room will help in access control and in preventing eavesdropping, recording, or breaking into the lab.
- The room's walls must be toughened. Having very advanced room access controls, but gypsum board walls, is not a very good idea.
- The basic security solutions, such as keeping access logs with time stamps, cameras, and security personnel must be provided if the lab is not already in a secured facility.

Most digital forensics phases don't require an Internet connection to run. Disconnecting the lab from the Internet is favorable for secrecy and to prevent infections or unwanted remote control by offenders who can change case results or damage evidence. However, some tasks will require an Internet connection such, as software updates. The lab should be provided with two separate networks, where one locally connects the analysis workstations, and the other one connects other computers to the Internet for daily research and updates and is provided with security solutions to help in preventing unauthorized access from the internet to the lab network.

Software

During this book's chapters, we chose to use all very effective, either free or open source tools in the wild. However, there are many commercial tools that can be purchased and added to the digital forensics lab in order to verify the results or perform some tasks in parallel.

Before using any tool, a verification process must take place first. We will verify the tool's functions by running this tool against preanalyzed evidence to make sure that it will produce the same results. After the tool passes this test, we can rely on its results in the future. An example of such tests is the acquisition process, where we calculate the hash of a resulted image from the new tool and compare it with the hash that we previously had for this evidence from the verified tool. If the hash differs, it means that this tools doesn't create a forensic image correctly, and we must not use it.

Also, verifying the results by different tools is a great way to be certain of the results that will be reported, especially for the sensitive cases, which required many analysis steps that depends on each other.

The tools required in the digital forensics lab usually categorized, but not limited, to the following categories:

- Incident response, including live analysis and evidence acquisition for different platforms
- Data recovery
- Media recovery
- Password recovery
- E-mail investigations
- Memory analysis
- Network forensics
- Browser investigation
- Mobile forensics
- Internet investigation

Note that some tools don't support all known filesystems, so you need to have different tools that understand and parse different filesystems (`FAT`, `NTFS`, `EXT`, `UFS`, and `HFS`).

Hardware

Due to the acquisition and the processing of large amounts of data in digital forensics, the analysis requires very powerful workstations. Some people prefer to work on servers, which will provide sufficient resources, including memory, processor, and storage.

Today, the budget to build a powerful machine is the limit. The more powerful machine you build, the more time you will save during analysis. Also, the reliability of the machine is very important. It will be very frustrating to work on a task for long time, then the machine fails and you lose all the work. For this reason, usually the forensics workstations come with a Xeon processor that is more reliable for such tasks.

Virtualization

Having multioperating systems is mandatory in digital forensics, such as different Windows versions and different Linux and UNIX distributions. Instead of having single machine for each operating system, virtualization gives us the ability to build different operating systems on the main operating system. In this section, we will briefly discuss the virtualization concept:

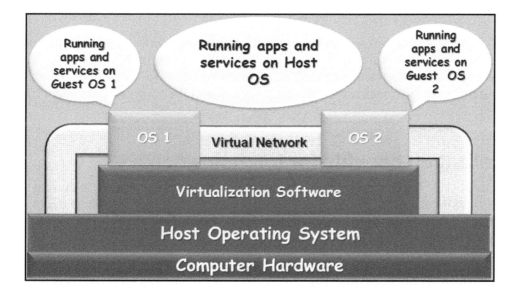

Figure 1: The virtualization blocks

In virtualization, what is actually virtualized is the computer hardware. Normally on the same hardware, we can't run more than one operating system concurrently. However, by adding an extra layer of software over the running operating system, called the virtualization solution, a virtual hardware will appear to be ready to install the new operating system. The new hardware is, of course, part of the main computer hardware, but virtually assigned to the new operating system. Every new virtual machine consumes part of the original machine resources.

The main operating system is called the HOST machine and any created operating system is called the GUEST virtual machine. The host shares all the computer resources with the Guests, even the network connection. As we can see in *Figure 1*, a virtual network connection can connect all the machines together with the Host and with each other. Also, a connection can only be shared with two Guests without the Host or between the Host OS with one Guest without the other. Many possibilities can take place in this approach. Sharing folders and files between the host and the guests is also applicable.

Backing up the guest virtual machine is very easy with virtualization. To back up a system, we need to take what is called a snapshot. A snapshot is a copy of the machine status at a specific time, including the hard disk changes and the memory. If the user decided to retrieve a previously taken snapshot without taking another snapshot of the machine, all the changes that took place from the last snapshot will be lost.

This is why virtualization provides a controlled environment, as this is needed during the analysis for testing or to run malicious code and monitor its behavior in what is called dynamic or behavior malware analysis. The investigator needs to take a snapshot before executing the malware, execute and test the malware, and then recover the system from the snapshot.

Virtualization benefits for forensics

In virtualization, everything is a file parsed by the Host operating system, including the hard disk and the memory. This makes the acquisition process much easier. If the case under investigation is related to a virtual system, the acquisition of memory, for example, will be just copying the memory file.

If the machine has previous snapshots, this will provide the investigator with different statuses of the machine from different times in the past, where the investigator can follow the machine's behavior to detect when the machine was, for instance, infected or compromised.

Every virtual machine has different files, and each file represents one resource as stated earlier. We will take the VMware software as an example and discuss the files that the program creates for each virtual machine:

- **Configuration file**: This is a VMX file, which stores the configurations of the machine itself, including hardware and network settings that the user has selected for this guest machine.
- **Memory file**: This is a VMEM file, which contains the running memory of the guest virtual machine.
- **Hard drive file**: This is a VMDK file, is the virtual hard drive of the guest virtual machine. It can consist of single or multiple files, according to the selection of the user while creating the virtual machine. In some cases, one guest machine can have multiple hard drives. Each hard drive will have a different file.
- **Snapshot file**: This is a VMSN file. When the user takes a snapshot of the guest machine, the state of the machine is stored in this file.
- **Suspend state file**: This is a VMSS file, the user can suspend the machine without turning it off. In this case, the memory of the machine is stored in this single file. When the user restarts the machine, this file is used to reload the machine memory.

There are other different types of files. All file types can be found in VMware website at https://www.vmware.com/support/ws55/doc/ws_learning_files_in_a_vm.html.

The distributed forensic system

In an enterprise environment or when the need for quick and remote analysis arises, the distributed forensic system can help. During the incident response, the investigator will be interested in collecting some data, such as running processes, registry keys, and user accounts in order to identify possible infection or test some IOCs. However, what if the physical access to the suspected environment is not possible in the meantime?

Many companies are now investing in producing live monitoring and analysis systems that can be deployed in an environment by installing a client on each machine in the network and have all these clients be connected to a server. The authorized investigator can access these machines from the server using the installed clients and acquire some data or build some statistics and perform some live and remote forensic analysis.

GRR

In this section, we will discuss the GRR Rapid Response framework, `https://github.com/google/grr`. GRR is an Incident Response Framework that is focused on Remote Live Forensics. It provides remote analysis using some famous digital forensics' frameworks such as TSK and Rekall. It consists of a server which can control a large number of clients at the same time.

We will run a demonstration to discuss GRR using a virtualization where we have two virtual machines. These are a Linux Ubuntu machine with the IP `192.168.153.142` and a Windows 7 Enterprise 64-bit machine with the IP `192.168.153.146`. The server will be installed on the Linux machine and the client will be installed on the Windows machine. For the Server-Client schema, both machines must be connected to the same network. We can use the NAT network configuration for both machines using any virtualization software and then test the connection between both machines.

Server installation

To install the server, you can follow the documentation at `https://github.com/google/grr-doc/blob/master/quickstart.adoc`. After you finish installing the server, it will ask you to initiate the server configuration, which it will use to build the clients for this specific server besides the admin username and password. For this exercise, the administration URL is `http://192.168.153.142:8000`, and the client frontend URL is `http://192.168.153.142:8080/control`.

Appendix A

Client installation

After making sure that both server and client can reach each other, we can proceed to installing the client on the Windows machine. For this exercise, we recommend that you disable the Windows virtual machine firewall. Open the following URL from the client machine `http://192.168.153.142:8000/#main=BinaryConfigurationView&t=_executables-windows-installers`, and enter the admin username and password:

Figure 2: Downloading the GRR client

This link will open the Windows clients directly. Our Windows machine is 64 bit, so we need to download the `GRR_3.0.0.7_amd64.exe` file. This client was configured to connect directly to the server at the Linux machine by the server IP, so make sure that there is no IP conflict in the testing environment. After downloading the client, we need to run it on the client machine with administrator privileges. Give it some time and then go to the server and open the admin URL again.

Note the following:

- The client can be transferred in any way, and not necessarily by opening the admin portal.
- In real life, if the client is really remote, the server must be published on the Internet with real IP. The Cloud can be used in such cases.

Browsing with the newly-connected client

After opening the administration URL, the clients will not appear directly. Therefore, we need to have any information about the client to search for it. According to GRR documentation, any information, such as the hostname, MAC, username, IP, and so on, will be enough to locate the client if it is connected. In our exercise, we will use the client IP `192.168.153.142`:

Figure 3: Search for client by IP

Double-clicking in the machine will open all the information about the machine, as shown in the following figure:

Figure 4: A newly-connected client

Appendix A

Start a new flow

To execute command on the client machine, we need to start what is called a flow. There are different types of flows in GRR, which are as follows:

Figure 5: Different flows in the machine

We will make one flow as an example by listing the processes in the remote Windows client. Select the flow under **Memory**, then select **AnalyzeClientMemory**. As we discussed in the memory forensics chapter, the plugin to list the system running processes in both Volatility and Rekall is the pslist plugin.

We will add this plugin in the requested plugins, as shown in the following screenshot:

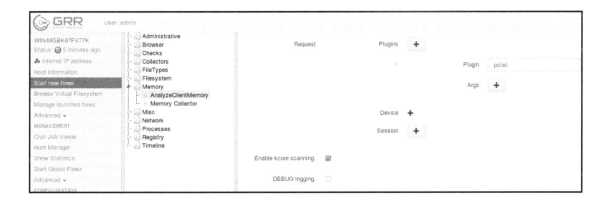

Figure 6: The request to run the pslist plugin on the remote client.

[279]

Building a Forensic Analysis Environment

The execution of such a command will take some time. After it finishes, the server will notify the administrator:

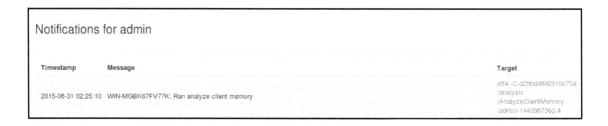

Figure 7: Admin notification of the results

Clicking on the notification will open the results of the analysis. The results will be the same as it shows in the Rekall output, as shown in the following screenshot:

Figure 8: The pslist plugin reuslts received in the server

Appendix A

GRR has many different usages, such as listing the files in the machine filesystem as seen by the normal operating system and by the TSK framework, where the investigator can notice any differences or recover deleted files.

The full documentation of the tool's capabilities can be found at `https://github.com/google/grr-doc/blob/master/user_manual.adoc`.

B
Case Study

Introduction

In this appendix, we will use an infected machine to illustrate how to conduct primary analysis on different types of evidence, and we will go through live analysis along with the post-mortem analysis.

Scenario

To conduct this analysis, we created a small virtual network with the following structure:

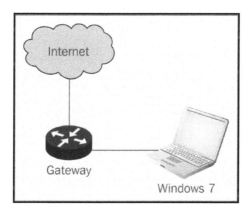

Case Study

All the scenario parts were created using virtualization, including the required Internet hosts to download the malware. The machine is infected with ZeusVM malware. The malware executable can be downloaded for educational use only from the Zoo at `https://github.com/ytisf/theZoo/blob/master/malwares/Binaries/ZeusVM/ZeusVM.zip`. The malware sample SHA256 after unzipping is as follows:

`b04637c11c63dd5a4a599d7104f0c5880717b5d5b32e0104de5a416963f06118`

`theZoo` is a project that was created to make the possibility of malware analysis open and available to the public. `theZoo` was created by Yuval tisf Nativ, and it is now maintained by Shahak Shalev.

You can download the malware sample, recreate or infect a virtual machine with this malware, and follow the analysis steps in this appendix.

The machine used in this scenario is Windows 7 Enterprise 64 bit.

Acquisition

As we discussed before, the best practice is to start the evidence acquisition before changing anything in the machine under investigation. The acquired evidence must be stored in the USB storage device or network share. In our case, a USB storage device can be used between the infected and the analysis machines, but it must be carefully wiped after the analysis. Network acquisition with another analysis Linux virtual machine over the virtual network will be efficient in our case as well. Network acquisition will be as discussed before in `Chapter 4`, *Nonvolatile Data Acquisition*. We need to acquire the memory and hard disk of the infected machine.

Exercise: You need to perform this step, as we discussed before in the acquisition sections in `Chapter 3`, *Volatile Data Collection*, and `Chapter 4`, *Nonvolatile Data Acquisition*.

Live analysis

Next, let's perform some live analysis on the infected machine in hand. This live analysis will give us quick results. It may overwrite some traces in the system, but in our case here, we have already acquired our evidence.

The running processes

Listing the running processes will allow us to notice any maliciously-named processes that may relate to malware behavior. We can list the running processes using the `native tasklist` command:

```
Image Name                     PID Session Name        Session#    Mem Usage
========================= ======== ================ =========== ============
System Idle Process              0 Services                   0         24 K
System                           4 Services                   0      2,692 K
smss.exe                       260 Services                   0        668 K
csrss.exe                      352 Services                   0      3,404 K
csrss.exe                      404 Console                    1     13,176 K
wininit.exe                    436 Services                   0      3,316 K
services.exe                   476 Services                   0      9,312 K
lsass.exe                      484 Services                   0     10,160 K
winlogon.exe                   500 Console                    1      4,820 K
lsm.exe                        528 Services                   0      4,872 K
svchost.exe                    636 Services                   0      7,568 K
svchost.exe                    700 Services                   0      7,104 K
svchost.exe                    784 Services                   0     14,656 K
svchost.exe                    872 Services                   0     48,624 K
svchost.exe                    900 Services                   0     27,740 K
svchost.exe                    288 Services                   0     16,672 K
svchost.exe                    396 Services                   0     17,416 K
spoolsv.exe                    372 Services                   0      7,804 K
svchost.exe                   1044 Services                   0     12,288 K
svchost.exe                   1160 Services                   0     11,432 K
vmtoolsd.exe                  1260 Services                   0     12,712 K
svchost.exe                   1748 Services                   0      5,424 K
msdtc.exe                     2032 Services                   0      4,596 K
svchost.exe                   2224 Services                   0      6,232 K
SearchIndexer.exe             2512 Services                   0     28,372 K
taskhost.exe                  2864 Console                    1      6,576 K
dwm.exe                       2884 Console                    1      5,056 K
explorer.exe                  2892 Console                    1     62,920 K
vmtoolsd.exe                  3056 Console                    1     18,352 K
firefox.exe                   2064 Console                    1    207,852 K
explorer.exe                  2256 Console                    1     10,452 K
DART.EXE                      1944 Console                    1     19,080 K
cmd.exe                       1412 Console                    1      2,476 K
conhost.exe                   2432 Console                    1      4,736 K
tasklist.exe                  2460 Console                    1      5,168 K
WmiPrvSE.exe                  1540 Services                   0      5,804 K
```

Case Study

We can also use `processexplorer` from Sysinternals. We will notice no malicious names, but we can see that there are two processes named `explorer.exe` within the system. One holds an ID of `2256` ran for compatibility with 32 bit images but its current directory is `C:\Users\<<UserName>>\AppData\Roaming\` as shown in the Process Explorer in the following screenshot. Also, please note that this process most likely will hold another ID if you ran the malware in a machine on your own:

Process	CPU	Private Bytes	Working Set	PID	Description	Company Name
System Idle Process	97.29	0 K	24 K	0		
System	0.11	116 K	2,696 K	4		
Interrupts	0.75	0 K	0 K	n/a	Hardware Interrupts and DPCs	
smss.exe		352 K	792 K	260	Windows Session Manager	Microsoft Corporation
csrss.exe	< 0.01	2,684 K	3,712 K	352	Client Server Runtime Process	Microsoft Corporation
csrss.exe	0.07	18,096 K	13,584 K	404	Client Server Runtime Process	Microsoft Corporation
conhost.exe		1,304 K	4,864 K	2432	Console Window Host	Microsoft Corporation
wininit.exe		1,312 K	3,476 K	436	Windows Start-Up Application	Microsoft Corporation
services.exe		4,920 K	9,512 K	476	Services and Controller app	Microsoft Corporation
svchost.exe		3,556 K	7,796 K	636	Host Process for Windows S...	Microsoft Corporation
WmiPrvSE.exe		2,196 K	5,816 K	416	WMI Provider Host	Microsoft Corporation
svchost.exe		3,720 K	7,336 K	700	Host Process for Windows S...	Microsoft Corporation
svchost.exe		12,844 K	14,776 K	784	Host Process for Windows S...	Microsoft Corporation
svchost.exe	< 0.01	47,264 K	50,156 K	872	Host Process for Windows S...	Microsoft Corporation
dwm.exe		1,692 K	5,080 K	2884	Desktop Window Manager	Microsoft Corporation
svchost.exe	< 0.01	21,796 K	30,964 K	900	Host Process for Windows S...	Microsoft Corporation
svchost.exe	< 0.01	9,212 K	16,488 K	288	Host Process for Windows S...	Microsoft Corporation
svchost.exe	0.01	27,112 K	17,056 K	396	Host Process for Windows S...	Microsoft Corporation
spoolsv.exe		6,656 K	8,048 K	372	Spooler SubSystem App	Microsoft Corporation
svchost.exe		11,564 K	12,384 K	1044	Host Process for Windows S...	Microsoft Corporation
svchost.exe		5,444 K	11,512 K	1160	Host Process for Windows S...	Microsoft Corporation
vmtoolsd.exe	0.04	7,700 K	12,912 K	1260	VMware Tools Core Service	VMware, Inc.
svchost.exe		2,144 K	5,476 K	1748	Host Process for Windows S...	Microsoft Corporation
msdtc.exe		3,388 K	4,868 K	2032	Microsoft Distributed Transa...	Microsoft Corporation
svchost.exe		3,084 K	6,444 K	2224	Host Process for Windows S...	Microsoft Corporation
SearchIndexer.exe	0.02	25,992 K	23,128 K	2512	Microsoft Windows Search I...	Microsoft Corporation
SearchProtocolHost.e...	< 0.01	2,032 K	7,372 K	1456	Microsoft Windows Search P...	Microsoft Corporation
SearchFilterHost.exe		1,456 K	4,464 K	716	Microsoft Windows Search F...	Microsoft Corporation
taskhost.exe		2,848 K	6,628 K	2864	Host Process for Windows T...	Microsoft Corporation
taskhost.exe	< 0.01	3,912 K	9,860 K	1288	Host Process for Windows T...	Microsoft Corporation
lsass.exe		4,280 K	10,180 K	484	Local Security Authority Proc...	Microsoft Corporation
lsm.exe		2,732 K	5,044 K	528	Local Session Manager Serv...	Microsoft Corporation
winlogon.exe		2,496 K	5,232 K	500	Windows Logon Application	Microsoft Corporation
explorer.exe	0.03	69,932 K	65,472 K	2892	Windows Explorer	Microsoft Corporation
vmtoolsd.exe	0.08	12,748 K	19,500 K	3056	VMware Tools Core Service	VMware, Inc.
firefox.exe	0.92	192,160 K	206,960 K	2064	Firefox	Mozilla Corporation
DART.EXE		10,264 K	18,688 K	1944		
cmd.exe		1,920 K	2,484 K	1412	Windows Command Processor	Microsoft Corporation
procexp.exe		3,460 K	9,188 K	2520	Sysinternals Process Explorer	Sysinternals - www.sysinter...
procexp64.exe	0.63	11,740 K	22,080 K	1444	Sysinternals Process Explorer	Sysinternals - www.sysinter...
explorer.exe	0.03	5,624 K	10,436 K	2256	Windows Explorer	Microsoft Corporation

To investigate this process more, we can use `ProcessActivityView` from DART tools to see which files are accessed by this process in real time. We will find this process access a file located and named `C:\Users\<<UserName>>\AppData\Roaming\Tyull\yquna.tmp`.

The folder name and filenames seem to be randomly created which is a typical malware behavior.

Then, if we try to scan the running system with the GMER tool, it will detect some injected code in the running process `2256 explorer.exe`, as follows:

Thread	C:\Windows\SysWOW64\explorer.exe [2256:2332]	00000000000008a6e3
Thread	C:\Windows\SysWOW64\explorer.exe [2256:2724]	00000000000aacd8
Thread	C:\Windows\SysWOW64\explorer.exe [2256:1276]	00000000000a01a6
Thread	C:\Windows\SysWOW64\explorer.exe [2256:2740]	00000000000a921c
Thread	C:\Windows\SysWOW64\explorer.exe [2256:2876]	00000000000a026d
Thread	C:\Windows\SysWOW64\explorer.exe [2256:2352]	00000000000a02d7
Thread	C:\Windows\SysWOW64\explorer.exe [2256:344]	00000000000a8f82
Thread	C:\Windows\SysWOW64\explorer.exe [2256:624]	00000000000a8f82

Network activities

Most of the malware samples out there need a network connection to complete their goal and connect to the attacker. By checking the network activities on the suspicious connection, we will notice that it listens for connections and port `37337`. Here, we must note that we already isolated the machine from the Internet and the internal network and such connections can't be completed:

Port `37337` is known for its wide usage in malware-related activities.

Case Study

Autorun keys

We also can check for the autorun keys in the system, which are used by the malware to preserve their existence in the system even after system reboot. We can do this using the Sysinternals tool `autorunsc.exe` or its GUI `autoruns.exe`. We can use the command-line version with the following options:

- `-l`: These are elements that start automatically at login (the default option)
- `-t`: These are assigned tasks
- `-m`: These do not display elements that are digitally signed by Microsoft
- `-v`: These verify digital signatures

```
HKCU\Software\Microsoft\Windows\CurrentVersion\Run
    Entry last modified: 11/3/2015 11:33 AM
    epqe.exe
        C:\Users\             \AppData\Roaming\Imyrug\epqe.exe
        c:\users\             \appdata\roaming\imyrug\epqe.exe
        2/16/2013 11:53 PM
```

Under the `HKCU\Software\Microsoft\Windows\CurrentVersion\Run` registry key, the location of this unknown executable is `C:\users\<<UserName>>\appdata\roaming\imyrug\epqe.exe`. Pay attention to the key last access date, which is old.

We can extract this executable for further analysis, such as reverse engineering and malware analysis, to make sure that it is malicious and understand its functionality. The same results can be found using the GUI version of the tool:

Autorun Entry	Description	Publisher	Image Path	Timestamp
HKLM\SOFTWARE\Microsoft\Windows\CurrentVersion\Run				10/29/2015 10:09 PM
☑ VMware User ...	VMware Tools Core Service	VMware, Inc.	c:\program files\vmware\vmware tools\vmtoolsd.exe	2/26/2013 2:56 AM
HKLM\SOFTWARE\Wow6432Node\Microsoft\Windows\CurrentVersion\Run				2/21/2016 8:19 PM
☑ Adobe Reader ...	Adobe Acrobat SpeedLaun...	Adobe Systems Incorporated	c:\program files (x86)\adobe\reader 9.0\reader\reader_sl.exe	6/12/2008 9:37 AM
HKLM\SOFTWARE\Microsoft\Active Setup\Installed Components				10/29/2015 11:04 PM
☑ Microsoft Wind...	Windows Mail	Microsoft Corporation	c:\program files\windows mail\winmail.exe	7/13/2009 11:58 PM
HKLM\SOFTWARE\Wow6432Node\Microsoft\Active Setup\Installed Components				10/29/2015 11:04 PM
☑ Microsoft Wind...	Windows Mail	Microsoft Corporation	c:\program files (x86)\windows mail\winmail.exe	7/13/2009 11:42 PM
HKCU\Software\Microsoft\Windows\CurrentVersion\Run				11/3/2015 11:33 AM
☑ epqe.exe			c:\users\ \appdata\roaming\imyrug\epqe.exe	2/16/2013 11:53 PM

So, the question now is what added this executable to the registry keys?

Prefetch files

To try to answer the previous question, we can start analyzing the prefetch files. From DART, open the WinPrefetchView tool. This tool will automatically parse the prefetch files of the live system and view their results in human readable format.

After spending some time in viewing the files and searching for the executable named `epqe`, we can find that `eqpe.exe` ran just two seconds after a file named `latest_report.pdf.exe` ran in the system, and at the same second the `Explorer.exe` started:

LATEST_REPORT.PDF.EXE-69E6ECF4.pf	2/21/2016 10:20:26 PM	2/21/2016 10:20:26 PM	26,964	LATEST_REPORT.PDF.EXE
EPQE.EXE-BCDAD835.pf	2/21/2016 10:20:28 PM	2/21/2016 10:20:28 PM	25,974	EPQE.EXE
EXPLORER.EXE-254441E9.pf	2/21/2016 10:20:28 PM	2/21/2016 10:20:28 PM	48,648	EXPLORER.EXE

As we can see, the first filename is very suspicious. It is located under `C:\Users\<<UserName>>\Downloads\latest_report.pdf.exe`. If we tried to search this location for this file, we won't find it. In the list of files used by this `latest_report.pdf.exe` file, according to `WinPrefetchView`, we will find the `epqe.exe` file used or created by this file:

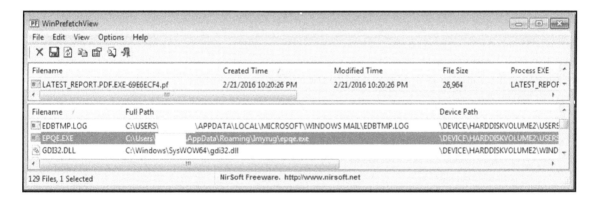

However, what made the victim download this malicious executable?

Browser analysis

The `last_report.pdf.exe` file may have been copied to the machine from another storage or over the network, but because it was located in the `Downloads` folder, it may be more reasonable to start investigating the browser history.

The installed browsers in the system were Internet Explorer and Mozilla Firefox. By investigating both with DART tools, we can find some interesting results from `MozillaHistoryView`:

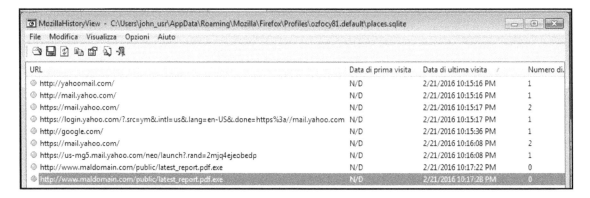

We can see that the file was downloaded from `http://www.maldomain.com/public/latest_report.pdf.exe`. However, we can see that the visit time was just after the user visited `mail.yahoo.com`, which increases the chance that the malicious link was sent to the victim in an e-mail.

If we have the ability to open the victim's mailbox to prove or refute this assumption, in our case, we will find the following message:

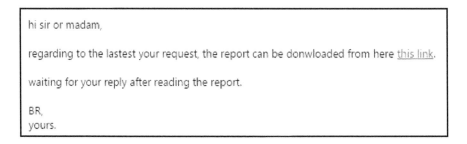

We can find this e-mail where the language isn't accurate and the link was added in order to display other text `this link` rather than the actual link:

www.maldomain.com/public/latest_report.pdf.exe

Note: The e-mail and browser history analysis results won't appear in your analysis if you run the malware within a machine on your own.

Postmortem analysis

Before performing the live analysis, we acquired the evidence. These were the memory and the hard drive. Let's see what we can get from this evidence.

Memory analysis

The memory is the working space for the operating system, and we can get many traces of any malware that ran within the system from the memory analysis. In this section, we will use the volatility framework to analyze the dumped memory file and try to get the same information that we got from the live analysis.

To get information about the profile of the memory file, we can use the imageinfo plugin:

Case Study

From the output, the image profile that we will use is `Win7SP0x64`. Then, let's list the running processes and the network connections, as we discussed in the memory analysis chapter:

```
> vol.py --profile=Win7SP0x64 psxview -f memory.raw
Volatility Foundation Volatility Framework 2.3.1
Offset(P)          Name                PID pslist psscan thrdproc pspcid csrss session deskthrd
---------------    ----------------    --- ------ ------ -------- ------ ----- ------- --------
0x000000003fb657e0 DART.EXE           1324 True   True   True     True   True  True    True
0x000000003deac8e0 svchost.exe        1044 True   True   True     True   True  True    True
0x000000003de0c960 svchost.exe         288 True   True   True     True   True  True    True
0x000000003e5e9060 lsm.exe             528 True   True   True     True   True  True    True
0x000000003fa2b060 dwm.exe            2884 True   True   True     True   True  True    True
0x000000003fa28b30 taskhost.exe       2864 True   True   True     True   True  True    True
0x000000003dc9e4a0 svchost.exe        1748 True   True   True     True   True  True    True
0x000000003de2cb30 svchost.exe         396 True   True   True     True   True  True    True
0x000000003f8a9b30 SearchFilterHo     2156 True   True   True     True   True  True    True
0x000000003de02b30 svchost.exe         900 True   True   True     True   True  True    True
0x000000003fdf7960 vmtoolsd.exe       3056 True   True   True     True   True  True    True
0x000000003deefb30 svchost.exe        1160 True   True   True     True   True  True    True
0x000000003e547740 wininit.exe         436 True   True   True     True   True  True    True
0x000000003e1d8060 svchost.exe         872 True   True   True     True   True  True    True
0x000000003df95b30 vmtoolsd.exe       1260 True   True   True     True   True  True    True
0x000000003e5b3060 winlogon.exe        500 True   True   True     True   True  True    True
0x000000004dd7060 firefox.exe        2064 True   True   True     True   True  True    True
0x000000003de881d0 spoolsv.exe         372 True   True   True     True   True  True    True
0x000000003e5f5b30 svchost.exe         636 True   True   True     True   True  True    True
0x000000003dd1a5b0 SearchIndexer.     2512 True   True   True     True   True  True    True
0x000000003e58d260 services.exe        476 True   True   True     True   True  True    False
0x000000003dd9b060 DumpIt.exe         1936 True   True   True     True   True  True    True
0x000000003f7e12e0 SearchProtocol     2760 True   True   True     True   True  True    True
0x000000003dd1b060 svchost.exe        2224 True   True   True     True   True  True    False
0x000000003fcbb3d0 explorer.exe       2892 True   True   True     True   True  True    True
0x000000003e7f53e0 svchost.exe         700 True   True   True     True   True  True    True
0x000000003e53bb30 lsass.exe           484 True   True   True     True   True  True    False
0x000000003dcf02f0 explorer.exe       2256 True   True   True     True   True  True    False
0x000000003df7bab0 msdtc.exe          2032 True   True   True     True   True  True    True
0x000000003f7ab2e0 conhost.exe        2536 True   True   True     True   True  True    True
0x000000003e14cb30 svchost.exe         784 True   True   True     True   True  True    False
0x000000003fabf580 dllhost.exe         300 True   True   False    True   False True    True
0x000000003e4cb500 csrss.exe           404 True   True   True     True   False True    True
0x000000003f09b310 smss.exe            260 True   True   True     True   False False   False
0x000000003e1cbb30 epqe.exe            292 True   True   False    True   False True    False
0x000000003e47f060 csrss.exe           352 True   True   True     True   False True    True
0x000000003ff32410 System                4 True   True   True     True   False False   False
0x000000003dc2e790 dllhost.exe        3064 False  True   False    False  False False   False
0x000000003f8f62e0 dllhost.exe        1064 False  True   False    False  False False   False
```

We will notice the two `explorer.exe` processes, but we can't see any hidden processes. There are two processes named `dllhost.exe`, which can be found in the psscan plugin's output only. However, these two processes were exited and their structures were still in memory, and they can be found by psscan plugin, as we can see from the output of the psscan plugin:

```
0x000000003f8f62e0 dllhost.exe        1064    636 0x00000000197d0000 2016-02-21 22:18:00 UTC+0000 2016-02-21 22:18:05 UTC+0000
```

Then, we can filter, based on the malicious connections that can be found in the system using the netscan plugin:

```
> vol.py --profile=Win7SP0x64 netscan -f memory.raw
Volatility Foundation Volatility Framework 2.3.1
Offset(P)   Proto  Local Address          Foreign Address                       State        Pid   Owner         Created
0x3dc48790  TCPv4  0.0.0.0:445            0.0.0.0:0                             LISTENING    4     System
0x3dc48790  TCPv6  :::445                 :::0                                  LISTENING    4     System
0x3dc6bc80  TCPv4  0.0.0.0:5357           0.0.0.0:0                             LISTENING    4     System
0x3dc6bc80  TCPv6  :::5357                :::0                                  LISTENING    4     System
0x3dc79670  TCPv4  0.0.0.0:49165          0.0.0.0:0                             LISTENING    476   services.exe
0x3dc79670  TCPv6  :::49165               :::0                                  LISTENING    476   services.exe
0x3dc7e740  TCPv4  0.0.0.0:56142          0.0.0.0:0                             LISTENING    1748  svchost.exe
0x3dc81b10  TCPv4  0.0.0.0:56142          0.0.0.0:0                             LISTENING    1748  svchost.exe
0x3dc81b10  TCPv6  :::56142               :::0                                  LISTENING    1748  svchost.exe
0x3dcc88b0  TCPv4  0.0.0.0:3389           0.0.0.0:0                             LISTENING    396   svchost.exe
0x3dccd8b0  TCPv4  0.0.0.0:3389           0.0.0.0:0                             LISTENING    396   svchost.exe
0x3dccd8b0  TCPv6  :::3389                :::0                                  LISTENING    396   svchost.exe
0x3dcf5ef0  TCPv4  0.0.0.0:37337          0.0.0.0:0                             LISTENING    2256  explorer.exe
0x3dcf6ef0  TCPv4  0.0.0.0:37337          0.0.0.0:0                             LISTENING    2256  explorer.exe
0x3dcf6ef0  TCPv6  :::37337               :::0                                  LISTENING    2256  explorer.exe
0x3de59760  TCPv4  0.0.0.0:49165          0.0.0.0:0                             LISTENING    476   services.exe
0x3e114d20  TCPv4  0.0.0.0:49152          0.0.0.0:0                             LISTENING    436   wininit.exe
0x3e11d1b0  TCPv4  0.0.0.0:135            0.0.0.0:0                             LISTENING    700   svchost.exe
0x3e11d1b0  TCPv6  :::135                 :::0                                  LISTENING    700   svchost.exe
0x3e126010  TCPv4  0.0.0.0:49153          0.0.0.0:0                             LISTENING    784   svchost.exe
0x3e126010  TCPv6  :::49153               :::0                                  LISTENING    784   svchost.exe
0x3e1261a0  TCPv4  0.0.0.0:49153          0.0.0.0:0                             LISTENING    784   svchost.exe
0x3e12a290  TCPv4  0.0.0.0:135            0.0.0.0:0                             LISTENING    700   svchost.exe
0x3e148350  TCPv4  0.0.0.0:49154          0.0.0.0:0                             LISTENING    484   lsass.exe
0x3e18c310  TCPv4  0.0.0.0:49154          0.0.0.0:0                             LISTENING    484   lsass.exe
0x3e18c310  TCPv6  :::49154               :::0                                  LISTENING    484   lsass.exe
0x3e4165b0  TCPv4  0.0.0.0:49152          0.0.0.0:0                             LISTENING    436   wininit.exe
0x3e4165b0  TCPv6  :::49152               :::0                                  LISTENING    436   wininit.exe
0x3e49a4f0  TCPv4  0.0.0.0:49155          0.0.0.0:0                             LISTENING    900   svchost.exe
0x3e49a4f0  TCPv6  :::49155               :::0                                  LISTENING    900   svchost.exe
0x3e4a0400  TCPv4  0.0.0.0:49155          0.0.0.0:0                             LISTENING    900   svchost.exe
0x3da65980  TCPv4  -:56408                -:443                                 CLOSED       2064  firefox.exe
0x3da9faa0  TCPv4  -:56511                224.0.0.252:445                       CLOSED       4     System
0x3dc10010  TCPv4  -:56514                224.0.0.22:443                        CLOSED       2064  firefox.exe
0x3dc3aa90  TCPv6  -:0                    1854:cb0c:80fa:ffff:1854:cb0c:80fa:ffff:0 CLOSED    484   lsass.exe
0x3dc6ecf0  TCPv4  -:56400                192.228.79.201:443                    CLOSED       2064  firefox.exe
```

We will find `explorer.exe` process's listening connections on port `37337`. So, let's focus on this process.

Let's dump this process and search for any interesting strings that can identify its function:

```
> vol.py --profile=Win7SP0x64 memdump -p 2256 -f memory.raw  -D ./
Volatility Foundation Volatility Framework 2.3.1
************************************************************
Writing explorer.exe [ 2256] to 2256.dmp
```

Case Study

If we run the `strings 2256.dmp | more` command, it will show many strings in the process dump file. Some of these strings, such as `Run` and `Runonce`, should make us think about registry keys. To list the registry keys in memory, we can use the hivelist plugin:

```
> vol.py --profile=Win7SP0x64 hivelist -f memory.raw
Volatility Foundation Volatility Framework 2.3.1
Virtual            Physical           Name
------------------ ------------------ ----
0xfffff8a000062010 0x0000000004c2d010 \REGISTRY\MACHINE\HARDWARE
0xfffff8a0000e1290 0x000000002f924290 \Device\HarddiskVolume1\Boot\BCD
0xfffff8a000514420 0x00000000337a3420 \SystemRoot\System32\Config\SECURITY
0xfffff8a000537010 0x000000003434b010 \SystemRoot\System32\Config\SOFTWARE
0xfffff8a0009c1420 0x0000000034459420 \SystemRoot\System32\Config\DEFAULT
0xfffff8a000c80010 0x0000000028e68010 \??\C:\Windows\ServiceProfiles\NetworkService\NTUSER.DAT
0xfffff8a000d12010 0x00000000280c5010 \??\C:\Windows\ServiceProfiles\LocalService\NTUSER.DAT
0xfffff8a001882010 0x000000003bb9c010 \??\C:\Users\         \AppData\Local\Microsoft\Windows\UsrClass.dat
0xfffff8a0018b7010 0x0000000000994a010 \??\C:\Users\         \ntuser.dat
0xfffff8a00320a010 0x0000000032aad010 \SystemRoot\System32\Config\SAM
0xfffff8a00800d420 0x00000000395b8420 \??\C:\System Volume Information\Syscache.hve
0xfffff8a00000d240 0x0000000002f82240 [no name]
0xfffff8a000024010 0x0000000004c6d010 \REGISTRY\MACHINE\SYSTEM
```

Now, we have the locations of the opened hives in memory. We can browse through these hives in memory using the printkey plugin with the virtual offset of the registry hive.

We can try different hives, but let's try the `ntuser.dat` hive of the system user. Check `Software\Microsoft\Windows\CurrentVersion\Run`:

```
> vol.py --profile=Win7SP0x64 printkey -o 0xfffff8a0018b7010 -K "Software\Microsoft\Windows\CurrentVersion\Run" -f memory.raw
Volatility Foundation Volatility Framework 2.3.1
Legend: (S) = Stable   (V) = Volatile
----------------------------
Registry: User Specified
Key name: Run (S)
Last updated: 2016-02-21 22:20:19 UTC+0000

Subkeys:

Values:
REG_SZ        epqe.exe       : (S) C:\Users\       \AppData\Roaming\Imyrug\epqe.exe
```

We can find the unknown executable in the memory as well. Now, let's try to scan for all opened files in memory and filter on this filename:

```
> vol.py --profile=Win7SP0x64 mftparser -f memory.raw --output=body --output-file=mft.body
Volatility Foundation Volatility Framework 2.3.1
Scanning for MFT entries and building directory, this can take a while
```

Then, convert the body file to the timeline file using the following command:

```
mactime -b mft.body > mft.tmline
```

The output will be a timeline of all the activities in the system. If we tried to filter based on the suspicious executable filename, we can get the same sequence that we got from investigating the prefetch files during live analysis:

```
Sun Feb 21 2016 17:20:26   504 macb  ---a---------I--- 0   0   46175   [MFT FILE_NAME] Windows\Prefetch\LATEST_REPORT.PDF.EXE-69E6ECF4.pf (Offset: 0x19a51c00)
                           456 macb  ---a---------I--- 0   0   46175   [MFT FILE_NAME] Windows\Prefetch\LATEST_REPORT.PDF.EXE-69E6ECF4.pf (Offset: 0x82576a8)
                           504 macb  ---a---------I--- 0   0   46175   [MFT FILE_NAME] Windows\Prefetch\LATEST~1.PF (Offset: 0x19a51c00)
                           456 macb  ---a---------I--- 0   0   46175   [MFT FILE_NAME] Windows\Prefetch\LATEST~1.PF (Offset: 0x82576a8)
                           504 macb  ---a---------I--- 0   0   46175   [MFT STD_INFO] Windows\Prefetch\LATEST~1.PF (Offset: 0x19a51c00)
                           456 macb  ---a---------I--- 0   0   46175   [MFT STD_INFO] Windows\Prefetch\LATEST~1.PF (Offset: 0x82576a8)
Sun Feb 21 2016 17:20:28   480 macb  ---a---------I--- 0   0   46182   [MFT FILE_NAME] Windows\Prefetch\EPQE.EXE-BCDAD835.pf (Offset: 0x5c89800)
                           432 macb  ---a---------I--- 0   0   46182   [MFT FILE_NAME] Windows\Prefetch\EPQE.EXE-BCDAD835.pf (Offset: 0x9da798)
                           480 macb  ---a---------I--- 0   0   46182   [MFT FILE_NAME] Windows\Prefetch\EPQEEX~1.PF (Offset: 0x5c89800)
                           432 macb  ---a---------I--- 0   0   46182   [MFT FILE_NAME] Windows\Prefetch\EPQEEX~1.PF (Offset: 0x9da798)
                           480 macb  ---a---------I--- 0   0   46182   [MFT STD_INFO] Windows\Prefetch\EPQEEX~1.PF (Offset: 0x5c89800)
                           432 macb  ---a---------I--- 0   0   46182   [MFT STD_INFO] Windows\Prefetch\EPQEEX~1.PF (Offset: 0x9da798)
                           440 macb  ---a---------I--- 0   0   46183   [MFT FILE_NAME] Windows\Prefetch\EXPLORER.EXE-254441E9.pf (Offset: 0x2e3dba68)
                           488 macb  ---a---------I--- 0   0   46183   [MFT FILE_NAME] Windows\Prefetch\EXPLORER.EXE-254441E9.pf (Offset: 0x5c89c00)
                           440 macb  ---a---------I--- 0   0   46183   [MFT FILE_NAME] Windows\Prefetch\EXPLOR~2.PF (Offset: 0x2e3dba68)
                           488 macb  ---a---------I--- 0   0   46183   [MFT FILE_NAME] Windows\Prefetch\EXPLOR~2.PF (Offset: 0x5c89c00)
                           440 macb  ---a---------I--- 0   0   46183   [MFT STD_INFO] Windows\Prefetch\EXPLOR~2.PF (Offset: 0x2e3dba68)
                           488 macb  ---a---------I--- 0   0   46183   [MFT STD_INFO] Windows\Prefetch\EXPLOR~2.PF (Offset: 0x5c89c00)
```

Then, we can try to recover the `latest_report.pdf.exe` from the hard disk image. Actually, the malware deleted that file and created the `epqe.exe` instead. But, what if we wanted to get this file and couldn't recover that file from the hard disk.

Network analysis

The network traffic is the most volatile evidence. For our scenario here, we dumped the network traffic during the attack simulation to a `pcap` file.

To analyze the network traffic, we will use the Networkminer tool that is installed within the Wine environment in our Linux analysis virtual machine.

Networkminer will parse the `pcap` file and view detailed information about the `maldomain.com` domain:

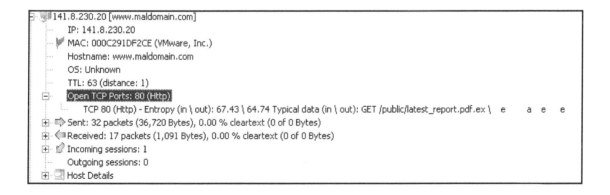

Case Study

It will also export the downloaded file with detailed information:

From the network traffic, we can export and analyze the first `latest_report.pdf.exe` executable file.

Timeline analysis

In this section, we will create a complete timeline of all the activities in the hard disk from the acquired disk image using log2timeline and the Plaso framework.

We will run all the parsers of Windows 7 against the acquired image. However, first, we need to get the offset of the `C:` partition in image using `mmls` tool from TSK:

```
> mmls image.dd
DOS Partition Table
Offset Sector: 0
Units are in 512-byte sectors

     Slot    Start        End          Length       Description
00:  Meta    0000000000   0000000000   0000000001   Primary Table (#0)
01:  -----   0000000000   0000002047   0000002048   Unallocated
02:  00:00   0000002048   0000206847   0000204800   NTFS (0x07)
03:  00:01   0000206848   0083884031   0083677184   NTFS (0x07)
04:  -----   0083884032   0083886079   0000002048   Unallocated
```

[296]

Then, we will use this offset with log2timeline. The process of generating the body file will take a long time because it parses the whole volume for any event mentioned in Win7 parsers:

```
> log2timeline.py -p --parsers win7 -z UTC -o 206848 tmline.body image.dd
[INFO] (MainProcess) Starting to collect pre-processing information.
[INFO] (MainProcess) Filename: image.dd
[INFO] (MainProcess) [PreProcess] Set attribute: windir to //Windows
[INFO] (MainProcess) [PreProcess] Set attribute: systemroot to //Windows/System32
[INFO] (MainProcess) [PreProcess] Set attribute: sysregistry to //Windows/System32/config
[INFO] (MainProcess) [PreProcess] Set attribute: osversion to Windows 7 Enterprise
[INFO] (MainProcess) [PreProcess] Set attribute: users to [{'path': u'%systemroot%\\system32\\config\\systemprofile', 'name': u'systemprofile', 'sid': u'S-1-5-18'}, {'pa
erviceProfiles\\LocalService', 'name': u'LocalService', 'sid': u'S-1-5-19'}, {'path': u'C:\\Windows\\ServiceProfiles\\NetworkService', 'name': u'NetworkService', 'sid':
: u'C:\\Users\\        ', 'name': u'          ', 'sid': u'S-1-5-21-1449995647-2107297555-1596967476-1000'}, {'path': u'C:\\Users\\         ', 'name': u'        ', 'sid': u'S-1-5-21
-760196112-1110'}]
[INFO] (MainProcess) [PreProcess] Set attribute: code_page to cp1252
[INFO] (MainProcess) [PreProcess] Set attribute: hostname to TOP-WS
[INFO] (MainProcess) [PreProcess] Set attribute: time_zone_str to UTC
[INFO] (MainProcess) Setting timezone to: UTC
[INFO] (MainProcess) Starting storage thread.
[INFO] (MainProcess) Starting to collect files for processing.
[INFO] (MainProcess) Starting to extract events.
[INFO] (Worker_0  ) Worker 0 (PID: 9642) started monitoring process queue.
[WARNING] (Worker_0  ) Unable to decode line ['d\x00\x01\x00\x00\x00H\x14\xbb\xbe\x90~\xe5\x19\xb4L\x91d\xd8\x950\xa5\x00\x00\x00\x00\x00\x00\x00'...] using UTF-8-SIG
[INFO] (MainProcess) Collection is hereby DONE
[INFO] (MainProcess) Waiting until all processing is done.
[INFO] (Worker_0  ) Worker 0 (PID: 9642) stopped monitoring process queue.
[INFO] (MainProcess) Processing done, waiting for storage.
[INFO] (StorageThread) [Storage] Closing the storage, nr. of events processed: 757437
[INFO] (MainProcess) Storage process is done.
[INFO] (MainProcess) Run completed.
```

Once this is finished, we can use the `psort.py` tool to view parts of the body file on our choice with the command line, as we did in the timeline analysis in Chapter 5, *Timeline*.

Or, we can convert the timeline body file into a CSV formatted file in order to view it with any spreadsheet program. The conversion will take some time to complete:

```
> psort.py -o L2tcsv tmline.body > tmline.csv
[INFO] Output processing is done.
[INFO]
******************************** Counter **********************************
[INFO]          Stored Events : 757437
[INFO]         Events Included : 757352
[INFO]       Duplicate Removals : 257152
```

Case Study

Once the conversion finishes, you can open the new file in, for example, Excel:

date	time	timezone	MACB	source	sourcetype	type	user	short	desc	version	filename	inode	notes	format	extra
#######	3:16:08	UTC	..C.	FILE	NTFS_DET	ctime	-	1/Users/Jo	image.dd:	2	image.dd:	22973	-	PfileStatP	fs_type: NTFS_DETECT allocated: True size: 0
#######	21:07:23	UTC	..C.	FILE	NTFS_DET	ctime	-	1/Users/Jo	image.dd:	2	image.dd:	22996	-	PfileStatP	fs_type: NTFS_DETECT allocated: True size: 0
#######	21:07:23	UTC	..C.	FILE	NTFS_DET	ctime	-	1/Users/Jo	image.dd:	2	image.dd:	22980	-	PfileStatP	fs_type: NTFS_DETECT allocated: True size: 0
#######	14:58:47	UTC	..C.	FILE	NTFS_DET	ctime	-	1/Users/Jo	image.dd:	2	image.dd:	23004	-	PfileStatP	fs_type: NTFS_DETECT allocated: True size: 0
#######	7:00:00	UTC	....	OLECF	OLECF Sur	Document	-	1Title: Inst	Title: Insta	2	image.dd:	27372	-	OleCfParser	
#######	14:46:54	UTC	...B	FILE	NTFS_DET	crtime	-	1/Program	image.dd:	2	image.dd:	58947	-	PfileStatP	fs_type: NTFS_DETECT allocated: True size: 684
#######	14:46:54	UTC	M...	FILE	NTFS_DET	mtime	-	1/Program	image.dd:	2	image.dd:	58950	-	PfileStatP	fs_type: NTFS_DETECT allocated: True size: 96418
#######	14:46:54	UTC	...B	FILE	NTFS_DET	crtime	-	1/Program	image.dd:	2	image.dd:	58951	-	PfileStatP	fs_type: NTFS_DETECT allocated: True size: 75573
#######	14:46:54	UTC	...B	FILE	NTFS_DET	crtime	-	1/Program	image.dd:	2	image.dd:	58950	-	PfileStatP	fs_type: NTFS_DETECT allocated: True size: 96418
#######	14:46:54	UTC	...B	FILE	NTFS_DET	crtime	-	1/Program	image.dd:	2	image.dd:	58953	-	PfileStatP	fs_type: NTFS_DETECT allocated: True size: 34705
#######	14:46:54	UTC	M...	FILE	NTFS_DET	mtime	-	1/Program	image.dd:	2	image.dd:	58949	-	PfileStatP	fs_type: NTFS_DETECT allocated: True size: 672
#######	14:46:54	UTC	M...	FILE	NTFS_DET	mtime	-	1/Program	image.dd:	2	image.dd:	58951	-	PfileStatP	fs_type: NTFS_DETECT allocated: True size: 75573
#######	14:46:54	UTC	...B	FILE	NTFS_DET	crtime	-	1/Program	image.dd:	2	image.dd:	58948	-	PfileStatP	fs_type: NTFS_DETECT allocated: True size: 683
#######	14:46:54	UTC	...B	FILE	NTFS_DET	crtime	-	1/Program	image.dd:	2	image.dd:	58949	-	PfileStatP	fs_type: NTFS_DETECT allocated: True size: 672
#######	14:46:54	UTC	M...	FILE	NTFS_DET	mtime	-	1/Program	image.dd:	2	image.dd:	58947	-	PfileStatP	fs_type: NTFS_DETECT allocated: True size: 684
#######	14:46:54	UTC	M...	FILE	NTFS_DET	mtime	-	1/Program	image.dd:	2	image.dd:	58953	-	PfileStatP	fs_type: NTFS_DETECT allocated: True size: 34705
#######	14:46:54	UTC	M...	FILE	NTFS_DET	mtime	-	1/Program	image.dd:	2	image.dd:	58948	-	PfileStatP	fs_type: NTFS_DETECT allocated: True size: 683
7/5/2000	21:12:14	UTC	M...	OLECF	OLECF Iter	Content N	-	1Name: Ro	Name: Ro	2	image.dd:	27372	-	OleCfPars	size: 8832
#######	16:47:08	UTC	...B	FILE	NTFS_DET	crtime	-	1/Program	image.dd:	2	image.dd:	58879	-	PfileStatP	fs_type: NTFS_DETECT allocated: True size: 878592
#######	16:47:08	UTC	M...	FILE	NTFS_DET	mtime	-	1/Program	image.dd:	2	image.dd:	58879	-	PfileStatP	fs_type: NTFS_DETECT allocated: True size: 878592
#######	19:49:58	UTC	M...	FILE	NTFS_DET	mtime	-	1/Program	image.dd:	2	image.dd:	58967	-	PfileStatP	fs_type: NTFS_DETECT allocated: True size: 46
#######	19:49:58	UTC	...B	FILE	NTFS_DET	crtime	-	1/Program	image.dd:	2	image.dd:	58967	-	PfileStatP	fs_type: NTFS_DETECT allocated: True size: 46
#######	13:44:50	UTC	M...	FILE	NTFS_DET	mtime	-	1/Program	image.dd:	2	image.dd:	58944	-	PfileStatP	fs_type: NTFS_DETECT allocated: True size: 1249
#######	13:44:50	UTC	...B	FILE	NTFS_DET	crtime	-	1/Program	image.dd:	2	image.dd:	58944	-	PfileStatP	fs_type: NTFS_DETECT allocated: True size: 1249
#######	13:44:50	UTC	M...	FILE	NTFS_DET	mtime	-	1/Program	image.dd:	2	image.dd:	58943	-	PfileStatP	fs_type: NTFS_DETECT allocated: True size: 6716
#######	13:44:50	UTC	M...	FILE	NTFS_DET	mtime	-	1/Program	image.dd:	2	image.dd:	58943	-	PfileStatP	fs_type: NTFS_DETECT allocated: True size: 6716
#######	21:46:52	UTC	...B	FILE	NTFS_DET	crtime	-	1/Program	image.dd:	2	image.dd:	58980	-	PfileStatP	fs_type: NTFS_DETECT allocated: True size: 58938
#######	21:46:52	UTC	M...	FILE	NTFS_DET	mtime	-	1/Program	image.dd:	2	image.dd:	58980	-	PfileStatP	fs_type: NTFS_DETECT allocated: True size: 58938
#######	16:01:08	UTC	M...	FILE	NTFS_DET	mtime	-	1/Program	image.dd:	2	image.dd:	58973	-	PfileStatP	fs_type: NTFS_DETECT allocated: True size: 7582
#######	16:01:08	UTC	...B	FILE	NTFS_DET	crtime	-	1/Program	image.dd:	2	image.dd:	58973	-	PfileStatP	fs_type: NTFS_DETECT allocated: True size: 7582

Then, we can use the Excel filtering tools to filter the output based on our needs, such as showing the prefetch analysis of the malicious files:

499807	2/21/2016	22:20:15 UTC	....	LOG	WinPrefe	Last Time	-	T(LATEST_REPORT.PDF.EXE was run 1 time(s)	Superfetc	2 image.dd:
499808	2/21/2016	22:20:18 UTC	....	LOG	WinPrefe	Last Time	-	T(EPQE.EXE was run 1 time(s)	Superfetc	2 image.dd:
499816	2/21/2016	22:20:18 UTC	....	LOG	WinPrefe	Last Time	-	T(EXPLORER.EXE was run 1 time(s)	Superfetc	2 image.dd:

Summary

After we finished the main book chapters, in this appendix we conducted a primary analysis and discovered malware in an infected machine. We used different analysis techniques, live analysis and postmortem analysis, and explained how to get the same results from both ways. Although, live analysis is easier, it is not applicable all the time. This is why we must be aware of both techniques for the real-life investigations.

Index

$
$Recycle.bin 194, 195

A
Advanced Forensics Format (AFF) 59
analysis, approaches
  about 12
  live analysis 12
  postmortem analysis 12
API hooking 240
attributes
  about 104
  non-resident 104
  resident 104
auto-run keys 157
autopsy
  about 119, 120, 122, 124, 125, 126, 127, 128
  URL 121

B
base block 149, 150
Berkley Packet Filter (BPF) 49
Blkcalc 118
blkcat 115, 116
blkls 118
block 99
Bro
  about 261, 262, 263, 264
  URL 267
browser analysis 290, 291
browser investigation 199
browsers 225
BrowsingHistoryView 206

C
cache, Firefox
  MozillaCacheView 224
Calamaris
  URL 255
clusters
  about 99, 100
  allocated cluster 99
  unallocated cluster 99
collection 83
Component Object Model (COM) 133
Content.IE5 209
Cookies.sqlite, Firefox 222
Coordinated Universal Time (UTC) 76
crash dump
  about 235
  kernel memory dump 235
  memory dump 235
CrashDumpEnable 236

D
data acquisition
  virtualization 69
Data unit layer (Block), Sleuth Kit (TSK)
  about 115
  Blkcalc 118
  blkcat 115, 116, 117
  blkls 118
DBX file 228
dd tool
  about 66, 67
  over network 67, 68
delete data 66
Digital Advanced Response Toolkit (DART) 56
digital crime 8
digital evidence 10, 11

Digital Evidence and Forensics Toolkit (DEFT) 55
digital forensics
  about 8
  acquisition and preservation 9
  analysis 10
  goals 11
  identification 9
  reporting and presentation of digital evidence 10
  subphases 9
Direct Kernel Object Manipulation (DKOM) 238
Direct Memory Access (DMA) 40
disk destroyer 66
disk wiping
  Linux 73
distributed forensic system
  about 275, 276
  GRR 276
Dumpcap 52
DumpIt 41, 42
duplicate data 66
duplicate disk 66
Dynamic Link Libraries (DLL) injection
  about 239
  reflective DLL injection 240
  remote 239
  remote code injection 239
dynamic linking 239

E

E-mail investigation
  about 225
  DBX (Outlook Express) 228
  EML and MSG files 226, 227
  other tools 230, 231
  outlook OST files 226
  outlook PST file 225, 226
  PFF Analysis (libpff) 228, 230
EnCase evidence file (E01) 59
ESEDatabaseView 219
Event ID.net
  URL 175
Event Log Explorer 174
event logging 165
event logs, extracting
  Event Log Explorer 174

event log, analyzing 176, 178, 179
Event Viewer 174
live systems 171, 172
offline system 172, 173
resources 175
event logs
  about 165
  application 167
  application log 167
  applications and services 168
  directory service 167
  DNS server 168
  example 176, 178, 179
  extracting 171
  file replication server 168
  forwarded events 168
  issues, resolving 166
  live systems 171
  offline systems 171
  security 167
  security event logs 168, 169, 170, 171
  security logs 167
  setup 168
  system 166, 167
  system log 167
Event Viewer 174
event, types
  error 170
  failure audit 171
  information 170
  success audit 171
  warning 170
evidence integrity
  about 71
  Acquisition 70
extended audit policies 170
Extensible Storage Engine (ESE) 218

F

File Allocation Table (FAT)
  about 100
  boot sector 100
  components 100, 102
  limitations 102, 103
  table 101

filename layer, Sleuth Kit (TSK) 112, 113, 114
filesystem layer, Sleuth Kit (TSK) 107
Firefox
  about 220, 221
  cache 224
  Places.sqlite 221
Foremost 128, 129, 130
forensic hardware duplicators 54
forensic image 54
Forensic Recovery of Evidence Device Laptop (FREDL) 22
FRED-L laptop 22
FTK image lite
  URL 58
FTK Imager 43
FTK imager
  about 218
  used, for imaging over network 61, 62, 63

G

GRR
  client, installing 277
  new flow, starting 279
  newly-connected client, browsing with 278
  server, installing 276
GUEST virtual machine 274

H

Handlin 71
Handling 71
Hard Disk Drives (HDD) 53
hard drive structure
  about 98
  data area 99
  filesystem area, in partition 99
  master boot record (MBR) 98
  partition boot sector 99
hard drive, live imaging
  about 54, 58
  FTK imager, used for imaging over network 61
  FTK imager, using 58, 60
  Linux, for imaging 65
Hbin and CELL 151, 152, 154
Helix 57
hive

mapping, to filesystem 141
HKEY_CLASSES_ROOT (HKCR) 135, 136, 137
HKEY_CURRENT_USER (HKCU) 140
HKEY_LOCAL_MACHINE 137
HKEY_USERS (HKU) 138, 139
HOST machine 274
hubs 47

I

icat 110
IECacheView 210
IECookiesView 213
IEHistoryView 206
ifind 111, 112
Import Address Table (IAT) 239
incident handling skills 17
  about 21
Incident Response (IR) process 54, 55
Incident Response CDs
  about 54
  DEFT 55, 56
  Helix 57
incident response CDs
  in live acquisition 65
Incident Response CDs
  in live acquisition 63, 64
injection 239
IR team
  about 13
  and Jump Bag 21
  personal skills 14
  security fundamentals 17
iSCSI
  used, for acquiring memory from remote computer 44, 45
istat 109

J

Jump Bag
  about 21
  live versus mortem 25, 26
  nonvolatile data 29
  registry data 30, 31
  software 25
  volatile data 26, 27, 28, 29

K

Kaspersky Forensics Agent (KPA) 44
kdbgscan 241

L

lab building, factors
  about 270
  environmental control 270, 271
  hardware 273
  hardware, virtualization 273, 274
  security 271
  size 270
  software 272
  virtualization, benefits for forensics 274, 275
Libolecf 227
library libpff
  URL 228
Linux
  disk wiping 73
live analysis
  about 12, 284
  autorun keys 288
  network activities 287
  running processes 285, 286, 287
Live Forensics approach 26
live response 35, 36
live systems 171, 172
log2timeline tool 84
logs
  exploring 253, 254, 255

M

malicious code 20
Master Boot Record (MBR) 98
  about 105
Master File Table (MFT) 99
  about 104
memory access, issues
  about 39
  DumpIt 41, 42
  FTK Imager 43
  tools, selecting 39, 40, 41
memory analysis
  about 240

volatility framework 240, 241
memory dump, sources
  about 234
  crash dump 235, 236
  hibernation file 234, 235
  page files 236, 237
memory dump
  small dump files 235
memory
  acquisition 38, 234
  network connections 238
  processes 237, 238
  structure 233, 234
metadata layer, Sleuth Kit (TSK)
  about 108
  icat 110
  ifind 111, 112
  istat 109
Microsoft Internet Explorer, cache
  Content.IE5 209
  IECacheView 210
  Msiecf parser (Plaso framework) 211
Microsoft Internet Explorer, cookies
  about 211
  favorites 213
  FavoritesView 214
  IECookiesView 213
  persistent cookies 212
  session cookies 212
Microsoft Internet Explorer, history
  BrowsingHistoryView 206
  files 200
  History.IE5 201, 202, 203, 204, 205
  IEHistoryView 206
  MiTeC History browser 207
Microsoft Internet Explorer, session restore
  about 214
  inprivate mode 217
  MiTeC SSV 215, 216
Microsoft Internet Explorer, WebCacheV#.dat
  about 217, 218
  ESEDatabaseView 219, 220
Microsoft Internet Explorer
  about 200
  cache 208

cookies 211
history 200, 201
IEHistoryView 206
WebCacheV#.dat 217
MiTeC Internet History browser 207
MiTeC SSV 215, 216
MozillaCacheView 224
MozillaCookiesView 223
MozillaHistoryView 222
MS TechNet
  URL 175

N

network forensics
  about 251
  network data collection 252
network-based data collection
  about 47
  Dumpcap 52
  hubs 47, 48
  switches 48, 49
  tcpdump 49, 50
  Tshark 51
  Wireshark 50, 51
New Technology Filesystem (NTFS)
  about 103
  components 103
  Master File Table (MFT) 104
Nirsoft.net
  URL 225
nonvolatile data 29

O

Offline Storage Table (OST) file 226
offline system 172, 173

P

page files 236
partition boot sector 99
Pelican
  URL 23
Personal File Folder (PFF) file 225
personal skills
  about 14

diplomacy 15
integrity 15
limits, knowing 16
oral communication 14
policies and procedures, following ability 15
presentation skills 14
problem, solving 16
stress, coping with 16
team skills 15
technical skills 17
time management 16
written communication 14
Personal Storage Table (PST) file 225
Places.sqlite, Firefox
  about 221
  MozillaCookiesView 223
  MozillaHistoryView 222
Plaso framework
  log2timeline 84
  Pinfo 84
  pprof 84
  preg 84
  pshell 84
  psort 84
  tools 84
Plaso, architecture
  collection 83
  preprocessing 83
  storage 84
  worker 83
Plaso
  about 82
  architecture 82
  results, analyzing 88, 89, 90, 92, 93, 94
  using 84, 85, 86, 87, 88
postmortem analysis 12
  about 8, 9, 291
  memory analysis 291, 292, 293, 294, 295
  network analysis 295, 296
  timeline analysis 296, 297, 298
prefetch file, Windows
  about 181, 182, 183, 289
  analysis 183, 184
preprocessing process 83

R

RawCopy
  URL 30
RecycleBin, Windows
  $Recycle.bin 194, 195
  about 191
  RECYCLER 192
RECYCLER 192, 193
registry analysis
  about 158
  MiTeC Windows registry recovery 164
  RegistryRipper 158, 159, 160
  Sysinternals 161, 162, 163
registry data 30, 31, 32, 33, 34, 35
registry files, parsing
  base block 149, 150
  Hbin and CELL 151, 152, 154, 155
registry files
  backing up 141, 142
  extracting, from forensic image 147
  extracting, from live system 143, 144, 146, 148
  parsing 149
registry hives
  about 135
  extracting 143
registry
  structure 134
RegistryRipper 158, 159, 160
Remote SPAN (RSPAN) 48
Request for Comments (RFC 3227) document 37
  evidence, list 37
root key 135
root keys
  HKEY_CLASSES_ROOT (HKCR) 135, 136, 137
  HKEY_CURRENT_USER (HKCU) 140
  HKEY_LOCAL_MACHINE 137
  HKEY_USERS (HKU) 138, 139
Russ Antony
  URL 175

S

SANS Reading Room
  URL 175
SARG
  URL 255
scheduled task 185
security event logs 168, 169, 170, 171
  about 170
security fundamentals
  about 17
  host or system security, issues 19, 20
  internet 18
  malicious code 20
  network applications and services 19
  network protocols 18, 19
  network security, issues 19
  programming skills 21
  risk 18
  security principles 17
  security vulnerabilities and weaknesses 17
security identifiers (SIDs) 94
shortcut files, Windows
  about 195
  analysis 196, 197
Sleuth Kit (TSK)
  about 79, 80, 81, 104, 105
  Data unit layer (Block) 115
  filename layer 112, 113, 114
  Filesystem layer 107
  metadata layer 108
  using 46
  volume layer (media management) 105, 106
snapshot 274
Squidview
  URL 255
storage 84
Super Timeline 82
svcscan 246
switch device 47
Switched Port Analyzer (SPAN) 48
switches 48, 49
Sysinternals 161, 162
system memory 233

T

tcpdump
  about 49, 50
  using 255, 256
Thumbcache Viewer 188
Thumbs DB, Windows
  about 186, 187
  corrupted Windows.edb files 190
  Thumbcache analysis 188, 189
timeline 75, 76, 77, 78
tools, memory access
  selecting 39, 40, 41
Tshark 51, 257
TZWorks evtwalk tool 172

U

Ultimate Windows Security
  URL 175
UTC 76

V

Virtual Address Descriptor (VAD) 249
virtualization
  in data acquisition 69
volatile data 26, 28, 29
volatility framework 241
volatility plugins
  apihooks 249
  connections 246
  connscan 246
  dlllist 243
  filescan 244
  getsids 243
  handles 244
  hivelist and printkey 247, 248
  imagecopy 241
  imageprofile 241
  malfind 248
  memdump 245
  mftparser 250
  netscan 247
  procexedump 245
  pslist 242
  psscan 242
  pstree 242
  psxview 243
  raw2dmp 241
  sockets 247
  sockscan 247
  svcscan 246
  vaddump 249
volume layer (media management), Sleuth Kit
  (TSK) 105, 106

W

Windows.edb files 190
Windows
  prefetch file analysis 183
  prefetch files 181, 182, 183
  RecycleBin 191
  shortcut files 195
  tasks 185
  Thumbs DB 186, 187
WinPrefetchView tool
  URL 183
Wireshark 50, 51
WireShark
  using 258, 259
worker 83

Z

Zoo
  URL 284

Lightning Source UK Ltd.
Milton Keynes UK
UKHW031852060320
359914UK00007B/1445